DATE DUE

THE MAKING
OF
Dr. Phil

THE MAKING
D^{OF} Dr. Phil

The Straight-Talking True Story of Everyone's Favorite Therapist

**Sophia Dembling
Lisa Gutierrez**

WILEY

John Wiley & Sons, Inc.

Published by John Wiley & Sons, Inc., Hoboken, New Jersey.
Published simultaneously in Canada.

For general information on our other products and services, or technical support, please contact our Customer Care Department within the United States at 800-762-2974, outside the United States at 317-572-3993 or fax 317-572-4002.

Wiley also publishes its books in a variety of electronic formats. Some content that appears in print may not be available in electronic books. For more information about Wiley products, visit our web site at www.wiley.com.

ISBN 0-471-46726-X

Printed in the United States of America.

10 9 8 7 6 5 4 3 2 1

CONTENTS

In every way, 2003 was shaping up to be among the best years of Phil McGraw's eventful life. With three best-selling self-help books already on the shelves, he had signed to write his next—about weight loss—for a reported $10 million advance, a staggering amount even for someone with his stellar track record. After more than two decades in Texas, he and his family had settled into a $7.5 million Beverly Hills mansion with all the trappings of luxury—a circular drive, library, guesthouse, three-car garage, and palm-tree-lined pool. He tooled around town in a $200,000 Ferrari, and was a regular on the talk show circuit, hobnobbing with the likes of Jay Leno, David Letterman, and Katie Couric. His face graced the covers of magazines from *Newsweek* to *Satellite Direct,* and his live "Get Real" seminars filled auditoriums around the world. At the same time, his Dallas-based legal consulting firm continued to thrive, even though he no longer had time to be involved in its day-to-day operations.

Perhaps most exciting of all, after a two-year stint as Oprah Winfrey's regular Tuesday guest, he was now hosting his own daytime talk show, to great acclaim. *Dr. Phil* premiered to such high ratings that even jaded industry experts were startled.

Given the charmed life he was leading, everybody expected McGraw to cap off his year of success with at least one Daytime Emmy nomination. After all, his show had more viewers and got more press than any other on the air that year. It did so well that by the time the nominees were named on March 12, 2003, *Dr. Phil* had already been renewed for another three years in 60 percent of its markets.

■ ■ ■

The Emmy nominations were announced during a live episode of *The View*, ABC's all-female talk program, which was created and frequently cohosted by veteran newswoman Barbara Walters. "If we are not nominated, this could be one of the most embarrassing moments on *The View*," Walters joked before the nominations were read.

McGraw was indeed nominated for, not one, but two awards—outstanding host and outstanding talk show. Most industry insiders agreed that McGraw had a better than good chance of taking both statues home. For one thing, two of the reigning powerhouses of the genre were out of the running this time around. Winfrey, the queen of daytime talk for as long as she'd been on the air, had removed herself from the competition in 2000. Her trophy case was already crowded with 15 Emmys. Rosie O'Donnell, another multiple winner, had abandoned her talk show the previous year and watched her eponymous magazine hit the skids as well. Aside from *The View*—which, to Walters' relief, *did* get nominated—McGraw's competition included Regis Philbin and Kelly Ripa, along with newcomer Wayne Brady (who took O'Donnell's time slot in most markets), and dark-horse contenders Lisa Rinna and Ty Treadway, hosts of an obscure cable show called *Soap Talk*.

McGraw had the added benefit of being a solo host. As Philbin and Ripa had learned in earlier years, cohosts rarely win because a voter who likes one might dislike the other. (After getting 10 nominations with former sidekick Kathie Lee Gifford, Philbin finally won a Daytime Emmy in 2001, when he was in between co-hosts.) And, to top it off, McGraw had the "Oprah juggernaut behind him," as one entertainment industry pundit put it. "The slam-dunk shoo-in for Best Talk Show Host is *Dr. Phil*," said Tom O'Neil, author of *The Emmys*, considered to be the definitive reference book on the awards. "It doesn't take a crystal ball to see that coming."

■ ■ ■

In the weeks leading up to the big ceremony, McGraw struggled to remain humble against the ebullient certainty surrounding him. He was the confident, odds-on favorite. He even made the talk show rounds in the days before the awards were to be presented, accepting plaudits and praise from fawning interviewers. "You got to know you were going to get them [the Emmy nominations]," gushed CNN's Larry King the night before the awards were to be handed out. The next morning, McGraw stopped by for a chat with Katie Couric on *Today*, who was equally enthusiastic.

"I hear the ratings are huge, so you must be, like, 'Yeah! I'm the man,'" Couric raved.

"Well, if you're going to do it, do it right, I suppose," McGraw preened. "I'm proud of what I've done. We've been on a year and I truly think that it's the highest and best use of television. I think we're giving people information they can use in their homes, every day for free. And I think that's a good thing to do."

■ ■ ■

Heavy winds and rain were predicted in New York on the evening of May 16, but daytime television's top stars were spared all but a dampening drizzle as they walked down the red carpet and into Radio City Music Hall. Fans crowded the streets outside, most hoping to see their favorite soap opera stars—the ultrabeautiful people who draw some of TV's most avid fans. The Daytime Emmys, after all, were primarily designed to honor the soaps. Yet CNN reporter Jason Carroll, stationed outside and providing color for the folks at home, observed, "You've got all these beautiful women out here and all these celebrities, and the one name that everyone keeps talking about is Dr. Phil."

All eyes were on McGraw as he arrived in black-tie tux, with Robin all a-cleavage in an olive strapless dress crafted by Dallas-reared Bradely Bayou, one of Winfrey's favorite designers. They took their seats inside the theater next to a glamorous array of soap stars and game show hosts. Bob Barker and Alex Trebek were there. So was Susan Lucci, the grande dame of soap stars, along with TV legend Art Linkletter and a plethora of famous faces who fill the small screen during daylight hours.

Award show emcee Wayne Brady—the comedian turned talk show host who competed with McGraw in both of his nominated categories—started the evening's festivities with an old school rap number. Decked out in a red tracksuit, he impressed the crowd (and, it seemed, himself) with his break-dancing talents. Brady was smooth and charming, and the audience was with him all the way. But even he acknowledged in his opening monologue that McGraw was the favorite to win that night.

"You would think that my family would have some faith in me," Brady told the audience. "But as I left the hotel, I kissed my little three-and-a-half-month-old baby and I was looking at her, you know, all this pride swelling inside of me. I said, 'Hey baby, who do you think is going to win?' Now my little girl has never spoken a word before. But she went 'ba . . . ba . . . ba . . . ba . . . badad-bada . . . Dr. Phil.'"

Cut to a close-up of a smiling and clearly confident McGraw in the audience. It was the first of several times during the broadcast that cameras would be focused on his familiar face.

■ ■ ■

This was a special year for the Daytime Emmys. It was the ceremony's thirtieth anniversary broadcast and, for the first time since going prime time in 1991, it would be on for three hours, just like its counterpart honoring evening programming. That meant McGraw had to wait through a lot of daytime TV's memorable moments, clip-filled tributes to nominated dramas, and an array of acting and game show awards, before attention turned to the categories that mattered most to him.

Finally, Sharon Osbourne, who was soon to host a syndicated talk program of her own, stepped out to present the award for best daytime talk show host. It was one of the two moments McGraw had been waiting for. Here, as he might say, was where the rubber hit the road.

Osbourne read the names of the five nominees—Wayne Brady of *The Wayne Brady Show;* Dr. Phil McGraw of *Dr. Phil;* Regis Philbin and Kelly Ripa of *Live with Regis and Kelly;* Lisa Rinna and Ty Treadway of *Soap Talk;* and Barbara Walters, Meredith Vieira, Star Jones, Joy Behar, and Lisa Ling of *The View.*

"I'm going to rub this for good luck," Osbourne said, stroking the envelope tenderly against her breast before breaking the seal and revealing the name inside.

"The winner is . . ."

The nominees—camera trained on their faces—held their breath.

". . . Wayne Brady."

The audience erupted in applause. Fellow losing nominees Barbara Walters and Kelly Ripa flashed big—and no doubt carefully rehearsed—smiles. But McGraw was stone-faced except for muttering a disappointed word to himself.

This was clearly a letdown, but all was not lost. The outstanding daytime talk show award was yet to come—after more drama awards, highlights, commercials, and a skit by the women of *The View* that included a punchline about McGraw's talents in the bedroom. This award was presented by "Judge Judy" Sheindlin (about whom McGraw has said, "I met her, and she scared the hell out of me"). Sheindlin first read the list of nominees in the outstanding talk show category: *Dr. Phil, Live with Regis and Kelly, Soap Talk, The View,* and *The Wayne Brady Show.* Then, she carefully opened the envelope and had a surprising announcement.

"Wow, I guess it wasn't such an easy judging," she said. "There is a tie."

McGraw no doubt felt secure that *Dr. Phil* was one of the names on the card in Sheindlin's hand. How could his show—with all the success and accolades it had piled up over the year—possibly lose?

"The first Emmy goes to . . . *The View.*"

The crowd cheered as Barbara Walters and a large crew from her show crowded the stage. After Walters was done giving thanks, Sheindlin returned to present the award to the other winning show.

"And the second Emmy goes to . . ."

McGraw was poised in his seat, ready to hear his name and make his way to the stage.

". . . *The Wayne Brady Show.*"

Despite having higher ratings and making more money than virtually all of the other nominees it was up against, *Dr. Phil*—and McGraw—would go home from the Emmys empty-handed on his first year out. It was a strikingly sour note in a year when everything was going so sweetly for this good ol' Texas boy who, in no time at all, had taken over Tinseltown.

■ ■ ■

McGraw's surprising loss—what some might even call come-uppance—may have been a shock, but losing big was hardly a new experience for him. Reaching high and falling lower has always been an integral part of McGraw's personal formula for success. By the time he sat among that glittering crowd in Radio City Music Hall, McGraw had failed nearly as often as he had succeeded. From childhood on, his life has been less a steady climb to the top than a series of fits and starts, with each new beginning bringing him to a higher level of accomplishment.

The only son of an ambitious but hard-drinking father, McGraw came from poverty and grew up in a family that pinched every penny and frequently moved from town to town. He was an undistinguished student and a bit of a bully as a boy. McGraw was married, divorced, and bankrupt before the age of 24. But he quickly pulled himself back together from these failures, and proved to be a talented college student who speed-studied his way to a doctorate in psychology. He spent a decade using his degree in a career he hated, cofounded a successful personal growth seminar business, and then got in trouble with the state's psychology licensing board. He decided to start all over again and teamed up with a lawyer friend to found what became a hugely successful litigation consulting firm. This ultimately led him to Oprah Winfrey and a job that would forever change his life in ways he probably had never imagined.

While McGraw likes to portray himself as just a folksy down-home doc who tells it like it is, he actually is a powerful character who leaves a trail of admiration, loyalty, respect, envy, dislike, mistrust, and gossip wherever he passes. Although McGraw refused to participate directly in the writing of this book, it's clear he is an ambitious, smart, and perceptive man who never fails at one endeavor without turning around to succeed brilliantly at the next. But with his win-at-all-costs approach, he has collected as many detractors as admirers along the way.

The story of Dr. Phil McGraw's rise to the top is not one of a well-thought-out and carefully executed plan, nor is it entirely a tale about the rewards of hard work—although McGraw is driven by the pursuit of success. Rather, it is the story of a brilliant opportunist with powerful survival instincts and a gift for quickly analyzing and sizing up any situation.

You may have heard the legend about the man who was blessed by Oprah's golden touch. But the true story about the making of Dr. Phil encompasses both embarrassing failures and promising opportunities that have been brilliantly capitalized on by someone with the brains—and nerves—to do what it takes to succeed. For McGraw, failure is always an option, but it is never an insurmountable obstacle.

Learning to Fly

Your life is not a dress rehearsal.

The night of September 1, 1950, didn't go quite as Joe McGraw had planned. The tall, thick-chested, burly young man was fresh out of college and couldn't wait to coach his first football game in the small town of Vinita, Oklahoma. He'd been the star of his own high school football team back in Texas. Now, at age 26, he was replacing Vinita High's winning football coach, who had brought two conference titles to the school. The pressure was definitely on. In Oklahoma—where football is king and boys proudly proclaim that they live and breathe the sport—winning is everything. And every game counts.

An hour before kickoff that Friday night, Joe's wife and high school sweetheart, Jerry, went into labor. The couple already had two little girls at home. This birth would finally bring them a boy, their firstborn son—the male child they, like most native Texans, had longed for.

At the town's tiny, 18-bed city hospital, Coach McGraw could do nothing but wait on the sidelines while his players readied for the big game. Fathers were not allowed in the delivery room back in those days. The two little McGraw girls—Donna and Deana—couldn't even be with their mom and dad because children, and their germs, were not welcome on the maternity ward.

Game time quickly approached. In less than 60 minutes, the moment McGraw had dreamed of for so long would become a reality. But, because of the impeding birth, questions plagued him. Would the Hornets have to play without their new coach? Might Joe actually miss the entire season opening game? And couldn't that new baby boy of his hurry up and make his arrival before kickoff?

As it turned out, Phillip Calvin McGraw, Joe's newborn son, had his own game plan in mind. In the first of many big entrances to come, he arrived in this world just 15 minutes before kickoff. As a result, his father missed his first game—the one he had looked forward to for so long.

"They [my parents] tell the story about how pumped he was for his first game," McGraw shares. "The kickoff was at 7:30 P.M., and my mother went into labor with me about an hour before that. He had to miss the game because I was born at 7:15 P.M. It was his whole life's dream, and I broke up his first football game."

Sue Sumner Secondine was among the few who got to hold the newborn future star. The local girl, who had just turned 16, was a nurse's aide at the Vinita hospital. Dressed in a white cotton uniform starched stiff as a board, the blond with the wide smile and pretty blue eyes hidden behind big glasses took temperatures and filled cups with water after school for 25 cents an hour.

She always made a point of checking on the babies of local teachers. After all, teachers are celebrities in small towns. Whenever a teacher or a teacher's wife had a baby, it was always special. But this baby was different. He was the *coach's* boy. "I look at Dr. Phil now and think, I held him as a tiny newborn," Secondine says.

When the four-bed maternity ward overflowed, nurses swaddled newborns and snuggled them in for the night inside dresser drawers in the nursery. McGraw may have spent his first night on this earth sleeping inside a piece of furniture. Quite a humble beginning for Oprah Winfrey's favorite psychologist, the host of one of TV's most popular talk shows, and a self-help author whose every book has been a huge bestseller.

The grandson of a butcher, Phil McGraw grew up in small towns and soaked up the rural talk-and-walk that imbued his personality and became his famous calling card as a shoot-from-the-lip advice guru. He spent much of his youth and adult life following in the footsteps of his ambitious father—a coach turned oil business salesman turned psychologist. But in the end, the son soared higher. Throughout life, there never seemed to be a town big enough to hold the ambitions of a man who would one day become known to the world simply as "Dr. Phil."

■ ■ ■

McGraw's family roots are sunk deep into the black waxy soil and sandy loam of rural Texas. Joe and Jerry McGraw dated and fell in love in high school in their small hometown of Munday, Texas. The town (population 1,500) sits on the rolling, mesquite-covered plains of Knox County in northwest central Texas, halfway between its bigger neighbors—Wichita Falls and Abilene.

Blessed with made-to-order soil for both farming and raising cattle, Munday's residents did both. Corn, wheat, and cotton could all thrive there. But by the 1930s, it was cotton that became the community's lifeblood. Like many of Munday's children, Joe and Jerry chopped cotton, a crop so vital that schools let out for two weeks during the harvest so youngsters could lend a hand in the fields.

The Depression and the Dust Bowl nearly destroyed the local cotton industry. Hundreds of acres of cotton fell out of production and farmers abandoned once-thriving farms. As the heavens rained dirt and their livelihoods fell apart, the people of Munday toiled hard to survive. "Times were tough for everybody, but we had good times," recalls Raymond Carden, who grew up with Joe and Jerry McGraw in Munday.

Joe and Jerry's parents were uneducated, but well acquainted with the worth of an honest day's work. Jerry's parents, with whom Phil spent summers as a child, made a particular impression on their grandson. Mabel Stevens, or "Nanny" as the family called her, stood a spunky 4 feet 11 inches. She ironed other people's clothes to bring in money for the family. Relatives recall how she liked to dip snuff, and how she worked it so enthusiastically that it would roll down her chin. Still spry well into her 80s, Mabel was known to regularly hike up her skirt and crawl over barbed wire fences to pick plums for her homemade jelly.

Just 3 inches shy of 7 feet tall, Mabel's husband of 68 years, Cal, towered over her. Cal owned a business in Munday, and just about everyone knew him. He ran the local freight warehouse where Phil McGraw later worked summers helping his grandfather load and unload cargo. Longtime residents remember Cal for driving his flatbed Dodge so slow down Munday's main street that he tied up traffic. High school boys running alongside the truck for fun could easily keep up. McGraw's grandfather rarely had to replace his truck's tires because he drove so slow they never wore out. Those who grew up around Cal in Munday still joke about this.

Cal and Mabel definitely didn't have a "normal" husband-wife relationship. In fact, McGraw says he first began thinking like a psychologist during those summers he used to spend with his grandparents in Texas as a little boy. He watched them closely and took mental notes on their relationship, later using his grandparents as an example of how some couples successfully defy traditional models of a healthy marriage. As quirky as their relationship may have seemed, Mabel and Cal were happy, he observed.

"They probably didn't speak to each other more than twenty-five words a week," he says. "They did not sleep in the same room, and their only common interest was survival. But even then I noticed that they did relate. No matter where we were or what we were doing they were physically very close and in most cases actually touching in some way."

■ ■ ■

Joe McGraw also grew up in Munday. He was named after his father, a butcher in a local grocery store. Growing up as the older brother to triplet siblings, Joe was just one of the boys in town. He and his friends passed their free time riding donkeys or playing hockey with a tin can and a stick in a vacant lot. One family member recalls that Joe earned the nickname "Spontaneous Combustion" when he nearly burned down the family barn.

Joe was different from many of the other boys he played with in that he was very curious about the world. In high school, "he was pretty good in his books," Carden reflects. "He liked to read. He read a lot . . . newspapers or anything."

Joe was also a jock at Munday High School. He played basketball, football, and ran track. In his senior year, he was already a big boy, standing just over 6 feet and weighing nearly 200 pounds. He was a running back with better than average speed on the football team. Carden was the quarterback, but Joe was the star of the team. In their senior year, they lost only one game to the team that eventually won the district championship. That was the beginning of a legacy of sports and competition that Joe would pass along to his only son.

Joe and Jerry got married before he shipped off with the Navy to serve in World War II. When he returned from his tour of duty, he announced to his family that he'd decided to go to college. Thanks to the U.S. government and the GI Bill, Joe and other returning soldiers could get money for college tuition and even a living allowance. Thousands of young men like him did just that.

No one in his family had ever gone to college, and the news exploded like a bomb. Uneducated relatives, accustomed to simply working hard to make their way in life, ridiculed Joe for wanting to play student. Schooling seemed like a waste of time to them when he could just go out and get a real job. But Joe was determined. Even though no one else in his family had ever gone past high school, he knew that a college education was the ticket to a better life for himself and his new bride, especially if they wanted to get out of Munday. So he ignored the criticism.

The two left for Oklahoma, where the University of Tulsa had offered McGraw a scholarship to play football. He couldn't know it then, but he was also blazing a trail for his future son. In the years to come, Phil McGraw would follow the same path, attending the same college to play the same sport.

■ ■ ■

Joe and Jerry took their Texas ways and rural outlook on life with them to Oklahoma. People often said that both McGraws, but especially Jerry, had a lot of country in them. Even today, the bright lights of Hollywood and stardom that shine on her son don't hold a glamorous appeal for Jerry, family members say. Jerry ("Granma" to Phil and the grandchildren) is just a country girl at heart who still lives in Texas.

Though Phil McGraw now lives far removed from his humble past—making his home in a multimillion-dollar Beverly Hills mansion and hobnobbing with celebrities—he goes out of his way to portray himself as just a good ol' country boy.

On a trip to Tulsa for a Junior League fund-raiser in 2002, the man who is famous for take-no-prisoners, in-your-face confrontations waxed uncharacteristically sentimental: "This is the heart of America," he told his audience. "This to me is the grassroots of America. People here know the value of a dollar, the value of hard work, and the value of family. This is where you can keep your feet on the ground. I'm proud to be from here and [to] have grown up here."

Joe struggled academically at the University of Tulsa, earning poor grades in almost every subject. He flunked out of his sociology class, got a C in general psychology, and barely graduated with a 2.008 overall grade point average. He got a mere three A's during his undergraduate years—in football, physical education, and a teaching class. Despite his disappointing grades, Joe was awarded a degree in education in 1950 and took the coaching and teaching job in Vinita, one of the oldest villages in Oklahoma. Vinita, Dr. Phil's birthplace, sits on Route 66, "America's Main Street," in former frontier country in the northeastern corner of Oklahoma.

Settled through the sweat and effort of cowboys and Cherokee Indians, Vinita was built along a railroad. In fact, it was the railroad companies that determined the askew placement of streets. Trains still frequently rumble through the town with throaty whistle blasts, blocking lunchtime traffic as they pass through.

"There isn't a true north and south, west and east street in town," says Sue Secondine, who still lives there. "Vinita doesn't run straight with the rest of the world."

Vinita is an oddly befitting hometown for a man who has carved out his own unique celebrity niche. In the early 1950s when the McGraws came to town, farming, oil, coal, and cattle were the town's main industries. Vinita was a lively little place then, with two dime stores, dress shops, shoe stores, small cafés, and three movie theaters. "The streets were full of people, especially on Saturday when the farmers came to town and did their trading," Secondine remembers.

The town hasn't grown much since the McGraws lived there, but the dress shops and dime stores have been replaced by small businesses like the Shout and Sack Deli, Happy House Fine Chinese Restaurant, and Loco Joe's Automobiles. Vinita is now home to several Fortune 500 factories and a minimum-security state prison.

Besides being a stop along Route 66, Vinita's main tourist attraction is the so-called world's largest McDonald's—29,000 square feet of Happy Meals and Big Macs that span the local slice of turnpike. The self-proclaimed World's Largest Calf Fry Festival and Cook-off, held every September, is Vinita's other claim to fame.

Though many of Vinita's residents know that Dr. Phil was born there, they don't make a fuss about it. By contrast, another Oklahoma native, cowboy humorist Will Rogers, is a special favorite son. Rogers has his own historical monument at one of the town's entrances and the turnpike and annual rodeo are named after him. Rogers attended college in town and still has relatives nearby.

■ ■ ■

Vinita High had a long tradition of successful sports teams before Joe McGraw came along. The school boasted state championships back to the 1910s in softball, baseball, football, and even women's basketball. Photos of the town's championship teams are preserved in glass cases at the town's Eastern Trail Museum.

As high-profile and important as the football coach's job may have been, there was little money in it for Joe. When Phil McGraw was born, his family lived in a tiny, frame house in a tidy neighborhood on the right side of the tracks. The house on South Scraper Street still stands today next to the Vinita Flag and Apron Company, maker of American flags and those colorful work aprons worn by employees at chain discount and home improvement stores. But none of the current neighbors seem to know that a celebrity was born on their street.

"Dr. Phil grew up like a lot of us," Secondine says. "It was a strong family. He grew up knowing what the world was about. I don't think he had anything handed to him on a silver platter. You grow up here knowing the value of a dollar."

At the old high school, which has since been replaced by a newer building, Joe also coached track, taught marriage and family classes, and put his psychology education to work as a guidance counselor. The yearbook describes his duties as "personal problems," which he helped many of his students solve. "He had a profound influence on everyone, which I didn't realize until later in life," says Eddie Berry, quarterback of Coach McGraw's team.

Former Vinita students remember Joe as a strict man with a kind heart. He greeted students in the halls with a smile and liked to tease the girlfriends of his players. Berry recalls how the coach took his team members on a field trip to Tulsa where he introduced the boys to football players and coaches at the university where he had once played ball. The small gesture was a big deal to the boys from Vinita.

But Coach McGraw had a tough side, too, that his players did their best to avoid. He was a blunt, no-bull, no-nonsense leader on the field. Tom Clanton, who also played football for Joe, remembers his coach's tendency to fiddle with the stem of his watch when he talked, a sure sign that he was thinking hard about something "and you better listen."

"He was somebody you respected," remembers Clanton, gray-haired now, yet still tall and slim—just like he was in high school when he wore jersey No. 41 and his friends called him Tommy. "He [Joe] told it like it was. He would never lie to you."

Girls tended to have a different reaction to Coach McGraw. "I was scared of him," Secondine says. "He was a big man. He was kind of gruff. I was in his study hall and I minded my Ps and Qs. I was a little old country farm girl and I was scared to death to get into trouble. He didn't take any guff off the boys in there either. He ran a pretty tight ship."

Not so tight, though, that he couldn't proudly invite his players over to view his newborn son. "I guess the last time I saw Phil McGraw he weighed about eight pounds," Clanton remembers.

His family has run Clanton's Café on Route 66 in Vinita for four generations. An eight-foot-tall red sign outside with white letters spelling "EAT" beckons hungry passersby. People from miles around visit the restaurant to enjoy its chicken-fried steak—fresh cut and hand-breaded, never frozen.

Inside, diners sit in maroon vinyl booths surrounded by darkly paneled walls that display framed photos of the town and the famous folk who have stopped by from time to time. Ronnie Dunn of the country and western duo Brooks & Dunn courted his wife in the booths there.

Clanton, recently retired from the restaurant's daily operations, wouldn't mind adding a photo of his high school coach's famous son to his collection on the café walls. It would take a place of honor alongside pictures of Mickey Mantle, who was raised 30 miles up the road, and another famous local—King Tut, the bull from the Elizabeth Taylor movie, *Giant*. "If he's half the man his dad was," Clanton says of Phil McGraw, "he's a pretty good man."

In Joe's first year, the team posted a losing 2–8 record, but Berry says the season was no reflection on the coach's abilities. He did the best he could with the players he had. Joe never had much of a chance to improve on this record. The McGraws didn't stay in Vinita longer than a couple of football seasons.

Berry and his teammates never knew why their coach left town so soon. They had no idea they lost him to a siren call. It came from the oil industry, which was just beginning to boom in the Southwest.

■ ■ ■

During World War II, oil exploration and field development slowed considerably because trained workers were in the armed services and steel was more urgently needed for the war effort. In the postwar years of the 1950s, the markets for oil and gas boomed, prompting a surge in drilling as companies began opening new oil and gas fields. These growing oil companies needed workers.

Lured once again by the possibility of a more lucrative living and better lifestyle for his young family, Joe left teaching and coaching for a job in this new, exciting field. Some of the best advice his dad ever gave him, Phil McGraw says, was to "create your own experience. Make a decision and pull the trigger." That's exactly what Joe did.

Living by what he preached, Joe pulled the trigger on yet another career path. He took a job as a salesman for an oil equipment company. The demands of this position required him to shuttle his family back and forth between towns in Oklahoma, Texas, and Colorado. Like the vagabond children in a military family, Phil McGraw, his two older sisters, and his one younger sister, Brenda, spent their childhood moving from homes on one dusty road after another.

Joe fathered his children the same way he coached the players on his team. He was a tough dad at home whose high expectations forced his son to grow up earlier than most children do, according to Phil McGraw's friends, who wonder whether he lost out on a real childhood because of it.

As the only boy, Joe's son had to do a man's share of the work in contributing to the family's well-being, whether it was mowing lawns, delivering newspapers, or eventually helping Joe in his new sales job. "We grew up in a lot of small towns . . . just trying to get by," McGraw says. "We were just really scrapping around for anything we could. We just did what we could to gather up enough money to get by on."

As tough as his father may have been, McGraw received a lot of loving from the women at home. His older sisters adored their only brother, and McGraw says that he was treated like a prince. They took him to school with them when he was 3 because they didn't want to leave him at home. Off he went, carrying his own little sack lunch. "He was the one and only and they just idolized him," mother Jerry says.

McGraw developed his now-famous tart tongue early on, not surprising considering the sense of entitlement the family bestowed on him as the only son. At age 3, he tried to teach one of his grandmothers, who was visiting, how to turn on the family stove. "He couldn't speak very well," his sister, Deana, recalls. "Finally, our grandmother said, 'Son, I can't understand a word you're saying.' Phil said very clearly, 'What, are you an idiot?'"

Before he was even in nursery school, McGraw was already telling it like it is, or at least how he saw it. "I think he has a lot of his dad's no-nonsense," says Secondine. "One thing I like about Dr. Phil is that everything is pretty much cut-and-dried."

That approach scores a lot of points with the kind of folks McGraw grew up around in Texas and Oklahoma, many of whom display the same regional tendency to cut quickly to the chase. They put a lot of stock in plain speaking and folks who don't varnish the truth. The only difference between them and McGraw is that McGraw is now making millions doing it.

He's always been a smart boy. "When Phil was little, he was basically just serious like he is now. He was determined with everything that he did. He was very intelligent," says sister, Deana.

■ ■ ■

As a youngster, and some would say later in life as a grown-up, McGraw's tendency to find trouble got the best of him. He was a Boy Scout for all of two weeks before being kicked out of his troop for throwing rocks at cars. His mom, the troop's leader, had to continue on without him.

He was never much interested in school either. It just didn't excite him. His mother recalls a visit from one teacher who said that little Phil needed to be challenged because he was so bored in school. "They suggested the piano, then they said after he learned it he'd never play it again because he was that bored with it. He'd conquer it and he would be through with it."

But there was one place McGraw was never bored. Like sports, flying would become another lifelong passion. Always aiming for the stars in one way or another, Joe was an avid pilot who somehow managed to work flight time into his day jobs. Flying was nearly second nature in the McGraw family. According to family members, one of McGraw's sisters could also fly a plane and two of his sisters married fellow pilots.

For McGraw, flying became such a guiding influence that whenever he talks about the most influential people in his life, the list always includes his father and two unforgettable pilots who crossed his path.

McGraw was a grade-schooler in the late 1950s when he met Gene Knight, a flying bootlegger. At the time, the McGraws were living in rural Oklahoma, where many counties were "dry." Because liquor sales were illegal, bootleggers like Knight were in constant demand. He made his living flying whiskey around Oklahoma. McGraw was in awe of this man who had such a great affinity for life. Knight was someone who loved his job and was so obviously fulfilling his passion. "Son, if you're not having fun," Knight was known to say, "change what you're doing!"

Joe McGraw was one of Knight's regular customers. On Saturday afternoons he and Phil would drive out of town and meet Knight in the middle of a big cotton patch, where McGraw remembers that even the local sheriff sometimes helped the bootlegger unload his cargo.

In McGraw's little-boy eyes, Knight must have been as dashing as Errol Flynn, tall and handsome in a leather flying jacket. One day Knight offered to take him for a ride in his old rattletrap plane. "As soon as we were airborne, I told myself, 'I'm gonna be a pilot,' and just as soon as I came of age, I got my license. I have been flying my entire life, a direct result of Gene Knight's influence," McGraw says.

By age 12, McGraw could handle the controls so competently that his father let him fly with him to deliver equipment to oil fields in Colorado. "I spent a lot of time with him flying in and out of those mountain landing strips up there," McGraw says. "I can remember going with him at 2 A.M. and we'd load something in the back and off we'd go in the dead of the night into the mountains . . . that's where I learned how to fly."

Later in life, McGraw took more lessons from a flying cowboy named Bill Solomon, a man who impressed him as one of the most sensible, down-to-earth people he had ever met. Even when he was talking about flying, Solomon seemed to be imparting lessons for life.

Solomon taught him that "when you are airborne, what you've got is yourself. You'd better depend on who you are. If you're in trouble, some guy 30 miles away in a radio room on the ground won't save you. It's you and the airplane. You'd better know yourself and you'd better depend on yourself."

McGraw, a man who has said with no apology that he considers himself the most important person in his own life, took the lesson to heart.

Like Father, Like Son

He's a role model not just because he was my father but because he overcame huge obstacles in his life. He taught me about vision and about never quitting. He showed me that no matter who you are, you can create a place of distinction in this world.

By the time Phil McGraw was 12, his father, Joe, was still trying to figure out what he wanted to do with his life. While searching for his true calling, he kept yanking his family from town to town, as he went from job to job.

Since the young McGraw moved just about every three or four years as a boy, he doesn't really have a place to call his hometown. One home blended into another into another, so much so that he can't even place some of his earliest memories.

"The earliest thing I remember I was three or four years old, I think, and I had on a little scrawny T-shirt and some scrawny shorts standing barefoot in front of a white frame house kind of out in the middle of nowhere," he says. "And I think it's where we lived in Oklahoma."

McGraw seemed to be hitting his own stride as he finished up his grade-school years in a suburb of Denver. That's where he and his family settled after his father took yet another job—this time flying drill bits and tools to oil workers in the Rocky Mountains. Easily bored in school, the boy was finally bringing home good grades. At the end of one school year, McGraw proudly won the Athlete of the Year award.

The McGraws lived modestly in suburbia in a three-bedroom, one-bathroom tract home with a one-car garage, just like everyone else's on the block. Like his father who had been "one of the boys" hanging out in Munday, Texas, McGraw was just one of the boys hanging out with the neighborhood kids in Denver, whiling away the hours racing bicycles with his friends and strategizing dirt-clod wars.

Then, there were those trips to the "Valley of Death," which stood in a big empty field in the neighborhood. A trench that was four feet deep ran from one end of the field to the other. McGraw and his friends built what could barely pass as a bridge over the ditch out of a single two-by-six board, and rode their bikes over the slim board at full speed.

This was no simple boyhood stunt for the psychologist in the making. It allowed him to discover at an early age just how powerful mind could be over matter. McGraw must have figured out how much success he could achieve if he simply envisioned it. If he could picture himself riding successfully across that board without falling—and focused on nothing else—he could do it. Trepidation and worst-case scenarios, on the other hand, were his enemies. If he rode up to the board thinking that he might slip off or miss it altogether, it would usually happen.

This apparent pattern has persisted throughout his life— tamping down emotions like fear to size up, break down, and overcome a challenge. He admits he's not the most emotionally expressive person. It is almost as if emotions get too much in his analytical way. "My approach is think through it, get a solution, and go to it," he says.

But over the span of McGraw's entire life, it seems there has been one emotion he's been unsuccessful at keeping in check. Even as a young boy, his anger has regularly gotten him into trouble.

McGraw does not like to have his opinion or his say challenged, according to former friends, and he can get mean when it happens. That may be why some observe that he seems more comfortable, confident, and charismatic in front of large audiences—where he has control of the proceedings—than he does in one-on-one settings. Personal, face-to-face moments have not always gone well for him in his life, even as long ago as grade school.

■ ■ ■

Falling into the Valley of Death was the least of McGraw's problems back then. When he reflects on the most defining moments in his life—a journey through the past he encourages others to take—he looks back on an incident so stunning that he claims it changed his self-concept for the rest of his life.

It began with a playground brawl.

A group of bigger, sixth-grade bullies started picking on some of the younger students, including McGraw, who defended himself by hitting one of his attackers in the face as hard as he could with a basketball. The fight ended when the boys were hauled into the principal's office, where McGraw was happy to see a teacher named Mrs. Johnson. She knew his reputation as a good student. He was certain Mrs. Johnson would defend him and put in a good word for him. But it didn't quite happen that way.

Instead of standing up for him, Mrs. Johnson yelled back. "Oh, you're Mr. Tough Guy, aren't you?" she berated him. "You don't take any guff off of *anybody*, do you?" Her reaction shocked

McGraw. How could she let him down this way? Could it be that Mrs. Johnson was trying to protect herself in front of the principal? Was she warning him not to make waves in her world, McGraw wondered?

"In a flash, it hit me right there in the principal's office that I could no longer assume that life was fair," McGraw says. "It was not fair. It was not objective. It became clear to me that the person I had to look to was me. The only person who 'had my back' was me."

Still processing this real-world slap in the face, an unfettered McGraw let Mrs. Johnson have it: "You're right. I don't take any guff from anybody. And that includes you!" The principal immediately suspended McGraw for three days.

McGraw claims that, from this moment on, he never again felt comfortable in any academic setting or, for that matter, any other place where someone tried to exert authority over him. One teacher's tirade in the fifth grade forever ruined the experience of school, he suggests; and indeed his future school days did not go smoothly. By his own admission, he likely wouldn't have made it through high school had it not been for the discipline of participating in sports.

■ ■ ■

Mrs. Johnson wasn't the only adult to show a young McGraw that even those he thought he could trust and felt closest to could let him down. Other harsh lessons came at home. The sales job his father took may have paid more than he earned as a teacher, but it also brought a new set of pressures to perform and to sell. As always, Joe pushed himself to a dangerous brink. Throughout his many careers, Joe's business socializing created contention between McGraw's parents that they never truly resolved, McGraw says. Wining and dining clients seemed to be part of every job Joe took. The McGraws often fought over how involved Jerry should be in Joe's business pursuits. He wanted her to be more social and to help him entertain clients, customers, and colleagues, but she wouldn't have anything to do with it. As much as Joe pressured her, the country girl said she hated entertaining.

The darker side of all that entertaining was that Joe began to drink too much. McGraw speaks freely about how much alcohol changed his father. He hated the drinking and didn't like the man his father became under the influence. It was so bad that McGraw says he himself has only touched a few drops of liquor in his life because of it, although former friends recall sharing drinks with him when he was a young adult.

"He was an alcoholic," McGraw says about his father. "I don't think he ever used that word, but everybody else did. I saw a brilliant, articulate, and caring man greatly diminished when he would drink."

Perhaps a blessing in disguise, the bottom began to fall out of the oil industry in the late 1950s when domestic demand for oil began to subside. Ever on the lookout for better opportunities, Joe could see that the end of the ride was near. He decided to dump his dead-end sales job and, along with it, the pressures that contributed to his drinking problem. Pulling the trigger once again on a life-changing move, he decided to go back to school in 1964 at the age of 40, this time to get his Ph.D. in psychology from the University of Oklahoma. The McGraws were ready to leave Colorado behind.

■ ■ ■

Wayne McKamie Jr., a psychologist who worked with Joe and Phil McGraw in the 1980s, says Joe made sacrifices for his wife and children, sometimes at their expense. "He was just a good ol' boy—very down to earth—and Phil saw in him this guy who literally knocked down all kinds of challenges to better himself educationally," McKamie says. "He certainly wasn't a traditional dad at all, because Phil pretty much raised himself when he wasn't there. His dad was in school and Phil was alone a lot."

Though McGraw says his dad never missed one of his sports games or school events, he has tried to avoid repeating any mistakes of the past with his own two sons. Once, McGraw even flew home to Dallas from New York just to see one of his son's basketball games and returned to New York the same night. "But, you know, you make a commitment, it becomes like a dare," he says.

McGraw says he doesn't take the job of fathering lightly and acknowledges that patience isn't something he always has in abundance. Also elusive is that precious balance between family and work that some say his own father couldn't find.

"One of the things I'm really nurturing in my life is the ability to say no 'cause I got a lot of people asking me for things and I've gotten better at saying no," he says. "But sometimes you get caught up in it and you look up and it's been two or three days and you haven't really spent the time that you need to with your child."

McKamie believes that his former colleague actually benefited in some ways from his nomadic childhood. Being forced to continually make new friends and fit into new environments nurtured his impressive chameleon-like personality, an asset that would help McGraw succeed in business as an adult, McKamie observes.

"If he went to the bank, he could talk bank language. If he went to the oil company, he could talk oil language. If he went to a law firm, he could talk law language," says McKamie. "I don't think he had any fear. He was never intimidated by anyone or anything. He'd walk right in like he owned the place.

"He can walk into any arena, he's used to that. I never thought he was a real outgoing individual, but at the same time new environments aren't something new to him, even today. Maybe it's what has prepared him for these new worlds he has conquered."

■ ■ ■

With Joe's return to college full-time, the family's income dropped dramatically. McGraw, who has made a fortune telling other people to listen to the wake-up calls in their lives, says one of his biggest came the day he realized that his family was poor. With his dad back in school again, "everything just stopped," McGraw says. "We were a family of four kids and we spent a lot of time wondering where we were going to get our next meal. And that was a wake-up call. When you live in an 'eat-what-you-kill' world, you'd better jack it up and get in the game. So I kind of got results-based at that point in my life, and have never been the same since."

Everyone pitched in to keep food on the table, even if it sometimes was just ketchup-and-mustard sandwiches for dinner. His mom took a job at Sears, while he and his dad delivered newspapers. "My dad said, 'Successful people will do what unsuccessful people won't,'" Phil's sister, Deana, recalls.

In those times, being successful meant rolling out of bed every morning at 4:30 to throw newspapers out of the family car, covering more than 50 miles each time. "I'd fold and he'd drive. It took us about 2½ hours every day, and then we'd have to do it again in the afternoon," McGraw says. "That was the time in my life when we were the poorest. It was the first time in my life I was aware I was poor."

Since then, McGraw has lived as though he's afraid of being poor again. One of the thoughts that motivated him to stick with the college psychology classes he hated so much was envisioning how much money he could make from it all someday: "I did take a lot of work at one time because I got so far behind in not taking school seriously that then I decided hey, you're going to school for you, buddy, not for anybody else. Your teacher doesn't care what kind of grades you make. You're going to sell this information very soon and the more you have the more you can sell."

While Joe was in grad school, the McGraws lived with Phil's oldest sister, Deana, and her then husband, Troy Linthicum, in Oklahoma City. "They moved in with us because money was tight back then," says Linthicum, who was married to Deana for about

13 years. "We bought the house they were living in and we told them they could stay with us."

Linthicum watched McGraw grow into a teenager—one with an appetite as big as his burly, linebacker physique, just like his dad's. By the time he was in high school, McGraw stood over 6 feet tall. "We lived close to a Sonic drive-in and he could eat three of those foot-long chili cheese dogs [in one sitting]," Linthicum says.

Apparently to McGraw, *free* food of any kind was even better, though it sometimes took petty larceny to get it. At the supermarket, "he was sly," Linthicum remembers. "He'd go back to the deli and say 'Give me a pound of gizzards.' We'd go down and get some bread and he'd start to eat those gizzards right there in the store." By the time they got to the checkout, the bag and gizzards were gone—leaving nothing left to pay for.

■ ■ ■

Scoring a free bag of gizzards was small potatoes compared with some of McGraw's other youthful escapades. As difficult as times were in Oklahoma, Joe still managed somehow to buy his son a new Yamaha 250 motorcycle when he was 13. Joe reminded him to drive it carefully since McGraw was too young to have insurance coverage. "And whatever you do," Joe told him, "don't let anyone else ride it."

Of course, McGraw let one of his buddies ride it two weeks later. The friend came "screaming down the street and hit a Buick Riviera at 80 mph on the side," McGraw says. "Almost killed him but didn't. 'Course it destroyed the motorcycle."

The worst part was yet to come—'fessing up to his dad. "Boy, you better tell me he took that motorcycle without your permission," Joe told him. For a fleeting moment, McGraw considered lying, but bravely decided not to. "Your telling me the truth when it'd be so much easier not to is worth more to me than that motorcycle or the cost," Joe replied.

The moral that McGraw should have learned from this incident: Always be honest. Apparently, the lesson didn't stick. Years later, Linthicum flew with McGraw down to the Bahamas on a trip that ended with another harrowing escape.

"We were having a good time down there," Linthicum says. "We rented a car, and right there at the rental place it says 'Do not take these cars on the beach and get stuck. If you do, you have to pay a towing fee.' And the first thing we did was got stuck on the beach."

They rocked the compact Pinto back and forth trying to free it. Linthicum, pushing on the outside of the car, kept yelling to McGraw in the driver's seat, "Put it in reverse, put it in reverse." Back and forth, back and forth, "put it in reverse, put it in reverse!" The stick shift broke right off in McGraw's hand. He stuck it out the window and yelled at Linthicum, "You put it in reverse!"

They wound up leaving the car stuck in the sand. When they called the rental agent and told him what happened, he said he was going to charge them for the wrecker fee. But he never got the chance. According to Linthicum, they caught a quick ride to the airport and ran to McGraw's plane. "That guy [the rental agent] was right behind us," Linthicum says. "We took off and looked down and he was still sitting there."

The McGraw spirit has always been unquestionably headstrong. In some ways, McGraw and his father were mirror images of each other, but in other ways they were quite different. Some believe that from early on, Joe may have tried to mold his only son in his image. But if that was the case, McGraw clearly was determined to do everything bigger, bolder, and better than his father. He wanted to be better and more successful in business, make more money, and be a bigger fish in a bigger pond.

As he grew older, Joe seemed comfortable with his life, with his psychology work, with his RV, and with his cigars. He didn't crave the country-club lifestyle, colleagues say. But his son sure did. Even as a child, McGraw swaggered through life as though he owned the universe. Some called it arrogance; others called it confidence.

"They're just a couple of characters," says McKamie. "Joe had this kind of personality that Phil can express at times. Joe could have you laughing so easily. He was just very personable."

McKamie first met both McGraws on a Wichita Falls tennis court in the early 1980s. McGraw and his dad loved tennis. Every workday ended the same way—on the court or on their way to a tennis tournament by 5 P.M. Football injuries and extra weight slowed down Joe in his later years, but he still competed fiercely.

McGraw's relationship with his father could get raw on and off the tennis court. When they argued, which was often after they went into business together, people found them intolerable to be around. They butted heads, as well as overblown egos, and people joke that they could argue about anything, even the weather.

"The thing about the McGraws, you either loved them or hated them," says McKamie. "They could be a little much. They were very strong personalities."

Another former colleague, Thelma Box, believes that a lot of the friction between father and son stemmed from things that happened during Phil's childhood, a closed book that the McGraw family rarely opens for public viewing. McGraw takes great care to talk as little as possible about many of the particulars of his upbringing.

"Phil does not believe in inner child work," says Box, who founded a series of motivational seminars with McGraw in Texas. "It's the real basic difference in our philosophy. He didn't believe in doing inner child work and so he never went back to do the healing on that.

"My feeling is, feelings buried alive never die. He buried all those childhood feelings and he's still dealing with them."

As much as the two men clashed, the McGraw sense of family loyalty remained strong. "When we argued, we argued passionately," McGraw admits, "but we were always shoulder to shoulder when we needed to be."

McKamie concurs that nothing could truly divide Joe and Phil. "Sometimes when they fought, it was horrible," he says. "But if someone came after them, or one of them was in trouble, they would protect each other, they would go to bat for each other.

"Phil, at some level, really admired his dad. He's more open today about it. When I [knew them] there was too much of a 'Who's going to run the show?' kind of thing [going on]."

Neither McGraw backed away from telling it like it was. That was a family trait. But their ways did not strike people as insincere or put on, McKamie says. What you saw was what you got with both men. "People in Texas can be big b-sers. That's something the McGraws were not," McKamie adds. "You can have a lot of bs with that, but the McGraws were straight shooters, and people liked that.

"They knew how to be respectful and carry themselves with that kind of integrity. They were just very daring, bold. And that will get you a long way with people, telling people what they need to hear. That is something they both had in common, but I do think that Phil took it to a whole different level.

"Phil was quite a motivator. He's a good people coach. But I would say the differences, from my point of view, are that Phil was more sensitive and broader in his scope in dealing with people from various factions in life. He had . . . a greater sensitivity to people. I feel like he learned a lot from his father."

It's no surprise to McKamie that Joe's former football players hailed him as a coach. McKamie later saw the same nurturing style in Joe, the psychologist. "He was a very dedicated man, as far as working with his patients, and very caring," he says. "But he was also very practical and used no-nonsense wisdom with his patients. He worked well with them and could motivate them."

Some of that motivational charm came from Joe's down-home patter. People say Joe could turn a phrase into a homily, making common sense colorful and quotable. Among the phrases from his father that McGraw often quotes: "Worrying is like rocking in a chair—it's something to do, but you don't get anywhere." And, "Don't let your alligator mouth overload your humming-bird ass."

■ ■ ■

McGraw's first step toward following in his father's career path came when his junior high football team played a team from the Salvation Army. That's the day, he says, that the importance of psychology became real to him.

"We were bad-ass. We had the black jerseys, the black helmets, and here these kids come wearing rolled-up jeans and loafers for football shoes," McGraw says. "They beat us like they were clapping for a barn dance. At that point I really got interested in why some people, with all the advantages in the world, don't do well, and those with no advantages can be absolute champions."

He couldn't shake this new fascination with winners. "I started getting interested in what makes people do what they do," he says. "Why were these kids who had none of the advantages so good, and those of us who had all of the advantages weren't so good?"

Why were some people superstars and others not? Whatever the answer, McGraw knew which camp he wanted to join. "I thought if I could ever figure that out that would be an unbelievable edge in life. I started studying success."

He studied hard, but on his own terms. He says he would go on to read all of his father's texts from graduate school by the time he ever hit college.

But before running off to the university, McGraw first had to survive high school. In the mid-1960s, Joe moved from Oklahoma to suburban Kansas City to complete his psychology internship.

Worried about the rough crowd his son was hanging out with in Oklahoma, he took Phil along so he could keep an eye on him.

One last time, Joe uprooted his son. That Phil McGraw was not happy about this move was apparent to his new friends in Kansas. "I think he was lonely, being away from home and his mother and sisters," says Rocky Hughes, who befriended McGraw when they were both sophomores.

McGraw's dread turned out to be well-placed. In high school, he seemed to forget the lessons he learned in the Valley of Death, where he could envision himself riding his bicycle over that skinny board and making it safely to the other side.

Before long, a pretty blonde would catch McGraw's eye, temporarily drawing his attention off his newfound goal to find success in life and ultimately causing him to fall.

Some people are really well-read and they took Latin, and they know the origins of words. I went to school and played football.

Phil McGraw stood head and shoulders above his high school classmates in suburban Kansas City. Already a strapping 6 feet 4 inches tall by the age of 16, he loomed large over his adolescent peers. When he walked down the halls, everyone took notice. His receding hairline was also memorable. It made him look much older than he really was. His mature appearance paid off when he and his under-aged friends sneaked into local bars trying to buy beer.

McGraw's Oklahoma drawl set him further apart from his midwestern classmates, some of whom teased him and accused him of sounding like a hick. But it wasn't just his physical presence that made McGraw stand out in the Class of 1968. Truth is, McGraw was hardly a standout student even though, as the new sophomore with the funny accent, he was certainly a curiosity.

In a class of some 750, there were lots of popular men on campus, and McGraw wasn't one of them. In fact, before his star began to rise, McGraw returned to Kansas City in 1998 for his 30-year class reunion. Later, many of his former classmates were shocked to learn that the man who would become known as "Dr. Phil" was the big, tall, expensively dressed bald guy they hardly even noticed at the reunion.

Few believed that the Phil McGraw they went to high school with was the Phil McGraw making regular appearances on *The Oprah Winfrey Show* and whose picture was showing up on magazine covers all over the world. "He called me the year of the reunion and he wanted to go out and have drinks," says high school friend Rocky Hughes, who graduated with McGraw. "He told me he'd been doing the *Oprah* show and I thought, 'Yeah, Phil, feed me some more crap.'"

Even now, as McGraw's former classmates try to reconcile the boy they knew so long ago with the man on TV, they can't help but wonder: Is his success merely a matter of being in the right place at the right time?

Some would say that in high school, McGraw earned his celebrity primarily through his relationship with a certain girl. For two years, he was the boyfriend of a bubbly blonde with brown eyes, who was the homecoming queen. Her name was Debbie Higgins, and she says McGraw was her first love. Higgins was the head cheerleader McGraw set out to woo and would later marry with disastrous results. Until recently, he rarely spoke of this relationship, only mentioning it in passing when pressed by reporters.

■ ■ ■

McGraw spent three years at Shawnee Mission North High School. One of Kansas City's largest suburban schools at the time, it was filled with kids from predominantly middle- and upper-middle-class homes. Former classmates describe their alma mater as an almost idyllic place—good people with good values and good work ethics. Kids knew right from wrong back then. When they were wrong, they owned up to their actions. As testament to its high academic standards, a large percentage of North's graduates went on to college.

Tradition and school pride ran high. After a likeness of the school's Indian mascot was painted on the floor outside the principal's office, students, out of respect, took great care not to walk across it. Stanchions still protect that precious piece of tile at the school today.

With strong football, basketball, and track teams, athletics ruled at North in the 1960s, and McGraw was one of the jocks. Sports were so important that practically everyone belonged to the pep club. Girls wore skirts and corduroy jackets in the school colors of red and black, and the entire student body attended afternoon pep rallies on football Fridays. The players always looked smart and cool in their letter sweaters. McGraw was no exception. For away games, students would pack into more than a half dozen school buses and caravan to enemy territory.

■ ■ ■

Since football was the most popular sport at North, the football team occupied one of the loftiest rungs on the school's social ladder. Players were known for crazy antics such as "hog piles," in which they'd throw themselves into a giant heap in the hallways to show off and express their team spirit. If a guy was on the football team, most people on campus knew who he was. McGraw played football every year at North, but the gridiron wasn't his only passion. He also liked basketball. But even though he was one of the tallest boys in his class, he never made the varsity team.

On the football field, McGraw was one of the unsung heroes on the line. Known for his aggressive blocking, he played both offensive and defensive tackle on the varsity team his senior year. North finished the season 9–0, becoming the unofficial state champs.

McGraw's coach and teammates remember him fondly as a hard worker. Along with the rest of the team, he endured two-a-day workouts during the preseason under the scorching Kansas sun. He was a disciplined player who abided by and respected the coach's rules, with no questions asked. Those who broke the rules got tossed off the team. This happened to one of McGraw's teammates. It was a punishment that made a big impression on McGraw and the others.

Being part of North's championship team gave McGraw a stability and direction in his young life that friends say he didn't have at home. McGraw contends that he probably would have dropped out of school his junior or senior year if it hadn't been for his coaches, who kept a tight rein on him.

"The thing I liked about him was his willingness to get things done," says classmate Ed Dallam, quarterback of North's 1967 championship team. "He just had that sort of determined look and was always ready to go."

Though not one of the stars on campus, McGraw was a tough competitor on and off the field. Those who knew him say he didn't like to lose in any situation.

In his senior year, he took a business economics class from Donald Alpaugh. The first-year teacher had only boys in his business classes. Like McGraw, many of them were football players, and they could be a little restless. "Some of those guys, including him, were kind of ornery," Alpaugh says. "I just remember them being a little feisty, not mean or anything."

During their senior year, Alpaugh helped his students stage a mock trial that offered an early flash of the confrontational, in-your-face style that would later become McGraw's trademark.

McGraw was the prosecutor. Richard Kenley was the defense attorney, defending another student who played the part of a teacher accused of student brutality. "As the trial went on, the fella I had was a very, very bad witness. Phil got him on the stand and just tore him up," Kenley remembers. As a last-ditch strategy, Kenley switched his client's plea to insanity. The move swayed the jury, which voted not guilty. McGraw was livid.

"He was almost jumping up and down," Kenley reflects. "He thought he had won. When he lost that case, he was just madder than a wet hen. He was intense. Intense is the word [that best describes him]. He just had that stick-to-itiveness."

■ ■ ■

It is surprising how reluctant many of McGraw's friends from high school are about dragging their memories of him into the open. Some don't have much to say about their former classmate because he was often an enigma to them. When they lived in Kansas City, the McGraws kept to themselves. Best friend Hughes didn't even know that Joe McGraw battled alcoholism during those years until he heard McGraw talk about it on a television biography program. "There were things in the family that weren't open to us," Hughes reveals.

Former friends choose their words carefully when talking about those years. Some describe the young McGraw as the strong, silent type, not someone who would strike up conversations easily with others. Others say he was a charmer who could turn it on when he had the spotlight, a characteristic they still see in him today.

More often, though, he's described as "being strung tight" and "very physical," like a bully with a short fuse. One picture of him in his high school yearbook shows McGraw snoozing in typing class with bandages wrapped around his hands because he had hurt them in a fight.

In one television interview, a CNN reporter asked McGraw whether he was a wild kid. "There were times," McGraw admitted. "In high school and college, my friends and I were pretty violent. It wouldn't be unusual to find us in a bar fight before the end of the night on a regular basis and that's not my proudest hour. I probably shouldn't be talking about that."

"And what did that do for you at that time?" the reporter wondered.

"Well, it got it out of my system, I can tell you that," McGraw replied.

"Was it because of anger that you had? We're going to do a little psychoanalysis here now," the reporter kidded.

"Yeah, do a little psychoanalysis . . . I grew up in locker rooms and my reputation was I'd fight a buzz saw if I had half a chance and that was just the dumbest part of my life," McGraw reflected. "But I got over it pretty quick and I've had no tendencies like that since that time. So I think it was a phase I went through."

From what he sees of McGraw's techniques with people on television, Kenley doesn't think his former classmate has changed much since then. "It's the same aggressive personality," he says. "But he's polished now. He has learned to speak. He must have had some good college instruction because he's very articulate now."

■ ■ ■

Former classmate Larry McCarthy, now a lieutenant colonel in the United States Army Reserve, recalls receiving an early dose of McGraw's toughness. During football season in the fall of 1967, McCarthy was working at a local grocery store one Saturday night, he says, when McGraw came in and bought a couple of quarts and six packs of beer. The town had just passed a law banning sales of beer to anyone under 21, and McGraw was clearly underage.

About an hour later, McCarthy recalls, McGraw came back, this time with girlfriend Debbie Higgins in the car. According to McCarthy, McGraw walked inside and casually bought more beer. When McGraw left, McCarthy told the clerk who rang up the order that he had just sold beer to a minor.

Apparently, when the owner of the store found out about this, he called McGraw's mother. McCarthy says she took him to the store and made him apologize to the owner—in front of the other employees—for breaking the law. On returning to school, an angry McGraw warned McCarthy that his days "left on the planet" were numbered for squealing on him. McCarthy, who told the head football coach how McGraw had threatened him, never spoke to the future celebrity from that point on. He never saw him in the store again, either.

McGraw has said that if it hadn't been for sports, he probably would never have finished high school. He couldn't have done it on grades alone. He was no rocket scientist in the classroom, though he gave everyone the impression that he was bright.

Studying was clearly not McGraw's top priority. "I don't think you could say he was a leader," says Kenley, who is somewhat surprised that McGraw made it so big. "He was one of the guys who was tougher than nuts, but I didn't look up to him as a neat person or someone who would be a leader later in life."

In the spring of 2001, North student Robyn Busch interviewed McGraw for a special edition of the school's newspaper featuring well-known alumni. McGraw's alma mater boasts several illustrious graduates, including former Arizona Governor Jane Hull and General Richard Myers, chairman of the United States Joint Chiefs of Staff. That Dr. Phil was an alumnus was not common knowledge among North students and teachers although Myers mentioned this fact in a commencement address at the school. Even McGraw's classmates say they are still surprised to hear—and often don't believe—that they went to high school with the famous psychologist. That may partly be McGraw's fault. He rarely mentions that he spent his formative years in Kansas.

Until Busch did her story, few of her peers realized they walked the same halls that McGraw had traveled some 30 years earlier. "My friends who had heard of him were amazed. They thought it was so cool that Dr. Phil went here," she says.

Busch was impressed that McGraw granted an interview to a 16-year-old high school student. His publicity people promised her a short, 10-minute phone chat. But once he got talking, she says, he stayed on the phone much longer. Busch was even more taken by his frankness about his high school days. In the interview, McGraw portrayed his life as a rags-to-riches story, telling Busch, "We were so broke we couldn't pay attention."

In the classroom, McGraw was not the most motivated student, he told Busch. He did not distinguish himself academically. He did well in classes that interested him and not so well in those he didn't like. As an example, McGraw told Busch he got an A in geometry and a D in algebra.

He joked with the student reporter that at the end of his high school days he received an award for worst attendance—in the nonfelony category. "One of the things I was surprised to hear was that he was a self-proclaimed poor student," Busch shares.

McGraw went even further by admitting that attendance was one of his biggest challenges. "I had a hard time getting to school and I had a hard time staying in school once I got there," he said. "I had a hard time being where I was supposed to be."

■ ■ ■

McGraw has written about how he had little or no supervision during his high school years, possibly because his father was so busy with his internship work. Before the McGraws moved into a comfortable, suburban split-level, father and son lived in a lower-income apartment complex next to the high school. When McGraw reflects on that time, he says he lived in apartments that often had no utilities because they couldn't afford them.

He has said he was embarrassed to be poor, and that among his friends he was the one with no nice clothes, no car, no money, and no prospects. But that picture doesn't ring entirely true with the people he knew then, who don't recall him being as destitute as he claims.

McGraw has also maintained that when he was a junior, a college football scholarship seemed within his reach. So, according to McGraw, when his family moved to Texas, he stayed behind—alone in Kansas—to finish high school. But if he was living by himself, his friends never knew it. In fact, then-girlfriend Higgins recalls that his mother and younger sister eventually moved to Kansas City from Oklahoma to join McGraw and his father.

■ ■ ■

P hil McGraw resembled his father in many ways. Both were tall and broad-shouldered, though the senior McGraw was much huskier than his lean son. They shared the same dry, wry wit and understood each other's humor, even when those around them didn't. "Joe would kid you and you really wouldn't know how to take it," says Hughes. "Then Phil would start laughing and you'd know you'd been had somehow."

Joe, the former football player and coach, was a big fan of the game, who loved to watch his son play. Afterward, the two McGraw men would sit around and deconstruct North's highly successful games. "They analyzed everything," recalls Hughes, who often sat in on those postgame discussions. "I guess it was kind of a family sport. When he told me he'd become a psychologist, it didn't surprise me at all."

That the junior McGraw would go on to college after high school seemed preordained. Father and son often talked about the plan for Phil to attend the University of Tulsa.

Hughes and McGraw lost touch with each other after high school, once McGraw left for Oklahoma. Before that, during their sophomore and junior years, they were inseparable. Both tall, big boys, they immediately hit it off. They often double-dated, cruised a popular hamburger joint in Kansas City's upscale Country Club Plaza shopping district, and hung out at teen nightclubs for fun. McGraw became an honorary member of the Hughes family, spending a lot of free time with Hughes's parents and brothers. "We ate like horses. Phil was just another mouth," Hughes says.

"Today we'd be playing video games. Back then we hung out and watched a little TV."

Because McGraw lived so close to the school, he and his football buddies would gather at his apartment in between those two-a-day workouts, munching on one of their favorite, cheap treats—buttered crackers that McGraw warmed in the oven.

■ ■ ■

When he wasn't in school, McGraw worked the night shift at the Hallmark card plant in downtown Kansas City—grunt work, as he calls it. The job allowed him, he has said, to indulge his passion for going on dates and tinkering with cars. Not that he ever had a hot ride. When he was a sophomore, McGraw's father bought him a 1959 Plymouth with a push-button transmission that couldn't go in reverse. "Then he had a 1955 Chevy convertible that did the same thing," Hughes laughs.

After getting off work at the sprawling Hallmark complex at two o'clock in the morning, he roamed the deserted streets of Kansas City with friends. "We were night owls looking for trouble, and we usually found some," McGraw wrote in *Life Strategies*. "A buddy of mine, who also worked at the plant, owned a Chevy Chevelle muscle car with over four hundred horsepower. After work, we liked to race around the deserted streets at ridiculous speeds, looking for a drag race with some other late-night moron with a hundred dollars to bet."

One of those late-night forays on the streets of Kansas City served up a life lesson that McGraw still frequently talks about. It was a lesson about those who get it—and those who don't—in life. He was in a car that was speeding over 100 miles an hour near downtown Kansas City with two others during the Christmas holiday. An angry cop pulled the teens over. As the policeman stomped up to the car, one of the boys inside panicked and took off running. The cop, even angrier now, yanked open the driver's door, grabbed McGraw's friend, and demanded to know the name of the boy who ran off. Unfortunately, McGraw's friend made a bad decision. In a voice dripping with sarcasm, he said, "Well, his name is . . . Sam Sausage! What of it?"

"In retrospect," McGraw reflected, "it was at that moment that I recognized this first Law of Life, and perhaps even formulated how to express it, because I remember thinking, 'Buddy, you just don't get it.'"

The cop punched his friend in the nose, then moved on to McGraw's other friend, who, unlucky for him, really didn't know the name of the kid who had run off. But he did "get it." With no attitude, and in all sincerity, he told the policeman that he did not know the boy's name, but he was certain it wasn't Sam Sausage.

"One guy did not get it, and he was kissing the pavement and would sport two black eyes for the next two weeks. One guy did get it, and he was still vertical and could see out of both of his eyes. Life just goes better when you are one of those who get it."

■ ■ ■

This big, tough, late-night cruising kid is the Phil that Debbie Higgins—the head school cheerleader—fell in love with. Her mother didn't allow her to date until she was 16. Even then the dates came slowly. She later discovered that her younger brother was leveling threats against boys at school who even dared to think about asking her out. She said yes to McGraw's offer because she figured he was too big to be intimidated.

Despite a rocky start—McGraw got her home five minutes late from their first date and she got grounded—Higgins and McGraw quickly became an item. Some of their teachers even referred to the couple as "Mr. and Mrs. McGraw."

Classmates remember that McGraw was an extremely possessive boyfriend. During their several, typical high-school breakups, other boys wouldn't think of asking Higgins out for fear of risking the hot-tempered McGraw's wrath.

Higgins grew up just a few blocks from where the McGraws lived in their split-level home. She didn't come from one of the wealthiest families, but she was certainly one of the friendliest girls in school, with a smile and a wave for everyone, not just the cool kids. The pretty girl with the shiny, Sandra Dee hair flip was definitely one of the most popular students on campus. Whenever she ran in an election, she would win.

In her senior year, Higgins was elected homecoming queen. The 1968 North yearbook shows a picture of the smiling queen dancing with her football player boyfriend, who was a whole foot taller, his face tilted down and gazing adoringly at her. In just a few years, those golden high school moments would be replaced by much more difficult times. Before long, Higgins and McGraw would marry. But the honeymoon wouldn't last long, and Higgins would later seek the help of a psychologist to get over her seemingly perfect relationship with McGraw. Not surprisingly, it wasn't Dr. Phil that she called.

4

Tackling the Rough Times

I think if you're going to get a divorce, you've got to earn your way out, and that means you've got to do all the work.

Debbie Higgins McCall sits in a radio booth in Kansas City across from shock jock Randy Miller. It is October 2002, three decades after she married her high school beau, who was then a young and unknown Phil McGraw. Days earlier, in an interview with the *Kansas City Star,* McCall revealed publicly for the first time that she was "Dr. Phil's" first wife. Now the locals are clamoring to know more.

Today's show is called "Ask Dr. Phil's First Wife." Miller promises his listeners a McGraw faux pas, which he calls a "Phil pas."

But first, he plays a clip from the *Dr. Phil* show of a woman complaining that her fiancé is not as "well-endowed" as she would like. Does size matter, she asks McGraw? No it doesn't, he assures her.

"You were married to the guy for four years. Does size matter?" Miller asks, baiting McCall.

Silence.

"Debbie?"

"I'm thinking," she answers. "I'm trying to think of something clever."

Hearing nothing but a pregnant pause, Miller quickly changes the subject.

Some listeners have a hard time believing that McGraw even has an ex-wife. Oprah's beloved, tell-it-like-it-is guru had a failed marriage? The man who complains that America's divorce rate "is just ridiculous?" The same guy who once told Larry King that Americans pull the trigger on divorce way too quickly is, himself, someone's ex? "You have to turn over every stone, investigate every avenue of rehabilitation you can before you quit," McGraw has said.

Yes, *that* Dr. Phil is the ex-husband of a woman who has decided to spill the beans on their marriage today to Miller's radio audience. McCall now works in a suburban Kansas City liquor store owned by her current boyfriend. She alleges that McGraw cheated on her and then left her, quite literally, in the middle of the night. She says that, as her husband, McGraw had more than a roving eye. Another part of his body roved, too.

These accusations catch many of McGraw's fans by surprise because he has spoken so rarely about his first marriage, which lasted less than three years. When he does talk about it, his manner is usually dismissive, as though the whole affair is hardly worth mentioning. "I was the big football player and she was the cheerleader," he says. "This was just the next thing to do [get married]." Comments like that eventually prodded McCall to tell her side of the story.

One of Miller's listeners, Sandra, confesses that it's strange for her to hear and heed Dr. Phil's advice now that she knows more about how he has led his own life. "You just hope he's had a life change to counsel others," Miller weighs in.

Another listener is eager to do some two-timing math. "I'm curious as to how old Dr. Phil was when you two divorced," the caller asks. "On his show yesterday he said he met his wife Robin when he was 23 and married her when he was 24."

The first Mrs. McGraw avoids the question about his second wife. "There are a lot of people who question that, but it's not worth my time to go back and figure it out," McCall asserts, the weariness obvious in her voice. "We were separated for about a year . . ." She hesitates, then finishes the thought. "It doesn't really make too much difference to me, because he did whatever he wanted with women anyway."

■ ■ ■

McCall had never spoken publicly about the marriage until a *Kansas City Star* reporter (and the co-author of this book) called her while researching a story about McGraw's high school years in Kansas City. The charming homecoming photo of them dancing in their yearbook—McCall with a tiara on her head, McGraw in a white dinner jacket—caught the reporter's eye. "I figured somebody was going to find me out," McCall told the reporter.

But by then, former high school classmates who knew about the two may have been writing about this side of McGraw. In an anonymous review of one of McGraw's bestsellers on an Internet site, someone wrote, "While you're telling other people how to live their lives, practice what you preach." The posting was signed, "A member of the Class of '68."

As McGraw grew more famous, friends encouraged McCall to speak up or, better yet, to call Oprah Winfrey and tell her about the man she had placed her trust—and money—in. Some even jokingly considered holding a class reunion of sorts right in Winfrey's studio audience.

For her part, McCall didn't want anything to do with him—she never even watched McGraw on TV or read any of his books—until he began mentioning the marriage in published interviews. She thought it arrogant of him to have never spoken of it before, sort of like Bill Clinton lying about having sexual relations with Monica Lewinsky.

"If he had mentioned our marriage from the very beginning," McCall says, "I think the public would have not made an issue of it and find it more endearing that he had some insight being involved in a failed marriage."

■ ■ ■

Thirty years after their marriage, McCall is no longer the dewy young cheerleader. She is thrice divorced, the mother of a grown son and daughter. She's still petite and slim, but her blond hair has darkened and lines of hard luck etch her face. Nevertheless, her big dark eyes still snap with perky, rah-rah spunk.

She seemed to be born with that spark, says Bill Higgins, who describes his younger sister as "a force that you absolutely couldn't hold down. She just had constant energy and was so bubbly. She had absolutely no enemies. Except, as a brother, you'd get nailed every once in a while with her mean side, because nobody can be that bubbly all the time."

His sister's streak of bad luck with men stretches all the way back to infancy. Debbie's father abandoned the family—including her mother, older sister, and brother—before her first birthday. Their mom then married a railroad engineer who "didn't have the money to support both his liquor and family," Higgins shares.

The family lived in a tiny, unassuming house in suburban Kansas City that McGraw visited often when he and McCall dated in high school. When the football player came calling, he pulled his convertible high up onto the steep driveway and, because the car had no reverse gear, slipped it into neutral to roll it back down the drive.

Higgins's little sister was quite the catch at Shawnee Mission North High School. "A lot of guys wanted to be my friend just to see Debbie," he remembers. "I let them know right away that I was not that way and that approach wouldn't work. It hurt my feelings after a while."

His sister's ultimate beau, McGraw, was a young man of few words and not big on chitchat. "We would never talk," Higgins recalls. "He ran in a completely different crowd. He ran with a guy . . . who actually spoke for him. He [McGraw] would just kind of walk around and be that physical presence and the other guy would be the loud-mouth clown.

"At 17, 18, he looked like he was 40 years old. And this was four years after the Beatles hit. His hair was way out of style and completely not hip."

McGraw set his sights on the popular cheerleader because he liked what he saw, friends say. Her brother suspects she was attracted to all that special attention from McGraw, because he certainly wasn't his sister's first choice as a boyfriend. McCall had a crush on another member of the school's football team. McGraw "wouldn't talk to anybody else except Debbie," Higgins says. "She thought that was real cool."

■ ■ ■

Though McGraw towered over his tiny girlfriend, verbally she could hold her own. "She had a real sharp mind and she could outwit him," Higgins says. "She could do that with me, too. As she grew up, that was her defense, her wit."

After they graduated, the high school sweethearts continued their romance long-distance as they went their separate ways. In the fall of 1968, Debbie moved to Springfield, Missouri, to attend Southwest Missouri State to study social work. McGraw, meanwhile, accepted a football scholarship at the University of Tulsa, in Oklahoma.

He arrived in Oklahoma full of gusto and guts, ready to tackle anything and everything. "Phil showed up with his sunglasses on, with a suitcase, 8-track tape player, and carrying his suit," remembers friend Ken Petruck. "He said 'I am Phil from Kansas City.'"

Even though Petruck had arrived first, McGraw informed his new roommate that he was taking the top bunk. "He pretty much conducted himself like he owned the place. And that's pretty typical of Phil McGraw," Petruck remembers.

McGraw played middle linebacker on the school's freshman team. But his sports dream didn't last long. An injury on the field left him partially blind. Not one to sit around and feel sorry for himself, McGraw studied about optic nerve damage and helped heal himself by wearing a patch over the good eye to help strengthen the weak one. "Being blind was just an inconvenience to him," says his sister Deana. "That's kind of the way Phil looks at stuff. You can stand around and bellyache or you can get it done and move on."

McGraw dropped out of school and moved back to Texas to be closer to his family. While he'd been away at school, his father began working in the psychology field under a licensed psychologist in Wichita Falls. Joe didn't become a licensed psychologist himself until 1973, after flunking his first two licensing exams. Even before starting his own practice, Joe McGraw made a name for himself as the only counselor in the area to make house calls by airplane, flying from town to town across west Texas. To make his own money, Phil McGraw took a job in the fledgling health club industry in Lubbock and, like his father, seemed to be a born entrepreneur. He sold memberships at one club and soon owned partnership interests in others. Before long, he would turn this experience into a business of his own with disastrous results.

■ ■ ■

In his private life, McGraw continued to woo Debbie Higgins. He had given her a promise ring after high school and both traveled back and forth between Springfield and Tulsa to kindle the fires of romance, she says. After two semesters Debbie ran out of money and moved home to Kansas where she enrolled in a local junior college and hairdressing school. McGraw, though, wanted her closer and asked her to move to Lubbock with him, where he was working at a health club.

Debbie will never forget the day she joined McGraw in Texas, and neither will the residents of Lubbock. On May 11, 1970, a tornado struck the town, roaring through at more than 200 miles an hour. The twister killed 26 people and injured at least 1,500 more as it cut a deadly swath across the town. Years later, when she thought back to the day, Debbie said the storm proved to be a sign of things to come.

Six months later, the young couple married in Debbie's childhood church—Southridge Presbyterian Church, in Roeland Park, Kansas. The wedding was a family affair. Debbie's sister stood with her as matron of honor and one of McGraw's three sisters was a bridesmaid. McGraw's brother-in-law served as best man. Higgins, Debbie's brother, was an usher. The only visible hitch of the evening came at the reception. The napkins for the wedding party were erroneously printed "Debbie and Ed."

Debbie looked like a storybook princess in an A-line gown with a cathedral length train, carrying a romantic cascade of white rosebuds and small mums. The next month, the community newspaper ran her wedding portrait on a special page spotlighting holiday brides. In the black-and-white photo, decorated on the page with holly leaves and ribbons, Debbie is flashing her trademark smile, a perky curl of hair kissing her cheek under her veil.

After a honeymoon in Vail, Colorado, the new Mr. and Mrs. McGraw returned to Lubbock. Debbie's mother in Kansas was unhappy that her youngest daughter had moved so far away, Higgins remembers. So the young couple moved back to Kansas two years later when McGraw returned to the state to open the Grecian Health Spa in Topeka. Very quickly, both the business and the marriage began to sour.

■ ■ ■

Though he had made a most attentive and romantic boyfriend, McGraw changed as a husband, Debbie says. Rarely demonstrative and affectionate, he did not part easily with the words "I love you." His take-charge personality began to overwhelm her as he tried to control her in ways big and small. She was not allowed to get involved in the business, let alone visit the spa building itself. He demanded that she always look nice for him, even to the point where he had her lift weights to bulk up her chest. He became unbearable to be around, Debbie says.

"Debbie was supposed to be this dutiful wife who just sits around and waits for him to come home, the typical '50s wife, kind of *Leave It to Beaver*. And she tried," her brother says.

Then the big chill set in. McGraw began to freeze her out, emotionally and verbally, Debbie says. According to her brother, McGraw would come home from work and wouldn't even talk to her, marriage turmoil that Debbie apparently only shared with her mother and sister.

Back in the Kansas City radio booth with Randy Miller, the woman now named Debbie McCall delivers the promised "Phil pas" for the day. She tells listeners that McGraw often told her that she didn't possess the mental capacity to carry on a conversation with him during their marriage.

"Wow. This is Dr. Phil, the guy who helps people?" disc jockey Miller wonders aloud. "The guy who helps build self-esteem? What a jerk. What a jerk."

McCall tells the story of a plane ride she and McGraw took during their marriage from Topeka to Wichita Falls for a family weekend. McGraw sat in the pilot's seat for the four-hour flight. Fed up with the lack of communication in their relationship, McCall decided to test him. She purposely said nothing to him during the trip. But he didn't say anything, either, flunking her test.

"We get to Wichita Falls, we said hello [to family], get to the cabin. Not one word. On the flight back, not one word," she recalls.

That's how a bad marriage goes bad, McCall says. "They beat you down, beat you down. And you start to question yourself."

■ ■ ■

Though she felt trapped and smothered in her marriage, McCall apparently confided in few people. Her own brother, her long-time protector, didn't even know much about what she was going through at the time. "I don't know anybody in the family, except mama, that she would have confided in," he says. Their mother is now deceased.

"Debbie didn't confide in me about those things because I was kind of a macho pig, too. I was very male-oriented. We [McGraw and Higgins] both thought that men ought to rule the roost, that kind of thing. It took me four marriages, but I got it right now.

"I don't think I went as far as he did, and I've certainly grown over the years, and he probably has, too," Higgins adds. "Neither one of us is the same person anymore."

But there was another problem with the marriage that McCall couldn't ignore: McGraw, she claims, was cheating on her. Friends called this behavior adulterous and called it to her attention, she says. Neighbors in Topeka told her they saw him bringing women to their home. McCall says that when she asked him about it, McGraw responded, "Don't take it personally."

"When I confronted him about his infidelities he didn't deny these girls and told me that it had nothing to do with his feelings toward me, to grow up, that's the way it was in the world," McCall says.

McCall and McGraw give very different accounts of how and why their marriage dissolved. He has portrayed the break as friendly. "You want to talk about immature? I had no idea then, and neither did she, and after a very short period of time we kind of looked at each other one day and said, 'What are we doing? I mean, we're just kids. We shouldn't be doing this anyway. Fortunately we came to our senses before we got very far down the road."

But that's not exactly how others who watched the relationship collapse remember it. "I don't remember her saying why they were getting divorced, except that I knew that he had been unfaithful, and back then that was enough for a divorce," Higgins says. "And then for him to be so blatant about it. It wasn't like he was hiding the fact that he was fooling around on her. And that made her even madder, of course."

Some onlookers weren't at all surprised that the marriage didn't last. A former friend of both McGraw and McCall describes her as being rough-edged and unpolished, not the kind of woman some would have expected the driven and motivated McGraw to marry. Others say that McCall was a stereotypical bubbleheaded cheerleader, and McGraw simply outgrew her. Whatever the truth, the two lacked the ingredients that McGraw tells his audiences today are necessary to salvage a critically wounded relationship: A willing spirit, long-term effort, and "the courage to accept that you can't control your partner, you can only make it easier for him or her to do right."

■ ■ ■

The marriage was annulled by a Kansas court in December 1973. Neither saw each other after the split until their 30-year high school reunion in Kansas City, the first either one had attended, as far as classmates can recall. "I think they just kind of stayed apart from each other," says a former classmate.

Curious high school pals watched the two closely to see how they would act around each other, but there were no fireworks—just pleasantries exchanged between the ex's and Robin, the second Mrs. McGraw. Afterward, McGraw called a female classmate and commented that he didn't recall his old high school being so blue-collar. "I think he's been on this fast track that's gotten ahead of him," she said. "I look at him now and see him on TV and really believe he's forgotten where he's come from."

But that's not entirely true, because McGraw wrote about that reunion night in one of his books, *Self Matters*. He cited some of his former female classmates as people who hold onto "labels" to give themselves an identity. Could he have been talking about a certain former head cheerleader? He wrote, "The 'pretty girls' may still have been pretty, but they sure weren't very interesting."

If McGraw was referring to his first wife, it wouldn't have been the first time she'd been stung by his plainspoken words. As McCall finishes up her guest stint on Randy Miller's show, the sympathetic disc jockey asks, "When you got out of the relationship with Phil, obviously that had to be tough. Didn't you feel like crap?"

"Oh yeah, it was like a death," she responds. "Then you internalize it and you say, what did I do wrong? The constant belittling . . . it was tough."

One listener wants to know what motivated McCall to come forward and talk about McGraw now. Some readers of the *Kansas City Star* article were angered that she was talking so publicly and harshly about the TV celebrity, suspecting her of cashing in on his fame. But McCall reassures Miller's listeners that she does not want to belittle McGraw, "but rather to specifically direct my attention to those who are in the same situation now that I was in when I was married to him.

"I can only speak about my past experiences, not from a professional point of view, but just from how I survived and have maintained a sense of humor about it," she insists. "I did not choose to be brought into the media's eye, but because of Phil's denial of our relationship for so long, it spoke very loudly that he was once again being disrespectful and dishonest about me. He preaches taking responsibility and I think it would be great if he would take responsibility for our relationship.

"Some people say this happened thirty years ago and I should be over it by now. I believe the amount of time that has passed is unimportant. Time is an illusion. Pain is pain. When our feelings and emotions are involved, it affects us, in one way or another, for our lifetime. I know I am a different person today because of all I went through with Phil. The good thing is, I like myself now."

She likes herself so much, in fact, that she's writing a book about the marriage. Instead of a tell-all, she says, it will offer advice to women on how to keep a sense of humor even after a failed relationship. Talking about her failed marriage has changed McCall's life dramatically, in some ways for the worse. Her newfound celebrity status has tabloids hounding her, offering money for the salacious details of her marriage to McGraw. One photographer even staked out her home in suburban Kansas City before knocking on her door one morning. She then hired a lawyer to help keep the press at bay.

Someday the former cheerleader will have a lot more to tell on her own terms. Her brother believes that three failed marriages have ruined love for her because now she is reluctant to marry her long-time live-in boyfriend. Debbie McCall, though, is far from being the only person left with hard feelings from personal dealings with McGraw, either now or in his younger years.

5

Let's Make a Deal

The principle of reciprocity simply says that you "get what you give." The manner, style and level you use to engage people will determine how they respond to you.

Back in December 1971, Jim McNeece and his wife, Linda, lived in a tiny, modest Topeka, Kansas, apartment. They were newlyweds in their 20s, and just starting out their new lives together.

When they heard about a new health club opening in the city's wealthiest neighborhood, McNeece recalls that he decided to take a look. The YMCA was the only other place in town to work out. An athletic 5 feet 10 inches and 180 pounds, McNeece liked to play sports and wanted a place to keep in shape for the softball season.

According to McNeece, when he visited the new Grecian Health Spa, a salesperson offered him what he referred to as a "lifetime membership." He explained that there still wasn't much equipment inside, because the club was so new. Even though the young couple couldn't really afford it, the McNeeces decided that the money was an investment in their health. They signed up, committed to remain members for at least a year, and began paying their monthly dues. In all, they handed over $1,300 to the spa during an 18-month period. McNeece still has the check stubs to prove it.

In less than a year, however, McNeece found out just how long—or short, in this case—a "lifetime" really is.

"I thought it was kind of neat to think it was a lifetime membership," recalls the 54-year-old IBM tech services employee, who still lives in Topeka. "They hadn't finished [the spa] yet. They said they were working on it. So I just went ahead and signed up, investing in the future. And boom, it was never finished."

The Grecian Health Spa—a club that closed its doors to the public and went bankrupt just two years after it opened—was run by a then 21-year-old Phil McGraw. After filing for bankruptcy, McGraw left Topeka. His customers and the landlady who owned the building say they weren't told that he was shutting the business down. This was McGraw's first business venture, and it ended with a spectacular thud. His business practices also came under scrutiny by the Kansas attorney general's office, in a review that ultimately helped change consumer protection laws in Kansas.

"*That* was Dr. Phil? Dad gum, I would have never even tied it together," said a stunned McNeece on learning who owned the now defunct health club. "I just took it in the shorts [losing money on the membership]. I told my wife, 'Bad experience. I won't let that happen again.' That's the last time we joined anything like that in the last 30 years."

■ ■ ■

Health clubs were all but unheard of in the 1970s. After all, it was only the very early days of a fitness craze that would eventually work this increasingly health-conscious country into a sweat. By the 1980s, people were spending more money on exercise equipment, diets, and health club memberships than ever before. It was during this decade that fitness gurus Richard Simmons and Jane Fonda became household names.

But the fitness industry hit a few speed bumps along the way. Most came in the form of mismanaged health clubs. By the end of the 1980s, under-capitalized and fly-by-night operations that sought to make a quick buck off the fitness fad were increasingly going under.

As his state considered regulating health clubs in 1986, William Webster, then Missouri's attorney general, noted, "The bottom line is that it is fairly easy to get into this business because you do not have a massive inventory. You get a few pieces of equipment, lease a facility, and you too can have a spa."

Apparently, McGraw was among the first to recognize that this field was ripe with possibility. As an entrepreneur, he took his cues from his father, Joe, who never seemed to pass up a chance to make an extra dollar.

In 1969, McGraw moved back to Texas after a football injury ended his stay at the University of Tulsa. He began working in some Lubbock health clubs, a seemingly natural fit for this former football player with such a large physical presence.

In 1971, McGraw, his father, and two friends from Texas formed a corporation called International Health Resorts Inc. McGraw was president, with 46 percent ownership.

It is unclear exactly why they chose to put a spa in Topeka, though the McGraws became familiar with the area when they lived about an hour's drive away in Overland Park, Kansas. Of course, that is where McGraw finished high school and met his wife, Debbie. Her family still lived in the Kansas City suburbs and apparently welcomed their return to the area.

In June 1971, International Health Resorts opened the Grecian Health Spa in Topeka in a building leased from Elizabeth Wooster-Petrik and her husband, Lawrence, who is now deceased. Like McNeece, Wooster-Petrik had no idea that the young man she had done business with some 30 years ago was TV's famous psychologist. He skipped town owing her rent and left her building in a state of disrepair, she contends. She and her husband claimed nearly $28,000 in unpaid rent and damages to the premises when the business went belly up. The bankruptcy court ultimately gave them a mere $843.18.

Bitterness tinges the former landlady's recollections as she recounts the celebrity's business folly at the expense of a lot of folks in Topeka. "I think people are being gypped," the 87-year-old Wooster-Petrik says of McGraw's current-day followers. "Once a gypper, you're not going to change colors."

Wooster-Petrik and her husband owned a building in Topeka's fashionable Westboro neighborhood. According to Wooster-Petrik, in 1971, a local real estate agent brought two men from Texas—Joe and Phil McGraw—to talk to them about renting the building. The father and son were unfamiliar faces to the landlady. She listened inquisitively as they told her about their idea for the business, which was unorthodox at the time.

Wooster-Petrik remembers being reluctant to lease the building to them because Phil McGraw, who would be running the club, was so young and obviously green at managing a business. But Joe assured her that the rent would be paid, and she took him at his word. He was *Doctor* McGraw, after all, even though he didn't fit the image of the impeccably dressed professional that Wooster-Petrik was used to being around. "He was a little rumpled, but I chalked that up to his traveling," she says.

■ ■ ■

The McGraws could hardly have chosen a better location for a private health club that planned to charge hundreds of dollars in membership dues. Westboro remains a neighborhood that Topeka's elite call home. The Tudors and impressive colonials with big lawns on shady, tree-lined streets give shelter to the city's movers and shakers, white-collar professionals, and families with long-time ties to the community.

In the 1970s, the neighborhood's small shopping area carried a fine pedigree as well, with upscale tenants that included a dress shop, children's store, and a gift shop where society brides registered their silver patterns. The McGraws rented two adjacent buildings. One was meant to be the athletic club; the other a spa with massage rooms, whirlpools, and steam rooms.

"It didn't take long to see they were having trouble," Wooster-Petrik reflects. The first sign came when rent payments stopped arriving after just a few months, forcing her into the role of nagging landlady. "I was there just about every day trying to collect rent," she says. Adding insult to injury, she had to pay a monthly finder's fee to the realtor who had hooked her up with the McGraws in the first place.

McNeece lived an easy bike ride from the club. He visited it two or three times a week, working out on the weight machines. Staff members were always helpful and seemed to know what they were doing, he says. But the club itself struck him as a bare-bones operation that certainly did not befit its wealthy surroundings. The spa was sparsely decorated—a deep purple carpet under all the exercise equipment was the most lavish decoration—and the machinery did not appear to be top quality. "Everything was kind of second-rate," he says.

"What got me going was they said they had a sauna and a whirlpool. Back then, 30 years ago, that was a big deal in Topeka, to go somewhere that was more private. Everybody in the world went to the YMCA," McNeece adds. "But it never came about. They never fixed it up very well. They just kept saying they were working on it. They kept saying, 'We're going to get some more money. Don't worry.'"

The spa was indeed quite barren, according to bankruptcy records that reveal what little the corporation claimed in the way of personal property. It listed miscellaneous exercise equipment worth $10,000, but with nearly $9,000 still owed on it. Miscellaneous office furniture and the carpet were also listed. The company even owed Sears for the curtains hanging over the windows.

Other than the steam boiler, some mechanical pumps, and $100 worth of office supplies, International Health Resorts claimed little else.

On one of Wooster-Petrik's trips to the spa to collect the rent, she says she found the building locked up and no one around. There was no sign in the window telling anyone what had happened. Phil McGraw had left the building—and town—she later found out, and left no traces behind.

McNeece learned of McGraw's departure much the same way. He says he found the building locked when he went to work out one day. The club closed on September 6, 1973, and filed for bankruptcy the following week.

■ ■ ■

The bankruptcy court in Kansas tried to track McGraw down in Texas by sending correspondence to his home in Wichita Falls: His mother, Jerry, had to sign for at least one registered letter. Other notices were sent to McGraw's attention at several health clubs in El Paso, Texas, but they were returned undelivered. His connection to those businesses is unclear.

McGraw apparently also left his first wife, Debbie, behind. Although she enjoyed the good life while the money was coming in, she claims she was left in the lurch when his business fell apart. "He left town in the middle of the night," says a friend of Debbie's who helped move her belongings out of the house she once shared with McGraw. "He owed a lot of people money." He and Debbie separated for good at this point. Their marriage was annulled a few months later.

A former friend of McGraw's offers a defense for McGraw and his business partners. "I don't think they set out to defraud people in the beginning, but they did," he says. "I don't think that was their intention. He [McGraw] and [his partners], they were young and they didn't know what was going on. They took all this money from memberships to the spa and spent it."

McNeece doesn't buy such explanations. "They told us they were going to fix it up. That's a misrepresentation," he insists. "In the end, they didn't tell anybody 'Hey, this isn't going to make it.' They just kept taking our money. I can't believe guys this smart didn't know what they were doing."

Billie Talmage, who owned the neighborhood dress shop across from the spa, bought the newly vacant building from Wooster-Petrik after McGraw left. She remembers that "it was a mess." There was a deep hole and a mound of dirt beside it in the basement, presumably the beginnings of a pool or whirlpool—a construction job the landlady had not been told about. Tons of dirt had to be hauled up out of the basement. Talmage had the building gutted and transformed it into her new dress boutique.

"When we went to sell to Billie there was a lien on the building because of this equipment that they had rented and didn't pay for," Wooster-Petrik says. She and her husband had to pay off the lien before they could sell the building.

The landlady wasn't the only one left shaken up. McGraw and his partners signed up hundreds of customers—just like the McNeeces—for lifetime memberships. Members were required to sign contracts committing them to pay monthly dues for a given term, regardless of whether the spa was actually in operation. McGraw and his associates then turned around and sold these membership contracts to local financial institutions for a percentage of each membership's value. Let's say a member committed to paying $50 a month for 12 months. The value of that contract to McGraw was $600, but it would take a whole year for him to pocket that entire amount. Instead, he would sell the contract—and the accompanying right to collect $600—to an outside financial institution for a smaller amount paid up front. So his $600 contract might net him an immediate $400 in cash. A clause in the membership agreement (which started with the phrase "for your convenience") both gave the spa the right to sell the contract to an outside financial institution and obligated members to pay these dues even if the health club went out of business. As a result, when the spa filed for bankruptcy, members were still legally liable for paying off their memberships even though the spa no longer existed, according to Emery Goad, who worked for the attorney general's office at the time.

■ ■ ■

The Kansas attorney general had begun fielding complaints from club members by the time McGraw left town. Goad was a young go-getter special agent in the office's consumer division.

When the first group of members to join began suspecting that the club would never be fully functional, they complained. "Obviously he was going to sign people up for as long as people were interested in signing up," says Goad, who now runs his own private investigation firm in Kansas. "So I went out to the spa one day with a subpoena for his books and records to find out what was going on, but never found anyone to serve."

Goad also wanted to know more about the spa's sales tactics. From the complaints, he perceived that "the big lure of the spa was really to women," he says. "Men were selling to women and they'd tell them how pretty they were and how much prettier they could be if they would lose weight. It was pretty clear to me from the people who were filing complaints that that's what was going on."

The Grecian Health Spa was one of many cases that caught the attention of Vern Miller's office in the early 1970s. Miller quickly established a reputation for being an aggressive, no-nonsense attorney general by leading one of the country's biggest organized drug raids in Lawrence, Kansas, six weeks after being sworn into office in 1971. Later, Miller made national headlines by declaring that airlines could not serve liquor to passengers while flying over Kansas airspace.

Miller was particularly focused on consumer fraud. During his four-year term, investigators in his office put a stop to scam artists such as the so-called Hong Kong tailors, who set up shop in motel rooms and took advance payments for tailoring custom suits. "The first time they would send you a suit that was worth more than you paid," Goad explains. "Then the next visit would be the big rip." In other words, after the first suit, the rest weren't worth the fabric they were made of.

In addition, Miller's crew investigated shady insect exterminators, who would dump cans of termites onto people's porches, then charge up to $500 for their services to get rid of the pests. They also cracked down on fraudulent trade schools (learn how to drive a big-rig for $700) that collected tuition but never trained anyone to do anything more than write them out a check.

In McGraw's case, he left Topeka one step ahead of investigators, who seemed determined to prove wrongdoing at the Grecian Health Spa. They never did, and charges were never filed.

"He [McGraw] rents this building, puts in a little equipment, puts in ads where you buy lifetime memberships," Goad says. "People would come in and they had professional salesmen who would flex their muscles and talk them into buying a lifetime membership, in those days for about $600 or $700. Everybody knew the spa was not up and running yet, but they knew it was coming. They just had enough equipment in there for bait."

After McGraw's club closed, financial institutions that had bought memberships from the club sued some members for unpaid dues. Some had their wages garnished, Goad says. The fact that the spa no longer existed was not a defense and did not excuse them from their legal obligation. A few years later, Kansas passed new laws to protect consumers in similar situations. "The Grecian Health Spa was one of the big inputs," in prompting the change, Goad adds.

Two years after McGraw's club closed its doors, the Federal Trade Commission launched a nationwide examination of health spa business practices. Complaints about high-pressure sales tactics and other abuses were pouring in. The FTC held public hearings and studied more than 6,500 consumer complaints about health spas across the country, mostly concerning incidents that took place between 1972 and 1977. The biggest problems, which persisted into the early 1980s, were spa closings like McGraw's in Topeka that left consumers with paid memberships and no place to use them or get refunds.

Yet, while the closings certainly caused headaches for consumers, the FTC concluded that many of these operations had not violated federal laws. They were often poorly managed, set up in bad locations, or suffered when customers simply lost interest. Nevertheless, state legislators kept busy during the early 1980s trying to protect constituents against health club scams. Both Missouri and Kansas eventually banned so-called lifetime memberships.

■ ■ ■

What exactly happened to McGraw's Grecian Health Spa? Some observers chalk up its failure to the inexperience of the men running it. They say McGraw's success at selling memberships went to his head and he lived way beyond his means on the profits. When the business went bankrupt, it turned over a list of more than 700 members, all of whom had been signed up in less than two years.

But the bankruptcy files also expose a textbook case of a business run badly. The string of creditors owed money was long and diverse. Many of the spa's bills were left unpaid. Three hundred dollars was owed to an Overland Park company for showers in the spa, and another $300 to a Kansas City, Missouri, business for lockers in the men's locker room. The spa owed money for newspaper and magazine advertisements, extermination services, electricity and phone bills, even bottled water. It owed money to hardware stores, sheet metal companies, electricians, and plumbers.

The selling of members' contracts to financial institutions was messy, too. General Finance Corporation (GFC) of Kansas was among the companies that bought the retail installment notes and contracts of International Health Resorts members, according to the bankruptcy filing. Once the sale took place, members were then legally obligated to make their future payments to GFC, and the health spa was entitled to nothing more until the contract term expired. But GFC claimed that the spa turned around and improperly continued to collect nearly $1,000 in dues directly from members, even after the sale.

"Claimant has contacted several of the members who are willing to testify that their payments were made directly to International Health Resorts Inc. of Topeka, Kansas," GFC asserted in court documents.

Member after member filed a claim for reimbursement and each complaint sounded very much like the next. One couple said they were due $500 because they had paid nearly $650 for a lifetime membership and had only been able to use the club for seven months. Another couple paid $500 for a two-year membership set to expire in March 1975. But the spa shut down in September 1973, "and its doors were closed to members, barring use of the facility by said members," the husband and wife wrote in their complaint.

There may have been accounting troubles as well. A former employee, hired to babysit the children of spa members, told the court that the business had not taken enough federal taxes out of her paychecks. She explained how she went to the spa to collect her check one day and found no one there. The business filed for bankruptcy the next day. Her claim totaled $73.20 in lost wages, and she enclosed copies of pay stubs to show the accounting inaccuracies. "Check stub No. 1 is what most of my checks were like, [with] just Social Security taken out," she wrote. "We called the accountant and he said he hadn't been taking out enough taxes. I don't know what was going on but I would like to know!"

A lot of people shared that same sentiment.

■ ■ ■

Some of those who knew McGraw in Topeka referred to him as "the doctor's son." He was living large, tooling around town in a new blue Chevy Corvette convertible. No more of those old beater cars from high school. He also had his own plane—a 1965 Mooney worth about $10,000 that he kept at the Kickapoo Airport in Wichita Falls.

About a year before the corporation filed for bankruptcy, McGraw had a new home built. One of his partners built a house right next door. McGraw's 1,700-square-foot, three-bedroom home was in a new development on Topeka's west side, a part of town that attracted a fairly affluent clientele—lawyers, investment bankers, and "some people who have moved on who are multimillionaires," according to a neighbor. McGraw's ranch house sat on a street not even two blocks long, on a hill that in those days overlooked picturesque, wide-open spaces. Later, a mall and other retailers moved into the area.

McGraw hadn't lived there long before the spa went under and he had to sell the home at a loss. For the man who bought the property after seeing the "sacrifice, must-sell" ad in the paper, it proved to be a good deal. All he learned during the transaction was a doctor's son from Wichita Falls had built the house. The real estate paperwork went back and forth between Topeka and Wichita Falls because McGraw had already left town.

McGraw had left his Corvette behind, locked up in the home's two-car garage. The new homeowner recalls the day the bank came to repossess McGraw's car. One of the "repo" men reached up and took the key from on top of one of the front tires and drove the car out. "If I'd known the key was there I would have driven it," the homeowner laughs.

A chiropractor moved into the house next door, where McGraw's business partner had lived. One night after work, the chiropractor arrived to find that a man had staked out the house and was waiting for him, thinking that he was one of the spa's owners. The man practically mauled the neighbor, yelling, "I want my money."

"They were angry and needed to take it out on somebody," says the man who bought McGraw's former home and still lives there today.

■ ■ ■

Though the spa's closing left a lot of people feeling ripped off and angry, there was very little public hue and cry. There were no newspaper headlines about the bankruptcy, unlike the ones that would herald the downfall of other health clubs in the years to come.

Goad believes that most Grecian Health Spa members simply chalked up the whole affair to a live-and-learn experience. Part of the reason was the amount of money involved. "[I]n those days [you] would pick a threshold where you could rip people off but they wouldn't come after you," he says. "Back then it was about $700. There is a threshold where it isn't worth the trouble."

That's exactly why McNeece didn't pursue the matter, even though he got nothing when the business received protection from the bankruptcy court. He, too, chalked the whole thing up to a learning experience and later turned to bicycling for his physical fitness. No more health spas for him. "Once you fall in a black hole you don't do it again," McNeece says.

Although there's no evidence that the partners intended to commit fraud, Goad—the former special agent—says that considering what McGraw has gone on to accomplish in his life he could at least offer some gesture to make amends for these past business blunders.

"He's got the money today and could dig up this litigation and say to those people, whoever is left, 'I'll give you your money back,'" Goad observes. "He could profit from this, ironically" with the resulting positive publicity that such a gesture would bring.

But sometimes, even money can't heal pain.

"I will never forget this the rest of my life," McGraw's former landlady says.

And neither will many others who were burned by McGraw before his abrupt departure from Topeka.

Studying Psychology

I almost quit every day. The faculty just jacked with you all the time . . . I remember telling one professor, "Either kick me out or get off my ass."

Perhaps chastened by the debacle of his first business venture, and certainly in financial straits, McGraw returned to his family in Wichita Falls, where Joe was finally enjoying the fruits of his many years of labor, having accomplished his goal of getting a license to practice psychology. Joe McGraw was now officially a "doctor." But the title was hard won.

College studies did not come easily to Joe. He barely graduated from the University of Tulsa, where his grades were deplorable. His undergraduate report cards were littered with D's, in everything from Hebrew history and English composition, to business math and intermediate French. He also had a weak academic start in those areas he would pursue later in life, garnering C's in general psychology and principles of sociology.

Sixteen years and a lot of life after receiving an undergraduate degree in education, Joe earned a master's degree in education and then a Ph.D. at the University of Oklahoma. This time, his dogged determination to succeed was evident. He had reversed his grades, piling up As in nearly all the courses in his major, stumbling into only one D—in history.

But earning an actual license to practice in the state of Texas proved to be a struggle. Joe flunked the written part of the two-part certification test given by the Texas State Board of Examiners of Psychologists in June 1970, and again in November 1970. He finally passed the written portion of the test in October 1972 by four points and passed the oral exam in January 1973, when the board certified him and granted him his license.

As Joe was getting his new practice going, his only son returned to town freshly separated from his wife, broke, on the radar screen of investigators from the Kansas attorney general's office, and seemingly at a loss for what to do next. Joe had an idea that was close to his heart: McGraw could complete his education, and they could establish a father-son psychology practice.

Either seeing the wisdom in the plan or simply wanting to please his father, McGraw enrolled in Midwestern State University, a small commuter college catering mostly to students within an 80- to 100-mile radius. McGraw joined about 4,000 others on the pretty campus of red brick buildings with red tile roofs. The university has always had an open enrollment policy, meaning that just about any student who applied was accepted. "If you could fill out the application blank, you could pretty much walk in," says George Diekhoff, Ph.D., current chairman of the school's psychology department.

McGraw's decision to stay in Wichita Falls might also have been affected by his chance meeting of Robin Jameson, a pretty and petite young woman a week out of high school, who happened to be visiting his sister one day. In Robin, perhaps McGraw glimpsed a different vision of his future. Add to that his first taste of business and personal failure, and McGraw was finally inspired to knuckle down to his schoolwork, setting his formidable mind to the task at hand. At the time McGraw enrolled, Midwestern didn't have a football team, so McGraw left his college athletic career behind and concentrated on his classroom studies.

■ ■ ■

Fulfilling Joe's wish, McGraw chose psychology as his major. Midwestern's psychology program was small, with only about four psychology professors on the faculty at the time. The focus of the program was primarily behavioral, an empirical-minded perspective that believes all human behavior is learned and can be unlearned. "Nobody was doing much analyst's couch and inkblots, for sure," recalls Diekhoff, in reference to the increasingly unfashionable Freudian perspective, which was built on unprovable concepts such as a caveman id lurking in the human psyche.

"As part of our grad training we often have to take courses of that type [Freudian], and those were the things Phil had trouble with—dealing with those third-order constructs that you couldn't see and you couldn't measure," recalls Donald Trahan, Ph.D., a psychologist in Beaumont, Texas, and a graduate school classmate of McGraw's. Instead, McGraw delved into a sort of "just do it" approach to human functioning and would follow the behaviorist path throughout his academic career and beyond. McGraw's Life Law #3—"People do what works"—is drawn directly from behaviorism; and shades of behaviorism also linger in Life Law #5—"Life rewards action" and Life Law #8—"We teach people how to treat us."

McGraw pretty much flew beneath the radar during his years at Midwestern, appearing in no yearbook class photos or listings, although if you look hard, you can find him on page 106 of the 1975 Wai-kun, the school yearbook. It is hard not to recognize him in the back row of a photo of Psi Chi, the psychology honor society. "Younger looking, but still Dr. Phil, moustache and all," says Dr. Everett Kindig, associate professor of history at Midwestern who had McGraw in one class. "His hair was receding even then, but he was nattily dressed, in turtleneck sweater and sport coat." After years as a lackadaisical student, McGraw was evidently now applying himself to his studies. "He was one of my good students," Kindig recalls. "He received an A, which I don't give out very readily."

McGraw graduated from Midwestern in 1975, having polished off three years' worth of coursework in just two, probably by simply tapping into his deep well of drive and ambition. "I assume he took a full load during the regular school year, went to summer school, and didn't change his major," says Diekhoff, who joined the Midwestern faculty in 1977. "That's really the only way going through this fast would be possible."

In the fall of 1975, he took several graduate-level courses in psychology, gearing up for the post-graduate education he would also blast through. For his graduate work, McGraw chose North Texas State University (now called University of North Texas), an 80-year-old institution undergoing a growth spurt. Internationally known for its jazz music program, the 500-acre campus is in Denton, Texas, about 35 miles north of Dallas. When McGraw was a student, the campus was a muddy maze of construction of new academic buildings, track facilities, music and art buildings, a library, and physical education buildings. The growing university had also recently taken control of the Texas College of Osteopathic Medicine and new graduate programs were being developed and approved.

The psychology department had just moved into an old dormitory that contained classrooms, psychology clinics, graduate student offices, and the main departmental office. This permitted a lot of interesting interaction among members of the department, according to Robert Wernick, Ph.D., a classmate of McGraw's. "If you were on campus, you were pretty much hanging out in that building most of the time," he says. Wernick, who now has a private practice in Coral Springs, Florida, says professors were very accessible, which was particularly notable to someone like himself who came from a large East Coast school with a commuter faculty.

"Here, we had faculty members who would occasionally invite students to their home or go out for a beer on Friday," he recalls. "It was nice. That part was very stimulating."

McGraw arrived at NTSU at an interesting time in the history of both its psychology department and the history of psychology in general. Behaviorism had held psychology in its thrall since the 1920s. But in the late 1960s, new research and theories started opening additional areas of study in the field. The humanistic perspective, which preaches a more holistic form of human potential, was placing considerably more faith than behaviorism in an individual's ability to make choices, change, and grow. (Some of the cuddly concepts McGraw most often scorns, such as the "inner child," were developed from this psychological perspective.) At the same time, cognitive psychology was beginning to probe the ways people think, asking such questions as how the memory works and whether there is a biological component in the way the brain stores and uses information. The behaviorists' contention that all human behavior is learned was being challenged by some of cognitive psychology's influential thinkers, such as Noam Chomsky, who asserted that the ability to develop language was not learned, but rather wired into the human brain.

In other words, in the 1970s, behaviorists were on the defensive.

This was perhaps especially true at schools like NTSU, where the cognitive and humanistic theories and research that had been coming down from loftier ivory towers were now being integrated into practice throughout clinical and counseling degree programs.

■ ■ ■

When McGraw entered the clinical psychology program at NTSU, the focus of the university's psychology department had recently been wrested from a group of radical behaviorists by other faculty members pushing to broaden the school's focus to include newer cognitive and humanistic perspectives. A tussle ensued, and things got snarky, as they sometimes do in academia. A new Center for Behavioral Studies was established, which annoyed some, says Fort Worth psychologist James Cannici, a friend and former classmate of McGraw's. When the two men started at the school, "There were still strong bad feelings about the split that had occurred," Cannici says.

"I wouldn't call it so much as a split as much as a function of the faculty that we had," Wernick adds. "We had a few pretty well-trained and well-entrenched behavioral faculty and then we had some other faculty that were more psychodynamic in their training and orientation. Those two groups don't see things the same way.

"As a student, it put you in a position, always thinking about pleasing faculty. It could get real interesting if you had a comprehensive exam and you had a committee with a real strong behaviorist and real strong psychodynamic and were trying to please them. I don't think there was an antagonism that a schism usually implies. It was more two different camps and it certainly wasn't too different than how I think it was in the profession at the time."

All this change and debate was taking place at school and in the field as McGraw embarked on his graduate studies. It provided a fertile Petri dish for his powerful and hungry young mind. The dissension among ranks and probable sniping that went with it also might have set the tone for McGraw's lifelong combative attitude toward other professionals in his field.

Today, McGraw likes to play up his contrary attitude toward those things his professors told him. Trahan says, "It was apparent that Phil thought pretty highly of his abilities and was very willing to tell you what his opinions were about things and how you were wrong if you disagreed with him." And in his introduction to *Self Matters*, McGraw proudly reminisces about having a contentious relationship with academic authorities. McGraw, referring to himself in the third person, wrote, "He remembered one of his favorite profs telling him he would never make it because he had an 'attitude' and refused to 'kiss ass.' He was told, 'You have too many options in your life to put up with this fiasco of dysfunction, you aren't near desperate enough to tolerate the abuse!' "

Nevertheless, McGraw flourished in this intellectual atmosphere and honed his debate skills in discussion with his professors and peers. Although harsh comments might have been made to McGraw by his professors privately, Cannici remembers McGraw's classroom debates with his professors as being civil and his commitment to the work sincere. "He had very strong opinions about things and he would not hesitate to speak up and challenge a professor and express his own point of view. I thought it was in a healthy and constructive way," Cannici says, adding that McGraw would also "organize study groups and was very dedicated to doing well in the program."

In their studies, McGraw and Trahan were both drawn to the behaviorist side of the discussion, "though perhaps he more than I," Trahan recalls. "As a general rule, I still agree with a lot of things he has to say, but I think he goes overboard." Cannici, on the other hand, was more taken with humanism. "[McGraw and I] engaged in what I would consider healthy dialog and difference of opinion," Cannici says.

Cannici also noticed that McGraw asked an inordinate number of questions in class, although he didn't seem to have any trouble mastering the material. At first, Cannici found this puzzling. But he soon understood the tactic. "It became apparent at the end of the first semester that he [McGraw] asked questions because he wanted to find out the exact answers—what the professors were looking for—so he knew what they wanted on the test," Cannici says. "I was impressed with that as an approach to dealing with professors in grad school."

Cannici vividly remembers the interest his classmate took in "the small person in the department, I mean the janitor and cleaning lady. He would take time to talk to them and check in with them in a way most people would not." This practice reappeared much later in McGraw's career, when he dropped in on crews building sets for his new television show, to see how the down-and-dirty work was going. McGraw says that his interest was deeply appreciated, describing how the guy who ran the shop told him, "I just want you to know, out of all the sets we've ever built, nobody has ever been here to look at their work. You're *not* in the way. They really appreciate it." At the same time, however, other staff members on McGraw's television show describe him as uninterested in some of his employees. Whether the interest McGraw claims to have had in the work of his construction crew was genuine, whether it was another venue in which he sought control, or whether it was a deliberate study in his ongoing education in human nature is unclear.

■ ■ ■

McGraw was determined to succeed at NTSU and didn't settle for good enough. Trahan started in the NTSU doctoral program a year before McGraw. As a graduate student, he taught an assessment lab in which students learned how to administer psychological tests. He recounts how McGraw came stalking over one day, mid-semester, upset over a grade he had just received from his young teacher. "By that time, Phil already had a strong A in the class, if not one of the highest grades in the class," Trahan recalls in a molasses drawl. "On this one assignment, I apparently gave him a grade that was a high B. Phil was extremely upset about that high B—not that it affected his average at all. That gave me the first indication that he was not only bright, but very aware of his intelligence. He had a pretty high opinion of his intelligence. I don't ever remember changing his grade, but I did assure him that this was not something he should worry about. Every class I had with him, he did well. I don't know that Phil ever made anything but an A."

McGraw enjoyed, to large extent, the life of a typical graduate student. He lived in an apartment, went to school basketball games and music events, and ate chili cheese fries and giant burgers at the Texas Pickup Café, a venerable NTSU hangout that burned down in November 2001. McGraw also played racquetball regularly with his friends. "I'm sure he won [when we played together]. He was much better and more athletic than me," says Cannici. "He's a hardcore tennis player and has been for a long, long time." Trahan recalls losing a match when he played racquetball with McGraw, but not by enough to satisfy McGraw's competitive nature. "It wasn't just that he had to win, he had to win big," Trahan says. "Anything short of that was obviously frustrating. Phil later commented to some other people, 'That Trahan guy really was good out there.' That's probably the only compliment I remember from him."

Yet McGraw also was an atypical student, continuing to commute to Wichita Falls in his small plane while most of his classmates drove around in beat-up cars. McGraw seemed to have multiple reasons for wanting to return home, including the pursuit of making money. Cannici spent several months flying between Denton and Wichita Falls with McGraw for a consulting business McGraw had set up on the side. "We would fly up from Denton in his private plane and we would consult with banks in Wichita Falls on their management practices—people skills, how to better manage the people you were responsible for, how to improve relationships among staff, and things like that."

Ever the entrepreneur, after a tornado devastated Wichita Falls in April 1979 (shortly before McGraw completed his studies), he and his brother-in-law, Scott Madsen, set up a construction company to rebuild houses around town in a typically brash McGraw fashion. "They knew about as much about construction as I did," a former psychology colleague in Wichita Falls recalls. "[But] they made a lot of money in that. They just subcontracted it [the work] out."

It's likely that McGraw also found good excuses to make the 230-mile round trip to Wichita Falls to continue courting Robin Jameson. In 1977, four years after they met, the couple wed. Robin then moved to Denton while McGraw completed his studies. Cannici says they lived comfortably in a modest two-bedroom flat on Eagle Drive, with only a counter separating the kitchen and living room. "They would make dinner together and so on," he reflects.

■ ■ ■

NTSU made it easy for students to work toward a master's degree and doctorate simultaneously. McGraw took advantage of this, completing his master's just one year after receiving his bachelor's—a nice accomplishment but by no means stunning or unique, his classmates agree. McGraw's thesis offers glimpses of the young man exploring concepts that would serve him well in his future courthouse adventures. It was titled "A Comparison of the Moral Judgements [sic] of Males and Females as a Function of Merging Sex Roles." McGraw's research involved giving men and women identical stories of a person committing a "moral transgression with mitigating circumstances" and having them decide if the perpetrator was guilty or if the mitigating circumstances excused the behavior. McGraw was able to conclude that "value orientation" (a person's values) had more effect on moral judgments than gender—a nugget that surely came in handy in his later career assisting with jury selections.

The thesis also speaks to the times in which McGraw was coming of age intellectually. In one of the scenarios that McGraw wrote for the experiment, a middle-aged owner of a small grocery store needs to hire a new clerk. Two qualified applicants appear, and the business owner hires the less qualified candidate because the more qualified one is a "hippie type" whom the businessman fears may alienate customers. In another scenario, a "man and his wife" wrestle with the decision of whether to have an abortion.

The paper includes a section outlining societal changes that would affect new research into gender differences. These changes included "More women pursuing what were previously considered to be exclusively male endeavors (corporate executives, police workers, truck drivers, R.O.T.C. involvement, etc.)" and "The emergence of unisex fashion (i.e., women wearing fewer dresses and more pants; men accepting more feminine styles including long hair, bell bottom trousers, silk patterned shirts, high heel shoes and purses)." McGraw also listed changes in morality that would affect outcomes, such as legalization of abortion, increased use of narcotics, and "changes in clothing which are in general more revealing (bare midriff, shorter skirts, the 'braless' look, as well as the open-shirt styles for men)."

■ ■ ■

McGraw was awarded his master's degree in 1976, just three years after he left Kansas and his first wife and decided to knuckle down in college. Moving on to his doctoral research, McGraw left gender issues and fashion reports behind. By this time, he had established a relationship with G. Frank Lawlis, Ph.D., a professor in the behaviorist camp who would become a friend, mentor, dissertation advisor, and eventual advisor to the *Dr. Phil* show. Lawlis is among the handful of people in McGraw's inner circle and now spreads McGraw's gospel through what are known as "Learn Dr. Phil Seminars."

McGraw frequently says of his friend and former professor, "Frank and I often debate about whether he taught me everything I know or everything he knows. Either way, he is, in my opinion, the leading authority in psychology today." It's a backhanded compliment, but in their NTSU days, Lawlis clearly influenced the thinking of this future psychologist.

Ten years older than McGraw, Lawlis might have recognized a bit of himself in his new student. Lawlis received his bachelor's degree at North Texas State University in 1962 and his doctorate at Texas Tech University in Lubbock in 1968, before returning to his undergraduate alma mater to teach. During his undergraduate years, Lawlis was a tackle on the Eagles, NTSU's varsity team. In 1959, he participated in one of the school's rare Sun Bowl appearances, alongside legendary running back Abner Haynes. Wernick remembers Lawlis as "a '70s kind of faculty member,"—in a sort of prototypical way—and "an interesting dude, a very bright guy." Like McGraw, Lawlis was young, smart, ambitious, confident, and good-looking, with fashionably long hair and hip sideburns. They both shared a fascination for the capabilities of the human mind.

Lawlis's primary interest was pain management using behavioral adaptations, which put him among the early practitioners in a burgeoning field now familiarly known as "mind-body." In one workshop at Caruth Memorial Rehabilitation Center in Dallas, Lawlis had pain sufferers plunge their hands into a wastebasket full of ice cubes. He told them, "With this ice, if you are anxious you can't hold your hand in there. If you relax and let your body absorb the cold, the pain will go away and your hand will become warm." In this particular case, all five participants did as they were told and all but one had the warming experience Lawlis predicted.

When McGraw arrived at NTSU, Lawlis was teaching primarily graduate level classes such as Introduction to Rehabilitation Counseling, Rehabilitation Motivation Problems, and Behavior Modification. He also worked with students on special projects and advised others on their master's theses and dissertations. In addition, Lawlis was among a group of faculty working to establish a degree program at the school in what was then called "clinical ecology" (today known as "behavioral medicine"), encompassing such techniques as biofeedback, imagery for disease treatment, and stress testing.

McGraw was drawn into the work Lawlis was doing. For his dissertation, McGraw conducted research on pain relief for rheumatoid arthritis using relaxation techniques and biofeedback, which help people obtain certain physiological states—such as lower or higher skin temperature—through psychological processes. McGraw's 24 research subjects, all women, lived in both Dallas and Wichita Falls, giving McGraw another good reason to fly between the two cities. McGraw would later maintain a biofeedback lab as part of his psychology practice in Wichita Falls.

McGraw's experiment included having research participants draw a normal joint, an arthritic joint, a picture of their disease, and an image of the treatment process. "Do this any way you want—real or fantasy—as long as it makes sense to you," the instructions read. With perhaps shades of McGraw's books to come, the instructions were packed with lists, exercises, and methods of self-examination. Research participants also completed a standard "locus of control" scale, which measured how much control they felt they had over events and experiences in their lives. This, too, was a building block of the later Dr. Phil philosophy that those with the will to do so can "manage" nearly everything in their lives.

McGraw's research probably didn't have the outcome he had hoped for. His relaxation techniques did not make research participants feel they had significantly greater control over their disease, nor was their pain significantly alleviated. "It is possible that some subjects may have perceived themselves as failing, a perception which may well have undermined an increasing sense of mastery or internal locus of control," McGraw wrote in his 122-page dissertation. "It should also be noted that many of the subjects had suffered for years and had been exposed to numerous treatments and 'cures,' and so were consequently not easily swayed in their perceptions or expectations." Here, McGraw had an early and frustrating run-in with the fuzziness of psychological research, along with the limitations of quick fixes, though he did buck up and take responsibility for the softness of his results. "The failure to determine any reliable changes in disease-related imagery is believed to be due to a lack of sophistication for both the subject and the experimenter," he wrote, in an uncharacteristic burst of modesty.

But nuanced results are certainly not unusual in psychological research, and McGraw's dissertation was approved and signed off on by Lawlis, a five-member graduate committee, the chairman of the department, and the dean of the graduate school.

■ ■ ■

For his mandatory internship, McGraw worked in the Waco VA Medical Center in Waco, Texas, a college town located about halfway between Dallas and Austin. By McGraw's own report, his time inhaling the scent of "thorazine-laced urine" in the halls of the Waco VA was miserable. In *Self Matters,* continuing his third-person narrative, McGraw reflected on doing time in Waco: "No less painfully, there had been the days, weeks, and months of dealing with a variety of insecure, 'emotionally interesting,' professors, many of them white-coated Napoleons who were all too eager to wield the power of their petty fiefdoms," he wrote. "Their torments had culminated in that unforgettable final year, when he walked the halls at school and put in his time at the hospital, armed with a signed letter of resignation on his clipboard, daring just one more anal-retentive, power-hungry mentor-turned-tormentor to say so much as 'boo' to him."

But in May 1979, all this was behind him. He made a collect call home from a pay phone in a parking lot, telling the operator "to be sure to emphasize that the call was from 'doctor' rather than 'mister'" McGraw.

He had put the Dr. in Dr. Phil, and now the newly minted Ph.D. and his young wife Robin would return to Wichita Falls to realize Joe McGraw's dream of having a practice together.

Pathways is one of the top two things I am most proud of.

Thelma Box led a sheltered childhood as the daughter of Gwendolene and Howard Peacock. Her mother was a school-teacher and her father, a Church of Christ pastor. Born in 1934, Thelma and her two sisters grew up in the quintessential small Texas town of Graham, about 60 miles from the McGraws' home in Wichita Falls. Though she finished high school, by age 15 Box was already married. She bore five children in the course of her 19-year marriage, the last one dying in infancy. That event put more stress on the already fraying relationship she had with her husband. "We were very young when we got married and there's not any doubt that we drifted apart," Box says.

Box tried to escape her marital problems by hiding in her work selling real estate and insurance, while also doing public accounting. But in 1967, she and her husband, who were living in the West Texas oil-field town of Midland, divorced. It was a harsh awakening for Box. At 35 years old, a shy and inexperienced single mother, she faced the prospect of an entirely new and challenging life.

Box had been struggling to get a foothold in her new status as a single mother for about four years when a sympathetic friend told her about a psychologist named Joe McGraw. McGraw lived in Wichita Falls, some 300 miles away, but flew to Midland one day a week to see patients there. Box decided to pay him a visit. "I saw Joe to get over all the trauma of divorce and all that," says Box in a lilting Texas twang. Joe was, she says, a good therapist and a "crusty old coot."

The relationship between the elder McGraw and Box extended beyond the office when she learned he had an airplane for sale. Box's son, Eldon, was interested in flying, and wound up buying the plane. "Somehow during that transaction, my son and Phil became friends," Box recalls. McGraw and Debbie were already divorced, and the two young men liked running around, "you know, checking girls" and such, Box fondly recalls.

Before long the Boxes and McGraws were socializing regularly, even more so when Box moved her family back to Graham, about 60 miles south of Wichita Falls. The two families had many dinners together, shared Thanksgivings, and took weekend trips.

■ ■ ■

When Box first began seeing Joe McGraw as his patient, Phil was still finishing his undergraduate degree in Wichita Falls before moving on to North Texas State University for graduate school. By June 1980, Phil had his doctorate from the North Texas State University, along with his psychology license, and had joined his father's counseling practice in Wichita Falls, a regional hub in the dusty Texas Panhandle. Home to Sheppard Air Force Base—the area's largest employer—the small city had a population of 94,000 at that time (it's only slightly more than that today). McGraw and his family ran with the fast set in Wichita Falls. "They led a colorful life [and] they were active at the country club," recalls Delores Jones, who knew the McGraws at that time. Like his dad, the younger McGraw established a

psychological practice catering to his country club cronies—
bankers, lawyers, realtors, and their families.

McGraw specialized in cognitive behaviorism, an approach that
treats thinking patterns and the behaviors they trigger. "People
would come in and say, 'I had a hard childhood, therefore I am
not doing well as an adult,'" McGraw explains. "A Freudian would
say, 'Let's work through your childhood.' I would say, 'That's fine,
but right now, you are an adult; you have a choice to stop yelling at
your kids.'"

Box respected the elder McGraw's skills as a psychologist and
when one of her teenage daughters started acting up, she called
him for help. Joe was unavailable at the moment but, says Box,
"Phil got on the phone and said, 'Well, I'll see you,' so I took my
daughter in. She [Box's daughter] liked him 'cause he was young.
She had seen Joe a few times, but she liked Phil better. So we
started going in to see Phil with some of the issues she was dealing with. I think Phil was a good therapist."

Still, Box adds, "Phil never liked one-on-one things." His dis-
satisfaction with the job was evident to her early on.

McGraw frequently denigrates his abilities at the work he got
himself into and says he quickly grew impatient and frustrated
with the job.

"Oh, my God! I got so tired of listening to people whine, I
could scream," he says. "I mean, I'd come in, a couple would sit
down in front of me and start bitching and whining, and, like, 10
minutes into it, I'm thinking, 'My God, I can't stand either one of
you. No wonder you can't get along.' That's not exactly what they
were looking for in a therapist."

McGraw ultimately concluded that one-on-one counseling just
wasn't his calling, even though his father had long looked forward to the day the two would go into practice together. "I'm just
not cut out for it," McGraw explains. "You know, I did it for a
while. I paid my dues. I've been there and sat in the office with

the therapist couch and done all that. But I don't have the temperament for it. A lot of people are looking for a baby-sitter. And I'm not very good at baby-sitting."

Some of the people McGraw counseled during his time in private practice are less critical of his skills, though they say he employed the same take-no-prisoners approach back then that he is famous for today.

Delores Jones, a bubbly, loquacious, and attractive woman, now in her 60s and living in Forth Worth, Texas, sought McGraw's help during an ugly divorce. (In the sometimes claustrophobic way of small towns, McGraw's best friend and soon-to-be business partner, Gary Dobbs, was the attorney for Jones's husband.) Looking back, Jones praises McGraw's skills. "He was abrupt but he got to the core of things," she says. "I was really down and in the dumps. He helped me see myself the way other people saw me. One of the things that astounds me is how young he was then. I was, like, 47; he was a baby. It never occurred to me then how young he was.

"I see him occasionally now on television, and he was exactly then as he is now," Jones continues. "He could be abrupt and say things strong, but he always had his arms around you, and I mean that in a philosophical way, not physically. You knew you were in a safe environment with him."

Jones had no inkling that McGraw was unhappy with his job as a therapist, and was hurt and disappointed the first time she came across a quote from him complaining about the burdens of his private practice. "When I read that he never liked counseling, I was just stunned. There was that remark [he made about being tired of patients who were constantly whining]. You *are* whining [in therapy]; you're hurting like hell. You're beyond whining; you're about comatose. I was very, very taken aback. I was so down on myself and he provided so much to me. And to look back on that time and think that perhaps it was just a chore [for him]."

Another longtime patient of McGraw's is similarly complimentary of his skills. "I think that he was incredible. I think he has a rare gift for getting to the heart of the matter. I watch his show every day when I'm home and what you see is what you get. I'm just so proud and pleased for him."

And Liz Brannan, who saw McGraw professionally for a short time when she was in her 20s, gives him credit for several important developments in her life. "He told my mother to buy me a new car," she fondly recalls. "He said, 'You can't expect Liz to go out and look for a job when she's driving that old Monte Carlo that's falling apart bolt by bolt down the street.' And I got a new car."

McGraw was treating Brannan's mother as well. "When it became clear to him that a lot of the issues I had were with my mother, he stepped back, as a good professional does, and said, 'I really feel I cannot be objective.'" McGraw instead referred Brannan to another colleague, Carol Meyers. "As a result, of that, I spent several years with Carol and she was a lifesaver," Brannan says. "The best thing Phil McGraw did was step out of the picture."

Brannan has nothing but good things to say about her former therapist. "He's brilliant," she says. "I respect and admire anybody who has a brain like that, and who can take what his brain has and put it into words so effectively. I admire a lot of things about Phil."

But some have a less favorable impression of the young doctor's in-office skills. Jones's close friend, Peggi Anderson, who turned to McGraw for help after the suicide of her 20-year-old son, expresses no admiration for him. The pain of that period lingers in her voice as she remembers trying to pick up the pieces after this devastating event. McGraw, she says, was not helpful.

"There were days when I was really suffering and I felt it was flat too painful to talk about. So I'd just turn the conversation to Phil, and he'd always talk about himself," she says. "If you've ever been to counseling, a good counselor will say, 'Well, we're really not here to talk about me, we were talking about such and such.' But he did not do that. If I didn't want to talk about something, I would just change the subject and he would tell me how great he is."

For example, Anderson remembers once sidetracking McGraw by asking him if he thought serial killer Henry Lee Lucas was a really sick person. "He said, 'Hell no, I think he's evil,'" Anderson recalls. "[He continued], 'During my internship, we learned that there are people who want you to think they're sick, but they're just mean. . . .' And he just kept talking."

■ ■ ■

Egocentric errors like this might have been early flags of McGraw's growing disenchantment with his chosen field. Whether his patients realized it or not, McGraw was chafing in the psychologist's chair. What he did enjoy was exercising the business and negotiating skills that would serve him well in the future, and that became a sort of a value-added element for his patients. For example, while helping Jones through the emotional pain of her divorce, he also assisted her in negotiating a financial settlement. "During my divorce, I felt ganged up on, but when you have Phil McGraw on your side, you're not afraid," Jones says. "When he went with me to a couple of meetings [with accountants], I felt safe."

At one point, Box's son, Eldon, hired McGraw to negotiate a series of bank loans for his faltering oil-field trucking business. "He is the most skillful negotiator I have ever seen," Thelma Box says. "He has a God-given gift, a combination of charm and charisma that can mesmerize a roomful of people." At that time, McGraw was also being called into court cases as an expert witness, an activity that sowed the seeds for his professional ventures to come.

Meanwhile, Box was getting back on her feet and found work as a real estate and insurance salesperson. She and McGraw recognized in each other a similar work ethic and entrepreneurial spirit. Box says McGraw frequently approached her with ideas for businesses they could launch together, usually having to do with real estate or insurance. But Box was already working in a job she was comfortable with and didn't want to take on another commitment. "I kept declining because I have always worked too many hours and too hard," Box says. "I wasn't really looking to get into another business [doing something else]."

In the course of her personal and professional growth, Box tapped into the self-improvement industry, attending motivational seminars by stalwarts Zig Ziglar and Dale Carnegie, to enhance her sales skills. Box then discovered that similar group techniques were being applied to the area of personal growth, in which charismatic speakers and teachers presented programs, exercises, and techniques for improving one's life in large group settings.

"I went to a lot of personal development seminars and I saw a lot of things happen in groups that didn't happen one-on-one [in individual psychotherapy]," Box says. Eventually, as she tells it, she had an inspiration for a business she could launch with McGraw—personal growth seminars for single mothers. "I saw what was happening," Box says. "My friends were getting divorced from one guy, and had little kids, and they'd jump back into another bad marriage because they were scared to death about making a living. I had a good life and didn't feel like I'd upset my kids' lives with a whole bunch of men going through it. So my original proposal was a program for single moms." With Box's real-life understanding of what her audience would need to hear and McGraw's psychology degree and powerful speaking presence, the collaboration seemed like a perfect setup.

Box says she approached McGraw with the idea, and that he immediately saw its potential as another way to make money from his professional skills. He had already experimented with pain clinics, weight-loss programs, executive recruiting, and expert witness testimony. But, according to Box, McGraw urged Box to widen the scope of her idea. "One of the things he and I talked a lot about [in counseling] was that I always view the world as either singles or couples. He helped me see the world as a world of people. He said, 'Well let's just do one [a seminar] for everybody, where single moms can come and find out they're not different.'"

McGraw had done similar self-empowerment work with small groups within his practice. Sometimes he'd invite Box to come in for a session "or two or three, just as a layperson, to basically tell them how great life can be even though you were divorced and had kids to raise," she recalls. "We had some processes and tools, as we call them, that worked. It was a really good relationship because he had the clinical aspect and I had the real life aspect."

Box also recognized that McGraw had the kind of personal magnetism that could hold a room. "Phil has charisma that does not come across on the television screen," she says. "He's a very charismatic guy." McGraw and Box soon launched their business, which they called "You." Box was content staying in the back of the room, contributing her ideas and thoughts, while McGraw took center stage as the main presenter.

"He was a quick study but he's not creative," Box says. "Most of the creative ideas, the new ideas, came from me. That's kind of my forte, to come up with a new idea or a new line. I read volumes. I see something in a book and think, oh we could do something with this. It may not look like what it started out originally, but I can come up with an idea. Phil's not creative in that way."

By combining Box's creativity and life experience with McGraw's charisma and clinical expertise, they built the framework for what would prove to be a successful and life-changing venture for both of them.

Nine months into the planning of the venture, Box was surprised to learn that she wasn't going into a 50–50 partnership with just one McGraw, as she expected. Instead, she recalls, McGraw informed her the business would be split three ways: among Box,

McGraw, and McGraw's father, Joe. At first, Box says, the younger McGraw simply suggested that they invite his father's input into the business. "I have respect for Joe; I didn't have a reason not to," Box says. But she was taken aback when McGraw informed her that Joe would be an actual partner in the venture. "It was, 'This is the way it is,'" Box complains. "I told him that I didn't think that was fair. I didn't think it was right. He [Phil McGraw] just said, 'Well, you can do it this way or we'll do it without you.'"

Box reluctantly agreed to the three-way deal and You Seminars, Inc., was established. This would be the first of several conflicts to erupt during their partnership.

■ ■ ■

The inaugural You Seminar was held at a small hotel in Wichita Falls in March 1983. It attracted more than 60 attendees— "people in his practice, my friends, our relatives, our neighbors, anybody we knew who we could get to come and see us," Box says. The seminar was presented in two parts. It began with a 26-hour weekend program that ran from Friday through Sunday. Attendees who completed this part of the program could then return for a later five-day seminar, with weekend follow-ups for those who wanted to take their training to the next level.

Box claims credit for the structure of the You Seminar programs, which eventually became known as Pathways. "I brought some ideas and things to the table. He [Phil McGraw] had the clinical aspect and he was a quick study, so we made changes after we started the basic model," she says. But McGraw was undoubtedly a factor in the seminars' success. He was both a psychological and a physical presence. He walked around the training room with his hands behind his back, sporting a serious glance and intimidating stare, not unlike the one he uses with guests on his television show today.

"The word 'God' was used with him a lot," says Jones, who attended several You Seminars. "He is charismatic. He's a handsome man, big and powerful. You can imagine, he was in his 30s, hard as a rock, a great big tall thing. You just felt that he was so in charge."

What occurred in those seminars is shrouded in a certain amount of mystery and confidentiality, largely because people were encouraged to share intimate matters. "We asked our people to remain confidential about the things that anybody else talked about," explains Box. "In the early days we also asked people not to talk about the processes we did. But we decided it painted the wrong picture so we stopped doing that. The reason we get accused of it being secret is because it's hard to explain since it's different for everybody. I can tell you exactly what we do, but that won't tell you what happens."

This closemouthed approach made some people nervous. Brannan, whose mother went to the You Seminars, says, "I started having some doubts because the people who were involved with those things were *so* involved. I think I had 'concerns' more than anything else." Brannan's mother told her nothing about her experiences in the seminars, so all Brannan knew about them is that they were, "intense."

The overall concept was relatively basic: Seminar attendees were urged to strip away self-deception, learn to do more of what worked in their lives, and replace those things that weren't working. It was similar to the message McGraw preached in his private practice and later on television and in books. In essence, Box says, seminar participants were encouraged to share their stories. "We talked about self-defeating games—the tapes you play [in your mind]—and learned to do more of what works in your life," she says.

Anderson says that even her dear friend, Delores Jones, reveals little to her about exactly what occurred at the You Seminars Jones attended. "I've heard people say we were naked," Jones shares with an incredulous chuckle. The seminars, Jones adds, did include such exercises as being blindfolded and falling backward into a teammate's waiting arms and sitting in a circle exchanging life stories. Another time, Jones recalls, participants were bused to a mall and instructed to strike up a conversation with a stranger, as an exercise in confidence building.

Box and McGraw originally intended to present two or three seminars a year; they didn't expect to develop what later came to be known as Pathways into a full-time business. But, Box says, "Pretty quickly, we were doing one [seminar] every month. And so we did, for almost 9 years, every month except December."

By the late 1980s, more than 1,000 people annually were paying up to $1,000 each to attend what was called "The Weekend" seminar with Box, McGraw, and his father. They also offered a five-day follow-up "Walk" for an additional cost. In later years, McGraw took over "The Weekend," while Box led the "Walk," and Joe McGraw ran the office and taught follow-up courses. As time went on, Box became more comfortable on stage, bringing a gentler touch than McGraw to the more sensitive discussions. "Thelma is not confrontational like Phil," Jones explains. "Thelma can get to the heart of things in a very gentle, yet pointed, way. She can really pull you up by your bootstraps."

■ ■ ■

At 69, Box remains busy and vibrant, a delicate and driven white-haired dynamo who still travels the world giving seminars. Looking back, she says she learned a lot from working with both of the McGraw men. She describes them as "two really tough clinicians."

"Phil was really, really smart and he has almost a photographic memory for recalling names and details and all that. If he doesn't recall it, he can bluff and make you think he does," Box adds. "I learned all the clinical aspects of dealing with people [that I still use today] from them one-on-one in the training room."

But Box and McGraw's different styles sometimes caused friction in the partnership. Pathways had a large number of volunteers who were such believers in the program, they donated their time to help spread its gospel. McGraw was hard on the volunteers, Box says. "He's unkind in the way he speaks to people. Phil and I had a different philosophy about that [how to treat volunteers]. He thought they ought to be beholden to us because we let them be there. I thought we ought to be appreciative because they were sharing whatever gift they had. If they flick the light switch at the wrong time, it's not that big a deal. Phil and Joe both would fuss at me. They said, 'It demeans you when you go around always saying thank-you to these people.' But I think you should say thank-you."

According to Box, McGraw's difficult manner got in the way of his first shot at Hollywood. A couple of television producers came to Wichita Falls with the idea of following seminar participants for a show. "They came in and did some filming and all that," Box remembers. "I don't know if this is the truth, but I heard that Phil was so difficult to work with, they didn't want to be a part of it."

■ ■ ■

All along, McGraw and his father kept their practice going until the late 1980s, when the two therapists both ran aground on similar rocky shoals. First, in 1987, a complaint against Joe was filed by a local banker's wife with the Texas State Board of Examiners of Psychologists. Records of the proceedings don't detail the problem, because Joe voluntarily turned in his license on July 20, 1987. Accompanying the license was a letter to the Board that read, in part: "Due to my deteriorating physical condition, please accept my resignation and the enclosed license. I do not anticipate ever reapplying for recertification or licensing before this board in the future, to be effective only upon your written approval set forth below." The board, having received this resignation, responded with an Order of Dismissal, dated July 23, 1987. The Board stated it would hold the complaint in abeyance unless Joe applied for recertification or relicensure, which he apparently never did.

Soon after, McGraw was called before the same Board in an apocalyptic episode in his own professional life—the full truth of which remains shrouded in rumors, denials, and conflicting information. A 19-year-old woman, who was in treatment with McGraw from about June 1984 through August 1984, lodged a complaint about him with the Texas State Board of Examiners of Psychologists.

The official complaint accused McGraw of "unprofessional conduct" and of having an "inappropriate dual relationship" with his female patient. According to documents filed in the case, the problem was "possible failure to provide proper separation between termination of therapy and the initiation of employment." In other words, the woman worked for McGraw in his biofeedback lab while he was still treating her. But the whisper among long-time McGraw watchers is that there was more to it than that.

One magazine quoted the woman as saying that McGraw sexually abused her. "He'd pull me down to sit in his lap while he was talking on the phone to patients, to other doctors—even his wife. He'd reach in my blouse and touch my breasts. He liked to rub my legs. He loved to rub my pelvic bone."

Another article included anonymous quotes, allegedly from the same woman, stating, "I was emotionally abused as a child and suffered from low self esteem." She accused McGraw of becoming overly involved, and grilling her for information about all aspects of her life. "If I was depressed or anxious, his first question was, 'Why didn't you call me?' Every time I felt bad, he insisted only he could fix me. He kept me totally dependent on him."

McGraw denies any sexual misconduct and insists he was only doing as the woman's family requested: Hiring her to keep a close watch on her. "The patient learned about that later, that family was involved and stuff like that, and took exception to it," McGraw says. "I file it under the adage: 'No good deed goes unpunished.'"

TV Guide quoted McGraw as insisting, "I have never so much as patted this woman on the back. It was absolutely and totally false. And it was fully investigated and dismissed." McGraw says he took a lie detector test that cleared him, but could not remember the name of the person who administered the test. The woman's parents, who still live in Wichita Falls, refuse to talk about what happened. McGraw waived a formal adjudicatory hearing and reached a settlement in this case with the Board of Examiners.

The Board's disciplinary action was stiffer than one would imagine a charge of inappropriate employment might warrant. It included a public letter of reprimand; a year of supervision by a licensed psychologist, to be approved by the Board; complete physical and psychological exams; and an ethics class. Then, McGraw was required to retake the state's jurisprudence examination. The severity of the discipline suggests an infraction far more serious than the dual relationship of therapist/employer, but the whole truth is hard to unearth from under both the official and still-whispered he-said, she-said accusations.

In Wichita Falls, these whispers among gossips are loud, about this case and about allegations of inappropriate relations with other female patients. But McGraw supporters insist it's all just talk.

"He may have done everything that anyone can come up with, but I just tell you I didn't see it," says Jones. "I never heard an ugly word about him."

"Some people just talk a little too much and there's no credence to it," says another former patient. "I *certainly* would not say that he was a womanizer. He was always a perfect gentleman."

Big, handsome, charismatic McGraw was either the victim of malicious envy, or unable to resist the temptations of his own personal magnetism. The Texas State Board of Examiners of Psychologists issued its official reprimand on October 21, 1988. Whether, as some suggest, a mob with pitchforks was gathering or whether, as McGraw tells it, he was simply ready to escape the practice that gave him so little satisfaction—McGraw was soon to leave his private practice and Wichita Falls far behind.

From the Couch to the Courtroom

I feel about litigation the way Patton did about war: God help me, I do love it so.

After a decade in private practice, McGraw says he had grown to loathe sitting in the psychologist's chair and pretending to be sympathetic to other people's problems. He was itching to escape the drudgery of psychotherapy. Pathways was successful, with McGraw providing charisma to the operation, but he was growing restless in that endeavor as well. "I saw the writing on the wall," Box says. "I knew that Phil was getting burned out. He was in the training room less. For several years we hired assistants to come in and help him out in the room. I got tired of training those people."

McGraw's interests were shifting in a new direction. He had dabbled in another venue for mind games—the courtroom—and found it to his liking. As an expert witness in divorce and personal injury cases, and in cases involving airplane crashes, he found a certainty in the courtroom that attracted him as strongly as the fuzzy science of psychotherapy frustrated him. "In law, 12 people go into a room, shut the door, hold an election and you've got a winner and a loser and they write a number down to go with it," he says.

McGraw was also facing disciplinary actions imposed by the Texas Board of Examiners of Psychologists. Though he denies the reprimand influenced his decision to give up psychotherapy, that and his own increasingly negative attitude toward providing it surely made 1989 seem as good a time as any to get out of a career he abhorred and into something for which he had a clear talent and an unabashed passion. "I hate that people get sued, but if they are, I love to be in the fight," he says.

McGraw's friend and neighbor in Wichita Falls, attorney Gary Dobbs, likewise was looking to put a new spin on his career. Dobbs, a former director of the State Bar of Texas, recognized McGraw's talent for seeing through people and being able to uncover their motivations, as well as his ability to break complex issues down into sound bites that juries could understand. "He's the best reader of people I've ever seen," Dobbs says. "You give him 15 minutes with anyone, and he can pretty much tell you who that person is. He can tell you character-wise, he can tell you personality-wise, what they are or what's bothering them, and in a very short time. That's a tremendous talent."

"Some people look at a person and see a maze," is how McGraw describes his gift. "I see a schematic diagram with a red arrow showing me where I need to go."

And so McGraw and Dobbs became partners in a new business venture. In 1989, they both moved 140 miles southeast to Dallas, the big city that lured restless young people living in small towns throughout Oklahoma and Texas. Dallas was a place of gleaming skyscrapers, ambitious people, fashionable shops, and—with the state recovering from the oil bust that sent its economy reeling— fields of green. Money, that is. Even today, Dallas is a wheeler-dealer city of entrepreneurs, where making and spending a buck are passions and business failure just means that you at least tried, and better luck next time.

In 1990, McGraw and Dobbs founded a trial consulting firm they named Courtroom Sciences, Inc. (CSI for short), in Irving, a fast-growing suburb west of Dallas. McGraw brought his psychological expertise and charisma to the company; Dobbs, whose license to practice law in Texas was suspended in 2003 for non-payment of state bar dues and the attorney occupational tax, came with legal knowledge, connections, and some suggest, mostly money. "The story always was that Gary had a lot of money from winning cases back in Wichita Falls in the oil business," says one former CSI employee. "He and Phil were friends and they started up this venture. Phil was to be the brains and Gary was to be the money and that's the way it was set up and pretty much the way it always was."

■ ■ ■

The field of trial consulting, which was born in the 1970s, suffers from an image problem. Like McGraw himself, trial consulting is equal parts psychology and show biz. The field is peopled by clinical psychologists, social psychologists, communications experts, linguists, marketing pros, and theater majors. Many view it with skepticism, according to Richard Gabriel, president of the American Society of Trial Consultants. But, as he points out, as the nation becomes more multicultural and the law more complex, attorneys increasingly need consultants to help them with the people side of the equation while they focus on the legal issues.

Trial consultants like CSI help attorneys understand jurors' mind-sets and motivations for more effective voir dire. They sell services such as attitudinal research to uncover jurors' preexisting beliefs. They also offer witness preparation. McGraw, with a mischievous grin, told David Letterman, "We don't coach them, we just teach them to tell the truth effectively." CSI employs artists and computer technicians who prepare graphic evidence for presentation to the jury. The company even developed a proprietary software program, called Trial Vision™, that aids attorneys in creating their own computer presentations. This software is "the bread and butter of their business," according to a former employee.

Among the cornerstones of CSI's business plan is a well-established Psychology 101 model of human cognition: "If you tell them [jurors], they retain about 10 percent of it [the information]," McGraw explains. "If you show them, they retain about 60 percent of it. If you show them and tell them, they retain about 80 percent of it. And then if you repeat it again at some point, pretty soon they start to get the essence of your case."

Trial consulting remains a field fighting for respect. A few years back, Simon Wood, an Ernst & Young auditor, hired CSI and McGraw. The auditor was accused of helping Cendant Corporation cook its books after an audit revealed accounting irregularities at the company in 1998. McGraw's job, by all accounts, was to coach Wood. In 2003, Judge William Walls said that McGraw should be required to reveal the substance of his discussions with Wood, implying that he didn't feel these conversations had the same protections as Wood's discussions with his lawyers. "It is unrealistic to assume, even for a moment, that a jury consultant is coming in to discuss things legal," Walls said. "It is, in effect, the cosmetician coming in to correct what may or may not be a pallor complexion." Ernst & Young's attorneys argued that such discussions were protected under attorney-client privilege. In September 2003, the court agreed

Gabriel points out that if McGraw had been required to talk, it would have cast a pall on the field of trial consulting. "If you start saying you can discover what was said, then there's no way that people can effectively prepare for trials."

■ ■ ■

For McGraw, the work of creating a courtroom production turned out to be as challenging and exciting as private practice was stultifying. "It's like being a producer-director of a movie," he says. "You get to design things in concert with some of the best lawyers in the world, and then you sit in the front row and watch it unfold." McGraw was good at his job. His insight into the minds of others brought something to the table that many lawyers could not. "He literally would walk into a room and sit down with 10 or 12 of the finest attorneys in the country and tell them things they had never realized," recalls Denver attorney Charice Miles, a litigation analyst for CSI for about seven years. "He did it all the time. He would come in and say, 'This is what your case is about, this is what you need to do, these are the five things you need to worry about, and this is it.' They'd sit there with their mouths open like, 'Oh my God, how did he do that?'"

"Phil had fermented into an even finer creator and operator," says James Cannici, Ph.D., who met McGraw in graduate school and worked briefly at CSI. "He had this tremendous operation at CSI, and he was a brilliant strategist and very creative. Although he co-ran it with Gary Dobbs, he was very much in charge and the inspiration behind it."

It was during this time that McGraw drifted further and further away from Pathways. In addition to being busy with CSI, his father's health was beginning to fail. Though McGraw and Box didn't have explicit discussions about the future of Pathways, "We had talked about the fact that we were going to have to make decisions about what we were going to do," Box recalls. "I thought that Phil would just want to bring in an employee, and I would pretty much continue what I was doing, with [the addition of the new worker]." Box also hoped that when McGraw was ready to exit Pathways, he would simply sell his interest to her.

Neither of those scenarios occurred. It was Joe McGraw who first raised his suspicions to Box. Steve Davidson, a philanthropist from Midland, Texas, had been filling in regularly as a Pathways speaker for the increasingly busy Phil McGraw. "Joe told me, 'I think Phil has made a deal with him or was going to make a deal with him [to take over Phil's interest in Pathways],'" Box says.

In reality, McGraw had already struck a deal, according to the *Dallas Observer*. On October 15, 1991, he reportedly sold his Pathways stock to Davidson for $325,000. The agreement stated that the sale was to remain confidential. A subsequent memo from McGraw emphasized that it should be kept secret from the public, Box, and even his own father "to minimize the inevitable pain of transition and disruption of support and enrollment." In fact, continuing a pattern that began long ago, McGraw apparently didn't get along very well with his father in the Pathways business from the start. During training sessions, McGraw reportedly seldom spoke with his dad, who often fell asleep in the training room and was, at times, more disruptive than helpful.

"He [Phil] sold his interest a whole year before he let me and his dad be aware of that," Box says. Joe's suspicions were confirmed by the audacious act of Davidson's secretary who, according to Box, faxed her documentation about the deal. "She just felt like I needed the information. She felt it wasn't right," says Box, who did not immediately reveal to McGraw what she had learned.

According to Box, the whole incident came to a head one day when Box and McGraw were in the training room. "[He] had one of his fits at me," Box says. "I told him 'This ain't working. I want you to buy me out or I want to buy you out.' I knew by that time he had already sold his interest but I didn't tell him that I knew." The matter wasn't resolved until later that day, after Box returned from a meeting with a business associate who urged her to act aggressively to remedy the situation. "In the past I would've let it drop," Box says. "But I went home and followed up. I [called McGraw] and said, 'It's time to call it quits. I want you to take seriously my request that either you sell out to me or let me buy you out.' The next correspondence I had was a fax from him telling me that they [McGraw and his dad] were negotiating to sell their two-thirds interest, and that the people [new owners] wanted to either buy me out or talk to me about being my partner." The fax arrived on November 16, 1992.

Box was incensed, insulted, and in no way willing to go into partnership with the new owners. "I knew both those guys. I didn't believe they were people with the same integrity level as me and I didn't want to be partners with them." In addition, Box claims, "I was privy to some of their correspondence and found out their plan was to keep me with them until I got them trained. Then they wouldn't have any more use for me and [could] get rid of me. So it was just a matter of walking out then or walking out now."

Box arguably had more at stake in the matter. While Pathways was merely a sideline for Joe and Phil McGraw, especially with CSI growing by the day, it was the way Thelma Box earned her living. Still, she chose to walk out sooner rather than later. "We had an announcement in December of 1992. They got up and made the announcement [in a seminar] and I got up and made mine. [I said] that by January, I'd be doing the same thing under a different name. I went out and became their competition. I maintained one-third ownership in Pathways for five years. Finally, one of them [the new owners] sold his one-third interest to another guy who got smart enough—a friend of mine helped him get smart—to realize that if he bought my one-third interest, he'd own two thirds and could get rid of the partner. At least I got money for my one-third interest."

■ ■ ■

"**P**athways Lifestyle Management" continues under the direction of McGraw trainee and lead facilitator Andy Lawrence. The web site for the Dallas-based company gives scant mention of Lawrence, but it plasters McGraw's name on every page, even though he remains involved only in the barest consulting capacity. The Pathways site also sells McGraw's ever-growing collection of books and tapes.

Thelma Box's name is nowhere to be found. The description of the training courses credits only McGraw and reads, "Founded by Dr. Phillip C. McGraw in 1985, the training uses Dr. Phil's famous 'no nonsense' approach to empower you to face and eliminate the barriers that stand between you and your success." Nor does McGraw ever mention Box in accounts of his climb to success. Her name does not appear in any of his books, and he never identifies her in media interviews. "Somebody told me a while back that he mentioned something [on television] about a woman who helped him get started, and that was a mentor. They thought he was describing me, but he didn't say my name," Box says, adding that she hears echoes of their early seminars in the advice and aphorisms McGraw spouts on television. "He needs to go to the seminar and get some new lines," she chuckles.

Box believes that if she were to telephone McGraw today, he would talk with her, despite the fact that she has been outspoken about her experiences with him. But even if he refused to talk, she is unconcerned. Box called him once, after his first book came out and while he was on *Oprah*, and the talk turned to her work with Choices. Box suggested that he refer people to her seminars "so they would get real and lasting help, as we both knew that he could not give them that in a few minutes," she says. He responded that they should get together over lunch to discuss the idea, she recalls, but when she called to set something up, he never returned the call. "My life is so good that I never ever made another phone call [to him]," Box says. "He doesn't know how to treat the friends he has."

While Pathways continued on its track, Box's gamble—quitting Pathways and striking out on her own at the age of 50—also paid off. She launched her own seminar company and now holds dozens of workshops annually in Dallas, Vancouver, and Calgary. "Maybe 70 percent of the [original Pathways base] went with me," she claims. "We never went back to the original numbers we had and it was a little bit of a struggle at first. But I never expected . . . to do that."

Box is circumspect about McGraw's success. "The truth is, I probably got more benefit associating with him than most people did. I don't want to be misleading about that," she admits. "My life has been great because Phil McGraw was in it and I think if he were honest he'd say the same about me."

■ ■ ■

By the early 1990s, McGraw was probably past caring about Box or Pathways. After all, he was building CSI, his successful new business. But just as CSI was getting on its feet, McGraw suffered a personal loss. By then, McGraw's parents had moved to Dallas as well. In 1993, Joe McGraw was diagnosed with heart disease. "He came by the house on the way back from the doctor and I said, 'Well, how'd it go?'" McGraw recalls. "And he said, 'Well, don't buy me any green bananas, I can tell you that for sure.' That was his way of telling me, 'I'm dying.'"

A devout churchgoer, Joe taught classes at the Irving Bible Church and completed graduate studies at the Dallas Theological Seminary just before suffering a fatal heart attack on August 22, 1993. He died while teaching Sunday School. But before his passing, this father and son were able to take stock of their sometimes strained relationship. "He and I had a chance to sit down and talk about everything we wanted to say and everything we wanted to do, and I have to tell you, I believe there was nothing left unsaid," McGraw attests. "And I took such peace from that."

In *Life Strategies*, McGraw recalled how Joe bared his heart to him before he died, telling his only son, "I love you. I am and always have been proud of you, even though I did not tell you very often, if ever . . . And now that I know I am not long for this world, I am truly sorry that I did not spend more time knowing you, being with you, and letting you know me."

Whatever grief he suffered, McGraw's pace didn't slow down. CSI had some lean years in the beginning, according to Dobbs, but it wasn't long before the endeavor was supporting McGraw in the style he preferred. Though he most likely arrived in Dallas with little in his pocket, by 1996 he was able to settle his family into a million-dollar, five-bedroom Italianate McMansion in a gated community a couple of miles from CSI's offices. The house was on a golf course and just steps away from the tony Four Seasons Resort, where he and Robin became members of the health club.

■ ■ ■

CSI today is a $20 million a year business housed in an undistinguished two-story building among other bland office parks in Irving. Past the spacious reception area with a vaulted ceiling, massive modular sofa, and a receptionist's desk that resembles a judge's bench sits a conference room with plump, tufted, black leather chairs. CSI's headquarters also include faux courtrooms in which mock trials are conducted for about $30,000 a day. McGraw's office, in particular, impressed one employee with its lavish decoration. "I've never seen an office that luxurious in my life," she says. "His own bathroom has a shower. I mean, that's not unusual for executive offices, but this isn't a multinational corporation here."

That may be, but CSI definitely runs with the big boys. Corporations pay upwards of $400 an hour for the company's expertise. Among CSI's corporate clients are half of the Fortune 500, including MCI, 3M, and all the major airlines. Exxon hired McGraw and CSI to work on the Valdez oil spill case to great effect. In 1996, CSI helped Exxon's legal team win a $400 million judgment from Lloyd's of London. The insurer originally refused to pay a claim for the massive cleanup costs that resulted from the spill. To secure this victory and get a court to require Lloyds to make this payment, McGraw and his team staged mock trials to mirror juries and assist in jury selection. "It is a tool that is available. And if you have a significant case, to not use it is like getting treatment without an X-ray, getting treatment without an MRI," McGraw says of CSI's techniques. "If that's available, if that's the state of the art and someone didn't use it in treating me, I wouldn't feel good about that. And if I'm going to trial in a significant matter and someone has scientific capabilities to ensure that I'm going to get a fair trial, I want it done."

CSI and McGraw also worked with the ABC television network when Food Lion sued the ABC news division for fraud, breach of duty of loyalty, trespass, and unfair trade practices (reporters had obtained jobs at the company using false resumes in order to expose the supermarket chain's unsafe food-handling habits). The fraud verdict in that case was overturned on appeal. Other charges stuck, although Food Lion was awarded all of $1 because the journalists trespassed, and another $1 because the journalists/supermarket employees breached their legal duty of loyalty to their employer. The miniscule penalties were perhaps testament, in part, to McGraw's consulting skills.

■ ■ ■

Though trial consulting is widespread and growing, the average trial consulting service is nowhere near the size and splendor of CSI. "There are some good ones out there and a lot of dabblers," says Miles. "There are probably about three or four companies in the country that actually do it to the level that we were doing it, with the complete package of graphic services, mock trials, and other services."

CSI has always kept a remarkably low profile in the media. Although CSI employees occasionally publish in industry journals or speak at seminars for the legal profession, the company's name rarely appears in the press, except in accounts of McGraw's rise to fame. Even then it's often only in passing. This is apparently by design. One observer claims that McGraw will test the loyalty of employees by staging telephone calls from people pretending to be members of the media.

Business comes to CSI by word of mouth. "All of it," stresses a former staffer. "There's no advertising done at all." Some referrals come from attorneys who have worked with CSI. Other times, corporate executives familiar with the firm refer their legal team to CSI with the express desire of staging a mock trial before making their way to the courtroom. While company lawyers who have never heard of CSI before are often reluctant to seek this outside help in the beginning, "they usually get on board once they see what it's all about," Miles says.

Dallas attorney Chip Babcock, who would later figure largely in McGraw's transition from the courtroom to the television studio, says, "I used to be skeptical, but Phil made a believer out of me. He has an innate ability to isolate people who would not see the facts the way you do. It's the most uncanny thing I've ever seen. He once told me he was never wrong."

"He [McGraw] has exceptional talent at helping lawyers be better teachers," says McGraw's own attorney, Dallas-based Bill Dawson, who has worked with McGraw since 1991. "I think he's far and away the very best at doing that that I have run into."

■ ■ ■

Typically, during McGraw's heyday at the firm, the work flow started with an attorney meeting with McGraw and Dobbs, who would then assign a CSI team to take on the case, Miles explains. Sometimes teams would have six months to work on a case; other times CSI would be called in a week before a case went to trial. Usually, Miles says, cases that CSI became involved in were for high stakes. "Frankly, it's extremely expensive, so we did not do little cases," she explains.

CSI also tended to work with lawyers representing defendants rather than plaintiffs, partly because of McGraw's trademark impatience. "I think suing is kind of whiny," he has said. "But also, practically, defendants are usually the deep pockets and they're the ones who can afford my kind of services."

In cases of this scale, success is relative. While attorneys who hire CSI might not always walk out the clear winners, neither are they usually complete losers. Asked about CSI's success rate, McGraw reasons, "Well, it depends on how you define success. I mean, we've had cases where a client was getting sued for $1 billion and a verdict was brought back against them for $3 million. That's a victory. Did we win the case? No, not in an outright sort of way. But did we damage control it down from some huge exposure to something that was economically viable and they could live with? Yes."

With the work he did at CSI, McGraw seemed to have found a perfect venue for his talents. He was clearly the mind behind the company's accomplishments. "The success of CSI rests totally on his shoulders," says Miles. "Everyone wanted him. He just had the charisma. It's like being next to a superstar. You want to be next to him."

McGraw knew he held the secret to CSI's success, and he made sure that everyone who worked for him did things his way. Judith Fletcher, a Plano, Texas, psychologist who took a break from private practice to work for CSI in 1999, said the job used her knowledge as a psychologist, but she still had to learn how to do things the McGraw way. "The people at Courtroom Sciences are not shy about saying that they pride themselves on teaching people how to do it the way he wants to do it," she recalls.

■ ■ ■

With the high dollar figures attached to the work that CSI does, it's not surprising that CSI is a high-stress workplace. As the boss, McGraw had an unfettered opportunity to unleash his demanding nature on employees. McGraw insisted that things be done his way, accepted nothing less than perfection, and made himself extremely disagreeable if he perceived a job to be substandard, according to several former CSI staffers. His demands, perfectionism, impatience, and infuriated outbursts created an atmosphere of fear, resentment, and anxiety, they say. Working at CSI was equal parts thrilling and terrible.

"He [McGraw] wasn't so much hard on people if a case was lost, but he was extremely hard on people if he felt a product CSI delivered was not done up to speed," a former employee recalls. "He was extremely tough on all of us. I have mixed feelings about that. I think the level of excellence that he expected from people, in a way, was great. It pushed all of us. I think he made me a better professional person. I just question some of his methods."

Working at CSI is an all-or-nothing commitment. Newcomers to the company are told to consider themselves on call, like a doctor. One employee recalls being paged at 3 A.M. "It was Phil, screaming at me."

"Phil engenders in that culture that you are his 24 hours a day, seven days a week, 365 days a year," says another former employee. "There's no time off. If you're a professional [as opposed to support staff], that's what you sign up for there. They own you. I wore a pager the entire time I worked there and if I ever, ever failed to answer a page, I got it big time."

"Sometimes you would go out of town for a three-month stint unexpectedly," Miles remembers. "A lot of single people would start a case with a boyfriend and by the time it was over, the boyfriend was long gone."

Fletcher recalls her own brush with unexpected travel, when she didn't even have time to go home and pack a suitcase or hit a cash machine for a trip to Los Angeles with a client. To make sure she had spending money for the trip, McGraw gave her the cash from his wallet and exhorted other employees to do the same until Fletcher had enough to see her through the trip. Fletcher recalls this incident warmly, although she ultimately found that her life could not support the demands of the job. "I had small children," she says. "I was really one of the only staff members with small children." When she learned she was pregnant with her third child after a couple of months at the company, her health became a factor.

"I lost 15 to 20 pounds that first trimester while working for Phil. I didn't tell anyone because the expectation is that you do what you need to do for the sake of the job. I wanted to do the job and I didn't want anyone making the assumption that I couldn't." Fletcher left the company after about six months, with no ill will. "People can interpret that as 'Ooh, that was such a big bad environment that you couldn't even tell them you were pregnant,'" Fletcher says. "But it was *my* decision. I want that clear."

Cannici, McGraw's grad school friend, called McGraw when he became restless in his academic setting. Cannici started at CSI a couple of weeks after their conversation, but found that about six months of the CSI pace was about all he could handle. "I didn't realize when I took the job that it would involve so much travel. It became a problem in terms of my family," he says. "But I enjoyed the work enormously."

■ ■ ■

Total commitment to the job is part of the CSI corporate culture. So is a sort of class system, according to a former employee. The litigation consultants were called "professionals." The "nonprofessionals" included denizens of the workroom—such as the secretarial pool, graphic artists, and computer technicians.

McGraw, Dobbs, and two other longtimers—Dennis Thompson and Lyndon McLennan—were the good ol' boys ruling the roost of about 50 mostly female employees. The women who succeed at CSI are tough, polished, forthright, and unafraid of a little salty language or bawdy humor. Says one former employee, "Interestingly enough, there are lots of really beautiful women that work there. There was really nobody who worked at CSI that was unpleasant looking, female-wise." But, the employee adds,

"There was never going to be any woman that was totally let in [to the inner circle]. These boys are bubbas to the core."

"[McGraw] has always said he prefers to work with women because the position we have is very detail-oriented and task-oriented," says Miles. "He felt that women did a great job at that." Miles disabuses the notion that McGraw preferred women employees because they're easier to intimidate. "His wrath was not directed only at women by any means," she says. "I think he likes strong women. If you're going to cry if he says something to you, I don't think he wants you to work there. But I don't want people like that working for me, either."

Still, Miles shudders when recalling McGraw telling people that their work looked like "an abortion." Another female former employee remembers that when McGraw was unable to get the copier to work, he would stand by it and bellow, "Could somebody get some goddamn ovaries in here to fix this thing?"

When McGraw was riled, he was uncensored. "There was yelling, there was cussing, there was ranting," Miles recalls.

"He's verbally abusive," another former employee complains. "He's called me a stupid bitch. It was so constant. Everybody who has worked at CSI shakes in their boots about Phil. That's just the way it is. I know that it's gotten worse over time."

But perks were also attached to the job. For those professionals who could withstand McGraw's outbursts, life at CSI was first class all the way. "He had catered lunches for our meetings; we flew first class; I stayed in every nice hotel in this country," says Miles. "He spared no expense because our reputation was to be the best and to be the best you had to act like it. There weren't going to be any cold sandwiches on a plate." For the nonprofessionals, life wasn't quite as cushy. A former employee recalls working on a trial in a town about an hour from CSI offices. While the professionals stayed in a hotel during the trial, this less exalted employee had to make the drive daily. And, she adds, the only time she ever flew first class was on a hop from Kansas City to Dallas.

Employees were usually paid well for their work—but there was a catch: Compensation was contingent on bonuses. This tactic is a classic motivator in the canon of behavioral management, a spinoff of the behavioral psychology McGraw focused on in school. "He would pay people minimum to moderate salaries, but you could earn more by earning bonuses," says Cannici. "He used a behavioral approach to compensation in a very effective way with his employees. You [only] had a moderate salary if you didn't choose to put in a lot of extra hours. I was working 60–70 hours a week."

As a litigation consultant, Miles says she earned a salary comparable to a secretary's, which was supplemented by quarterly bonuses of anywhere from $10,000 to $30,000. Employees could earn a lot, but wouldn't know in advance exactly how much. Financial planning, Miles notes, was impossible.

"It was extremely unfair," says Miles, who traces the beginning of the end of her tenure at CSI to the day she asked for raises for everyone and was branded a troublemaker. "You never knew what you were getting paid. You could work for three months and if you weren't in favor that day, maybe you didn't get a bonus. It was completely discretionary. So then, you'd basically been working for half your salary for the past three months. It was very odd. But then, barring any problem, every three months you got a big check."

Miles never received her final bonus after being asked to leave the company because she was "rocking the boat." She recalls other times when employees were told that other expenses would take precedence, resulting in smaller bonus checks. "There were times [when we were told] that, 'We're buying equipment for the office' and 'Gosh guys, there's not enough to go around,' and it [the bonus] would be smaller than expected."

Miles was skeptical of the reasons given for the smaller checks. "It's a little hard to explain when you [McGraw and Dobbs] pull up in your new Mercedes. We all knew where the money was going." Another former employee complains that the company kept slow past-prime computers to produce what should have been state-of-the-art work. This made substandard products more likely, for which employees were blamed. "A new computer is, what, $1,500?" the employee points out.

■ ■ ■

People who worked for McGraw at CSI have complicated, conflicting feelings about him. Many who leave the company do so feeling battered and abused. One former employee laughs at the idea of starting a support group for former CSI employees, but admits that there is already an informal one, of sorts. Although McGraw's brilliance sparks admiration, his perfectionism and verbal brutality leave lingering bitterness.

"It was very much a love/hate relationship," says Miles. "I admired him but I hated him. I respected him but I thought he was a pig. You know—the way most charismatic successful people are portrayed."

"He's funny, he's brilliant, he's the smartest person I've ever met in my life, hands down. And he can manipulate the shit out of anyone," says another former employee. "Phil is a cult personality, end of story. He is phenomenal. It's really impressive, and that's why he's done so well."

Yet, the same employee continues, "He's like an abusive husband. You love him and he's so nice and he's great, but he just beats you up every once in a while. But you keep going back to him."

Those who knew McGraw at CSI, however, point out that whatever other inappropriate behavior McGraw displayed, his reputation for womanizing appeared to be behind him and his devotion to Robin and his sons was evident to all. "I think he learned his lesson when he was young about this stuff," suggests one former employee.

■ ■ ■

Despite the atmosphere, many CSI employees stay with the company a long time. According to a former employee, "They constantly infused in us 'You can't go anywhere else, you're never going to make this kind of money, there's no company like CSI.' That's kind of a control tactic."

She adds, "I think a lot of people who work there, myself included, want to belong, they want to do well, they're pleasers. It embarrasses me to admit it, but it's very cult-like. They believe it's their only route, they believe they can't do anything differently, they think they can't do any better. I have a much different perspective on it now that I've left."

There is no denying that proximity to McGraw is heady and educational. Fletcher, who returned to private practice after leaving CSI, credits McGraw with helping her become a better businessperson. "I make very good business decisions now compared to before because of what I learned there."

And the work was clearly exciting. "Some attorneys have one or two cases that are cases of a lifetime," says Fletcher. "At Courtroom Sciences, every attorney you work with is working on the case of a lifetime."

Such was the case for Dallas attorney Chip Babcock, who came to CSI with his case of a lifetime, which was also to start a new chapter in McGraw's life.

Oprah Comes Calling

*There's something that I call the "Oprah factor." The "O fac-
tor." It just takes everything you do and it just goes up by an
order of magnitude that is overwhelming.*

On April 16, 1996, an episode of *The Oprah Winfrey Show* set
off a chain of events that would change the course of
McGraw's life yet again.

The world was gripped by fear of Mad Cow Disease. In Eu-
rope, thousands of cows were being destroyed and Americans
saw grisly images of the slaughter nightly on the television news.

Winfrey taped the show, titled "Dangerous Foods," on April 10,
about a week before it aired. The guest experts Winfrey presented
to her 15 million viewers included Howard Lyman, a former
rancher turned vegetarian and director of the Humane Society's
Eating with Conscience Campaign, which encourages an organic,
meat-free diet. Although the cattle industry was represented, the
antibeef images presented on the show were shocking and potent.
One exchange between Winfrey and Lyman went like this:

Mad cow disease, Lyman told Winfrey, could make AIDS look
like the common cold. When Winfrey pressed him, he described

how cows often die in the night, and how those dead cows would be ground up and fed back to other cows—like cannibals, he said.

Winfrey: Now see? Wait a minute. Let me just ask you this right now, Howard. Do you know for sure that the cows are ground up and fed back to other cows?

Lyman: Oh, I've seen it. These are USDA statistics. They're not something that we're making up.

Winfrey: Now doesn't that concern you all a little bit right here, hearing that?

Audience: Yeah!

Winfrey: *It has just stopped me cold from eating another burger! I'm stopped!*

■ ■ ■

In a Chicago hotel not far from the studio where *Oprah* is taped, Texas cattleman Paul Engler heard these words denouncing the food on which his fortune was built. "I never see *Oprah,* but I just happened to turn it on," Engler says. "I was entranced—I couldn't believe what I was seeing. It was so wrong, it was so judgmental. I knew it was going to have an impact on our industry."

There's no doubt that in today's pop culture universe, when Winfrey talks, people listen. Just ask Wally Lamb, Anita Shreve, Jane Hamilton, or any of the other authors who watched their books become bestsellers after Winfrey featured their titles on her book club. When cattle futures plummeted following the show, some industry watchers blamed the drought on Britain's mad cow scare. But cattlemen in Texas placed the blame for the crisis on Winfrey. They called it the "Oprah Crash."

Engler, who owns the cattle company Cactus Feeders, and Bill O'Brien, owner of Texas Beef, initiated a lawsuit against Winfrey, Lyman, and Harpo Productions, citing the False Disparagement of Perishable Food Products Act. This Act bars the vilification of perishable food products without scientific proof. The cattlemen sued for $12 million plus punitive damages, accusing Winfrey and Lyman of "lambasting the American cattle industry." Engler estimated that his company lost $7 million in the aftermath of the show.

Winfrey hired Charles "Chip" Babcock, a blue-eyed, baby-faced Dallas attorney with a silver mop of hair, who had extensive experience defending the media. Babcock's previous cases included defending Amway Corporation when Procter & Gamble accused it of spreading false rumors about that company's involvement in Satanism. He also defended Dallas television station KXAS, which was sued for fraud, defamation, negligence, invasion of privacy, and trespassing by Dallas Cowboys player Eric Williams, after the station reported what ultimately turned out to be a fabricated rape accusation against him. (The Amway suit was dismissed; the KXAS case was settled out of court.) Winfrey called Babcock, "One of the greatest lawyers, not just in terms of his ability to argue the case and to defend the case, but just a great heart."

■ ■ ■

To Winfrey's dismay, the case was to be tried in Amarillo, a cattle town in the rugged Texas panhandle. Winfrey feared a rough ride ahead, as a wealthy and successful black woman going up against the good ol' boys of Texas in a community where cattle is central not only to the region's mystique and self-image, but also to the livelihood of much of the population. "Oprah was scared to death about coming to Texas, the heart of cattle country," says Amarillo-based attorney Robert Garner, who was on the defense team.

Winfrey could not afford a false step in such a loaded confrontation. To add to his arsenal, Babcock hired Courtroom

Sciences, Inc. (CSI), and Phillip McGraw, with whom he had worked in the past.

"The big value he [McGraw] gives to me is he makes me think less like a lawyer and more like a real person," Babcock says. "Lawyers, time and again, forget they are trying a case to real people. You go through months and sometimes years of only talking to other lawyers, including the judge, who's also a lawyer."

McGraw didn't watch Winfrey's show often, but he said, "You can't be in this solar system and not know who Oprah Winfrey is." Whereas CSI may have taken cases in which McGraw was more of a figurehead than an active participant, a case of this magnitude had McGraw written all over it. "Phil stayed very close to cases that he knew were winners and stayed very far away from cases that he thought were dogs," is how a former CSI employee puts it. "That way when we lost, he didn't have any blood on his hands."

Prior to the trial, McGraw flew to Chicago to meet with Winfrey. The meeting didn't start well. On arrival, McGraw was told by one of Winfrey's assistants that he could have one hour with the star.

"Excuse me," McGraw responded. "It isn't *my* ass being sued. If that's all the time she's got, then I don't want to be a part of this."

Winfrey ultimately gave McGraw all the time he needed, and the two powerful personalities bonded, "in the first three minutes," as McGraw recalls.

"No one gave us much chance of winning in Amarillo because it's so dominated by the cattle industry," Babcock observes, but McGraw urged Winfrey to go in for the win. "I told her, 'If you're on the right side of the facts, then you're gonna win and the line to sue Oprah is gonna get a whole lot shorter'" he says.

McGraw has intimated it was his perspective that initially turned the case into a first amendment issue. "Think about it," he claims to have told Oprah. "Do you want to be the one that comes in and proves that, in fact, your beef supply is at risk, when everybody in the community makes money—tax money, school money, salaries—off the beef industry? That didn't fit right in my ear."

But some critics say that McGraw's taking credit for making it a first amendment case is disingenuous at best. "Chip Babcock is one of the best first amendment lawyers in the country and I think he would be very offended to hear that," says Charice Miles, an attorney who worked at CSI at the time. "But he [McGraw] is responsible for turning Oprah around in that case because she was a very angry, defensive woman. He turned her into the kind of woman that a jury would want to vote for and would want to help."

Winfrey flew down to CSI's offices to participate in mock trials and to prepare for the case. These trials revealed that Winfrey's fatal flaw in the courtroom would probably be her evident horror, disgust, and disbelief over being put through the ordeal. The mock panelists could see it in her eyes. Instead of presenting the warm personality that helped make her the queen of daytime television, she was coming across as hostile and suspicious. "One juror said to her, 'You look at us like we're a bunch of snakes and we're not,'" Babcock recalls. "'We're just here trying to honestly decide the case, so you don't have to be afraid of us.' And it was true. She was darting glances at them like they were a bunch of pythons over there."

"She came across poorly, in a state of disbelief that she was being sued," is how McGraw describes Winfrey at the mock trials. With McGraw's coaching, Winfrey was able to present a more sympathetic face to the jurors. McGraw further helped with the actual jury selection and with the coaching of witnesses. McGraw, characteristically, was driven to win the case. "Coming in second in a $100 million trial is not an option," he said.

■ ■ ■

Jury selection for the trial began January 20, 1998, and Amarillo locals clamored to be chosen. The circus kicked into full swing when Winfrey arrived in town. "She's here!" an Amarillo television reporter shouted into his microphone as Winfrey walked off a Gulfstream Jet, her two cocker spaniels in her arms, and stepped into a waiting black Chevrolet Suburban with tinted windows. "Oprah is here and she has just waved right at us!" the reporter exulted.

The trial was the most sensational event to take place in Amarillo since Fort Worth millionaire Cullen Davis was tried for murder there in the late 1970s. The news media, ranging from the *New York Times* to *Entertainment Tonight*, took over the town. Each morning, Winfrey—sedately dressed in a dark business suit and sunglasses—waved to her fans as she climbed the courtroom steps surrounded by a cadre of briefcase-toting attorneys, including Babcock, and other members of her legal team. McGraw, too, was never far behind.

Outside the courthouse, dozens of news satellite trucks blocked sidewalks. Vendors sold dueling "Amarillo Loves Oprah" and "The Only Mad Cow in Texas is Oprah" bumper stickers. Ministers prayed for both sides of the case, frat boys from West Texas A&M University grilled burgers, and protestors from People for the Ethical Treatment of Animals worked the crowd dressed as cows. The courtroom—inside and out—was the place to be for the news media and local curiosity seekers alike. "Seats were tough to come by," Babcock recalls. During voir dire, one potential juror burst into tears, admitting how much she loved Winfrey, losing any chance she might have had to sit on the jury.

Instead of putting her show on hold for the duration of the trial, Winfrey set up shop in the Amarillo Little Theater. After finishing up in court, she went to the theater to tape, where the ordeal she was enduring during the day was never mentioned, for good reason. "Well, I'm in Texas. I guess you heard. You also heard I'm not allowed to talk about why I'm here. So I ain't saying nothing about it," she announced during the opening of her first show in Texas.

Texas-born Patrick Swayze welcomed Winfrey to town on that show with a "cowgirl starter kit," including a black hat and a pair of Lucchese cowboy boots. Celebrity guests such as Celine Dion, John Travolta, Kathy Bates, and David Schwimmer were among the stars who trekked to Texas to be on the program. The mood was as fun and festive as ever. Seats for the show were as in demand as seats for the trial, and Winfrey made sure, whenever possible, to wrap loving arms around the state that had brought her to court. She even focused several shows on all things Texas. The people of Amarillo, for the most part, enthusiastically returned her affection.

In the center of this media maelstrom was McGraw. No one knew who he was at the time, but news footage of Winfrey entering and leaving the trial always seemed to include a big bald guy either walking alongside her or following close behind. "We thought he was security at first. He was this big guy who was always next to her, and he'd glare at us," remembers journalist Skip Hollandsworth, who covered the trial for *Texas Monthly*. "He was taking notes in the courtroom, and even though Chip ran the trial, I always got the feeling that he was the guy studying the jury." At the time, Hollandsworth reported, journalists were informed that McGraw did not speak to the press. And, he adds, "Someone told me that *Texas Lawyer* [a regional magazine] would call, and he never gave an interview. Never. He was adamant that CSI not get publicity. And if you think that this is the way he ran his business five years ago and made such an easy transition into the world of the modern celebrity—it's sort of curious."

McGraw's perpetual proximity to Winfrey was irritating to others working on the trial. "He wasn't the lawyer, Chip was, yet he would practically shove Chip out of the way and would stand next to her," Miles says.

In the meantime, McGraw and Winfrey were forging what would become a close and financially rewarding relationship.

Like many people before her—women, in particular—Winfrey was mesmerized by her charismatic consultant.

■ ■ ■

Winfrey is reputed to have an ego that rivals McGraw's, which suggests a likelihood of clashes between the two of them. But McGraw's colleagues at CSI witnessed no such tension and, in fact, found Winfrey to be as warm in person as she is on TV. "From my impressions, she really listened to what he would say," Miles recalls. "He was one of the first people to have the courage to sit down in her face and say, 'This is what you have to do.' She's a very nice person. She was as gracious as she appeared on television."

"Oprah is exactly who you think she would be," says another former CSI employee. "In retrospect, I have to wonder why she didn't see through Phil more. She's an incredibly giving person, incredibly emotional. I think it's the reason America connects with her. She's innocent, childlike. It took Oprah a while to see who she was dealing with. In my estimation, Phil had total command of that relationship."

Winfrey, McGraw, Babcock, and others in the case's inner circle settled into what became known as "Camp Oprah," aka the Adaberry Inn, a three-story bed-and-breakfast on the outskirts of town. Winfrey rented its nine suites for the duration of the trial and surrounded the inn with 24-hour armed guards.

"We were behind enemy lines up there, let me tell you," McGraw recalls. "There were death threats. There was a porte cochere in front of the house draped with canvas, and this bulletproof Suburban would pull in under the canvas, and we would get in it. A number of times, the Suburban zoomed off to the courthouse, and about five minutes later Oprah and I would go out the side door and get in my rented Toyota, and we would just go and drive around and wind up at the courthouse. We talked a lot."

The intimacy that develops when people are thrown together under fire, as well as the slumber camp ambience of Camp Oprah, helped cement the relationship between Winfrey and the man she was soon to launch on her public. "You get really close to someone when you live with 'em," McGraw says. "There were a lot of late-night sessions when we would just talk about copin' with all the stress and I shared some of my views and she found it helpful."

Camp Oprah was the setting for the tender scene that McGraw used to open his first best-selling self-help book, *Life Strategies*. It happened late at night, he wrote, and started with a gentle tap-tap-tapping of a single fingernail on the door to his room. A distraught, pajama-clad Winfrey had come to McGraw for counsel.

"Sitting on the floor across from this woman I had come to admire so very much, I searched my mind and heart for the right thing to say," McGraw writes. "We had been talking, analyzing, and working for some time now, but Oprah continued to struggle with the why of it all. What I knew was that, regardless of 'why,' we were here and she was in the crosshairs. Finally, I just took her hand and said, 'Oprah, look at me, right now. You'd better wake up, girl, and wake up *now*. It *is* really happening. You'd better *get over it* and get in the game, or these good ol' boys are going to hand you your ass on a platter.'"

He continued, "She looked me in the eye. And with a resolve I had not heard in all our previous work together, said, '*No, they will not.*'"

McGraw says the instant he heard this, he was convinced the cattlemen had lost their case. Winfrey agrees that this "get real" moment not only helped her regain her inner strength, but also gave her an edge in the courtroom.

"It is Phil who gave myself back to me," Oprah says. "Because . . . when I first started this trial, the thing that was hardest for me was to be myself."

■ ■ ■

At the end of the six-week trial, the jury decided against the cattlemen, ruling that Winfrey, Harpo Productions, and Lyman did not make false or disparaging remarks about the cattlemen or their business. Winfrey and Babcock were quick to credit McGraw for his contributions to the defense. "Without Phil on the Oprah case, I'm not sure we would have prevailed," Babcock says.

After the trial, McGraw let Winfrey know she had dodged a bullet, telling her that most media cases like hers are decided in favor of the plaintiffs. "Eighty percent of the cases are lost at the trial level and then 80 percent of those are reversed at the appellate level, but we didn't think you needed to know everything about it [before the trial was over]," McGraw said.

Back in Chicago, the first thing Winfrey did was take off the gag that Judge Mary Lou Robinson had imposed on her during the trial. Winfrey devoted an entire show to her ordeal in Amarillo. The program aired on February 27, 1998. Among the guests was McGraw, who made his first appearance on the *Oprah* stage when Winfrey introduced him as part of her entire legal team.

By this time, Winfrey was smitten with McGraw. Some of his colleagues already suspected that more would come of the relationship. "I knew that Phil was going to try to parlay that thing any way he could," says a former CSI employee. "Of course, I would, too. I don't blame him for that. The thing is, it was easy to do with Oprah. That's the way it is. You've heard that story about how he was in her room that night, helped her through the difficult thing, and all that. That's what he does."

■ ■ ■

Whether he planned it that way or not, McGraw found a powerful advocate in Winfrey, whose own plan was to share her new guru with the world. Winfrey told McGraw that she wanted him to appear as a guest on her show. "One day she said, 'You know what? You don't have the right to not be sharing your perspective and what you know,'" McGraw recalls. "[She said] 'I know you don't like it, but you don't have the right to do that, and I want you to share it with people' . . . It was 'I think you have something to say and I have great place to say it.' It was kind of a free-fall. 'Let's do this and see where it goes.'"

On April 10, 1998—two years, to the day, after she uttered the words that led her to court and McGraw—Dr. Phil hung his shingle on the *Oprah* show as a featured guest for the first time. Winfrey was lavish in her introduction.

"My next guest is here to help lead you in the right direction," she told her audience. "I've chosen him because he is the person who helped me the most getting through my trial in Texas on a daily basis. Without Dr. Phil McGraw, I don't know how I could have gotten through it. He is a trial strategist who is also one of the best psychologists I've ever run into, and I've talked to many, many, many psychologists over the years doing this show. And I said to Phil at one point during the trial, if I ever needed therapy, he would be the one I'd go to, and he said, 'I don't take clients.'"

McGraw didn't take clients, but he did take on Winfrey's enormous audience. During that first appearance, McGraw and Winfrey talked about asking oneself hard questions, about making commitments, about willpower and goal setting, about winners and losers, about losing weight, about finding relationships, and about getting over past hurts and getting on with your life—subjects that would soon become familiar McGraw themes. He told one guest—a woman who was raped at 13, became bulimic, attempted suicide, and said she hated herself—that he didn't believe her when she said she wanted to stop wallowing in self-pity and get on with her life. And in a refrain that McGraw fans could chant in their sleep, he told another woman, whose husband of 25 years left without explanation one day, that she was responsible for teaching him how to treat her. It was typical McGraw tough talk, but accepting it was hard for Winfrey's audience, accustomed to her nurturing style. Winfrey's fans were not impressed, nor were her producers.

"We had e-mails and letters saying, 'Oprah, how dare you let him talk to people like that?'" Winfrey says. "I think people thought he was abrasive, the fact that it was unlike me to allow someone like him to come on the show and say the things he was saying in the way he was saying them . . . and they told me about it. I think at first, we even had questions [about] whether we were going to continue with him."

But Winfrey, with confidence in her own Midas touch, is not easily swayed by anyone's opinion but her own. She brought McGraw back on the show. This time, however, she included an explanation of the McGraw style in her introduction. "Phil was just doing to them [on the previous show] what he did to me—telling it like it is," she told her audience. And the tactic worked. "Right after the second show, we had huge numbers of people writing in saying, 'Dear Oprah, I want Dr. Phil to tell me like it is,'" Winfrey says.

■ ■ ■

Before long, McGraw was getting real on *Oprah* every Tuesday, becoming her first guest with a permanent recurring appointment. McGraw's brand of therapy was less twelve-step than one-liner. McGraw said, "You either get it, or you don't," and Winfrey's audience loved it. Ratings for Tuesday editions of *Oprah* jumped more than 20 percent after McGraw became a regular.

For McGraw, the gig was a smooth and ideal set-up. "It's like riding a Rolls Royce," he says. "Everything is done for you."

And the Winfrey/McGraw, good cop/bad cop balance worked perfectly. Winfrey's kindly manner counteracted McGraw's antagonistic style and in-your-face opinions. "I get really intense sometimes and she'll say, 'Calm down, big boy.' She'll break the tension," McGraw said. Winfrey remained McGraw's

number-one cheerleader, always ready to say "amen" to her protégé's insights.

"You're planning for the wedding but not for the marriage,"
McGraw once told a couple planning to wed.

"Mercy, that is a good statement! That is so good! Jeez!" Winfrey extolled.

On stage together, McGraw and Winfrey were tag-team therapists, a two-headed self-help creature, perfectly in sync with
each other.

"This is what happens in a parent-child relationship," McGraw
told Rochelle, who was on the show because her husband was tired
of her controlling ways. "And, John, this is where you're cheating
your wife by letting her do this to you—because in every parent-
child relationship, what happens? Children grow up . . ."

"And rebel," Winfrey interjected.

". . . and they become independent, they rebel and break
away," McGraw continued without missing a beat.

Winfrey may be the only person on earth who can contradict
McGraw without reprimand. In an "Ask Dr. Phil" episode, McGraw
was about to tear into a woman whose marriage was strained because her new husband disliked her cats, which she called her "fur
children."

"But, you know, everything has two sides," McGraw said. "And
if he's married to the crazy cat woman, you know—I mean, you
say your 'fur kids,' your 'fur children' and—and that sort of . . ."

At this point, Winfrey, known to be passionate about her
own furry roommates—cocker spaniels Solomon and Sophie—
jumped to the woman's defense. "There's nothing wrong with
that," Winfrey offered.

McGraw conceded. "I understand, I understand," he said.

"Don't even try to go there," Winfrey instructed. McGraw immediately backed off.

McGraw started presenting several multipart series on the
show—on weight loss, on marriage and money, on relationships,

and a 10-parter called "The Get Real Challenge." In this series, 42 people spent five days locked in a room with McGraw, with the goal of turning their lives around in one way or another. Winfrey described it as "an intense, confrontational, emotional experience created by Dr. Phil to force people to get real about their lives." And, she added, "The group was kept in the dark about the schedule, all part of Dr. Phil's master plan, which included the rather unfriendly team he brought to assist him." (One participant described the helpers as being like morticians. "They're dressed all in black, and they never smile. That's a bit scary and intimidating.")

By the time the "Get Real Challenge" was first announced on Oprah.com in spring 2000, the nation was clamoring for McGraw. Fifteen thousand people applied for the privilege of having him verbally smack them around.

"May I ask you something?" one participant ventured on the first day of the challenge.

"No, you can't ask me something," McGraw replied. "I don't answer questions in here to begin with, and I'll tell you why. Eighty percent of all questions are statements in disguise, and any answers you're going to get in this room, you're going to find and create on your own. I'll guarantee you that."

In the end, of course, the participants testified to the power of Dr. Phil.

Don, who was molested by a priest as a child and kept people at a distance ever since, found his way out of this self-imposed isolation. "I just feel free," he said. Julie, whose husband was accused of molesting nine children, including her own, divorced the beast, lost 30 pounds, and cut her hair, "and she thanks Dr. Phil for it," Winfrey reported. Yolanda, who was badly abused as a child and close to suicide, rediscovered her will to live. Her story made Winfrey and even McGraw wipe away a tear. "I do believe I see a mist in Phil's eyes. Dear God, it's a new day," Winfrey teased him about the public display of emotion.

■ ■ ■

It was during his years on *Oprah* that McGraw first started living the life of a celebrity: He was parodied on *Saturday Night Live* and made his initial appearance on a sitcom by conducting a group therapy session on the short-lived comedy *Norm,* starring Norm MacDonald. McGraw also continued his work at CSI, flying back and forth from Dallas to Chicago for the tapings. "I don't foresee ever being completely unplugged from this [CSI] 'cause it's addictive," McGraw says.

His CSI employees were not dazzled by his burgeoning fame, for various reasons, including a ho-hum feeling about seeing McGraw on television when they saw him in person nearly every day. "I respect him, I admire him, but he's just like the rest of us. He's a person. At CSI we didn't have people gathered round the TV watching him because he was going to walk down the hall tomorrow," says Plano, Texas, psychologist Susan Fletcher, who worked at CSI during the time McGraw was a regular on *Oprah.*

Another former employee is less benevolent and remembers that McGraw's outbursts increased along with his fame. "As he got involved with Oprah and started doing the show it just got worse and worse. Phil's ego—he could never get it through the front door anyway—got worse. He became more and more abusive to people."

But whatever those closest to him thought, McGraw was racking up legions of fans through his appearances on *Oprah.* Before long, McGraw's fame would outgrow even his once-a-week gig, and new vistas of fame, notoriety, and control were about to unfold before him.

I'm not the kind of guy who believes life can be summed up in a cute phrase.

Publishers had their first taste of Oprah Winfrey's astonishing power to move books in 1994. That's when Winfrey's personal chef of five years, Rosie Daley, wrote a cookbook filled with Winfrey's favorite healthy and easy-to-prepare recipes. Although Winfrey didn't get any royalties from the book, she credited Daley's cooking with helping her to slim down. Winfrey also posed for the front cover photo and devoted an entire episode of her show to the cookbook.

In the Kitchen with Rosie immediately shot to the top of every major bestseller list. Bookstores couldn't keep up with the demand. Many were out of stock for days, sometimes weeks, while publisher Knopf went back to press several times. This slim book containing just 50 recipes wound up selling some 6.7 million copies at $19.95 each, becoming one of the best-selling cookbooks of all time. Daley, who was cooking at a health spa in San Diego when she first met Winfrey, quit her job with the talk show host after the book made her a millionaire.

Winfrey did it again two years later—this time with her personal trainer, Bob Greene. His book, *Make the Connection: Ten Steps to a Better Body and Better Life*, featured Winfrey's picture and name on the cover below his. It, too, was the topic of one of her shows. Greene's book raced up the charts, just like Daley's, selling 300,000 copies its first week and becoming the best-selling nonfiction book of the year. Other self-help experts such as relationship coach John Gray, inspirational speaker Iyanla Vanzant, and financial wizard Suze Orman were also beneficiaries of what eventually came to be known as "the Oprah Factor."

■ ■ ■

The Oprah Factor proved to be more powerful than anyone had realized when Winfrey launched her on-air book club on September 17, 1996. The ongoing feature brought together authors and panels of women to discuss books selected by Winfrey. A self-described passionate reader, Winfrey encouraged her vast television audience to read along with her.

Nobody was prepared for the tsunami that Oprah's Book Club would instantly rain on the publishing industry. Jacquelyn Mitchard's *The Deep End of the Ocean* had an initial print run of about 68,000 copies when it was released in June 1996. Three months later, after Winfrey chose the book as her first selection, publisher Viking printed and shipped an additional 100,000 copies, which proved to be woefully inadequate. Within two months of its book club debut, the number of copies of Mitchard's novel in print jumped to 750,000, and then quickly topped 1 million. The book spent 29 weeks on *Publishers Weekly*'s nonfiction bestseller list and now has about four million copies in print.

All this was just the beginning. A combination of newcomers and literary stalwarts—including Anita Shreve, Maya Angelou, Joyce Carol Oates, and Toni Morrison—all found themselves professionally and financially buoyed by Oprah's endorsement. When Wally Lamb's first novel, *She's Come Undone*, became a bestseller after being an Oprah's Book Club selection, publisher Harper-Collins printed a respectable first run of 250,000 copies of his second novel, *I Know This Much Is True.* After Winfrey featured that book as well, it went back to print four times within weeks of its initial release. Jonathan Franzen, author of *The Corrections,* created a media maelstrom just by declining the honor of appearing on Winfrey's show to discuss his novel after it was selected for the book club.

The power of Oprah to sell books may have been news even to Winfrey herself. "It's pretty stunning," admits Karen Jenkins Holt, editor of *Book Publishing Report.* "I think even she was surprised by it. She has an unprecedented rapport with her audience that gives her this authority that I think even she was shocked to find out she had."

After recommending 44 titles, almost all of which made it to the top of the bestseller charts, Winfrey ran out of steam and ended the first incarnation of her book club in April 2002. In June 2003, she started another one devoted to the classics, which immediately vaulted John Steinbeck's *East of Eden* to the top of the charts—just behind Harry Potter and over Hillary Clinton's still-new memoir—both of which broke sales records of their own during this same time.

■ ■ ■

Yet of all the authors Winfrey has supported over the years, perhaps none has benefited more than Phil McGraw. Because of her winning track record, when Winfrey urged her popular regular Tuesday guest to write a book of his own in 1998—accompanied by a clear intent to endorse it—you could say he was already halfway to the bestseller lists before putting a single word on paper. If there was such a thing as a surefire hit in publishing, this was it.

McGraw negotiated his initial two book deals with the help of an attorney. He sold his first book, *Life Strategies: Doing What*

Works, Doing What Matters, to editor Leslie Wells of Hyperion Publishing (an imprint of the Walt Disney Company) for what industry insiders estimate was a seven-figure advance. Hyperion was
well aware of the value of an endorsement from Winfrey, since it
also published *Make the Connection,* the first book by her personal
trainer Bob Greene.

By all reports, McGraw wrote *Life Strategies* himself, with help
from Jonathan Leach, an English teacher at Cistercian Prepara-
tory School in Irving, Texas. He also received some assistance
from CSI staffers and others. "I swear to God, I think he wrote it
in, like, a week," says attorney Charice Miles, who worked for
McGraw at CSI at the time he was preparing the manuscript. Hyperion released *Life Strategies* on January 7, 1999, with an initial
printing of 350,000 copies.

In his debut effort, McGraw introduces readers to his 10 "Life
Laws," including "You either get it or you don't" and "Life is managed, it is not cured." He describes the world as a courtroom, ". . .
a microcosm of life. In any trial, somebody is trying to take something away from somebody else. So it is in life." And he points out,
somewhat bleakly, "Life *is* a competition. They *are* keeping score,
and there *is* a time clock." The writing style is blunt, the personal
anecdotes folksy. The lessons contain no humbug, and the voice is
100 percent McGraw. Reading his book "was like talking to him—
the language, the rhythm, the vocabulary," says Delores Jones, a
former patient of McGraw's when he was in private practice. "It
[his way of talking] has stayed the same."

The review of *Life Strategies* in *Publishers Weekly,* the bible of the
bookselling industry, was dismissive. "While McGraw's presentation may play well on the small screen, it suffers on the page from
lack of focus, awkward writing and a relentlessly hectoring tone,"
the review read. But McGraw's fans, rebels against the ivory
tower, didn't care about the critics. They were ready for some hectoring, and they wanted it straight up. *Life Strategies* debuted at
number three on the *Publishers Weekly* bestseller list. The initial

350,000 press run had to be quickly supplemented by an additional 50,000. A week after its release, Winfrey featured the book and McGraw on her show. By the end of 1999, *Life Strategies* had sold more than 670,000 copies. By 2003, more than two million copies of the book were in print.

The book's success was due largely to the Oprah Factor, according to John Hogan, editor-in-chief of *Pages* magazine. Nevertheless, he doesn't altogether discount McGraw's appeal for the book's quick rise. "He was significantly different," Hogan observes. "He's more confrontational and abrasive than other self-help authors. People were tired of the feel-good kind of thing and needed a kick in the pants."

■ ■ ■

"McGraw hit the stage culturally at the perfect time for someone like him," adds Dallas writer Skip Hollandsworth, who has ghostwritten a number of self-help books in the past and was hired to edit McGraw's second title, *Relationship Rescue.* "The self-help world was just coming off a long love affair with this inner child movement. All the self-help authors were talking about how we were victims of the dysfunctional family. Oprah, who is as quick to spot a personal empowerment guru as anyone, had all those people on her show. They were all touchy-feely, sensitive, gentle types of approaches and the audience for it was getting tired. This whole 'finding your inner child' movement was getting tiring. And here comes McGraw."

Hollandsworth got the job of working with McGraw after interviewing the doctor and writing a brief profile of him for *Texas Monthly* magazine, for which he is an executive editor. McGraw was pleased by the experience and outcome, and called Hollandsworth for help when he found himself falling behind on his *Relationship Rescue* deadline. For about three months, Hollandsworth spent several hours a day sitting with McGraw in his home office, which was located right off the front foyer. The office had no door, so that as he worked, McGraw could watch and participate in the comings and goings of his family.

Hollandsworth brought his laptop, and the two worked from transcriptions, typed by CSI staffers, of McGraw's tape-recorded musings. "He would dictate into a little hand-held tape cassette the stuff he's thinking," Hollandsworth explains. "This was a guy who was stunning in his ability to talk out a book . . . His language was so good and precise straight off the bat that my job was just moving things around, typing a few sentences, organizing things here and there, and shaping it. But it wasn't ghostwriting in any real traditional sense. I have ghost-written self-help books before and there have been a few times in which I've really had to basically write the book. There's lots of authors that will just sort of talk awhile and let the ghostwriter somehow fashion a book out of it. McGraw would lay out the chapters, he would come up with all those little formulas, and I have never seen anybody so fast on his feet. I've never seen anyone so articulate."

McGraw was not the man or the mind Hollandsworth expected to encounter. "He was really much smarter and had a far greater intellectual heft when it came to these issues of psychological behavior than I ever expected. I thought he just sort of shot from the hip and did this kind of old 'Texasy' tell it like it is thing, and that is his nature. But it comes from all this study."

Though Hollandsworth has heard many stories about McGraw's controlling nature, his experience didn't back them up. "This is what tickled me," he says. "I would launch into my own particular rant or tirade about what should be in the book, even if it was completely antithetical to what he wanted, even if it was against the theme. And the thing I always remember is, McGraw never interrupted. He let me make my point, and he listened and he thought about it. This was what was fun about him. There was a great intellectual exchange."

Hollandsworth sometimes won the debates, perhaps persuading McGraw to tone down an overly adamant argument. And he enjoyed the debates thoroughly, both for the intellectual exchange and because of McGraw's way with words. "When we would have these debates, these lines would roll out of his mouth that were totally spontaneous and they were hilarious," Hollandsworth recalls. "They were this mixture of folksy rustic Texan and smart-ass one-liners. They just would fly out of him. He was good, he was really good."

At the same time McGraw was demanding of his editor. On occasion, recalls Hollandsworth, after McGraw spent time with his family and the kids were in bed, he would be ready to go back to work, phoning Hollandsworth as late as 10:30 at night.

As always, McGraw ultimately called all the shots. "He was tough," Hollandsworth says. "He never hesitated to tell me when I was screwing up. He used to mockingly call me a whiner 'cause I would complain about changes he wanted to make, and he sort of saw through me. He called them the Hollandsworth whine alerts. It was really fun."

The pace and intensity of working with McGraw quickened Hollandsworth's pulse. "It was thrilling," he says. "There was a charisma about showing up at his office, and I got addicted to it."

The product of Hollandsworth's work with McGraw, *Relationships Rescue,* followed *Life Strategies* to number one on both the *New York Times* and *Publishers Weekly* bestseller lists, though to date it has not sold as many copies as McGraw's other books.

In *Relationship Rescue,* McGraw reassures readers, "If your relationship is in trouble, big trouble or small, I'm going to tell you straight-up how to fix it" before launching into 254 pages of advice, anecdotes, quizzes, and exercises that break relationships down by the numbers. The book is subtitled *A Seven-Step Strategy for Reconnecting with Your Partner,* and the overview includes McGraw's Five Tough Questions (question 3: Knowing what you now do about your relationship, would you still get involved with the same person if you had to do it all over again? Why?). It includes 10 myths of relationships (Myth # 1: A great relationship depends on a great meeting of the minds, and Myth #6: A great relationship lets you vent all your feelings). The book also offers readers other crisply quantified concepts and strategies.

As he worked on each new book, McGraw seemed to nurture his brand name, publishing a workbook and self-discovery journal to go along with *Life Strategies,* and writing a companion workbook for *Relationship Rescue.* In 2001, McGraw released an audio program called *Dr. Phil Getting Real: Lessons in Life, Marriage, and Family.* The four-CD set was taped before a live audience and is published by Hay House. Not surprisingly, the CD quickly became—and remains—Hay House's top-selling title.

In 2000, McGraw signed with literary agent Jan Miller to represent him in future book deals. Miller's self-run agency, Dupree/Miller and Associates, is located in Highland Park Village, a posh Dallas shopping center far from the lunch loop that drives the New York publishing industry. Despite her unconventional geographic location, Miller has managed to carve a niche for herself within the self-help genre, representing such megastars as Steven Covey of *Seven Habits* fame and firewalker Tony Robbins. She also represents Maria Shriver and Winfrey's boyfriend, Stedman Graham. With McGraw added to her impressive roster, Miller would soon become the leading literary representative of psychological self-help authors, catering to a category that rings up sales of some $600 million a year.

Though she ignored interview requests for this book, Miller is, by all accounts, shrewd and driven, just like McGraw. Given his personality and his win-at-all-costs business style, McGraw certainly seemed a compatible match for his tough new agent.

■ ■ ■

As his own star in publishing continued to rise, McGraw decided to launch the ultimate branded product: his son, Jay. According to Phil McGraw, he decided to write a book for teenagers because, as a result of his appearances on *Oprah,* he was getting e-mails from teens about problems in their lives. Jay sat in on a meeting with the publisher as they were developing a concept for *Life Strategies for Teens.*

"When the subject came up at a meeting with the publisher, I had to stand up and say no," Jay said. "My dad is bald, he's a cue ball, he hasn't seen hair in 30 years. So I had to say 'No way, dad, let me do it so that the teenagers can understand it and relate with what I'm saying.'" At this point, the publisher supposedly jumped on the idea of having the young McGraw translate his father's wisdom into the language of teens, with Dad writing the book's foreword.

"The people at Simon & Schuster are great," Jay says. "They were ecstatic because there isn't a book out there [like this] for young people by a young person. We've all got enough parents and teachers telling us what to do and they agree with that."

Life Strategies for Teens was published in December 2000 by Fireside, Simon & Schuster's paperback division. Simon & Schuster had already successfully explored the father-son theme by publishing *Seven Habits of Highly Effective Teens* by Sean Covey, the teenage son of Steven Covey—and a fellow client of agent Jan Miller.

It wasn't until April 2000, months after Jay's book was in bookstores, that Simon & Schuster proudly announced it had signed Dr. Phil McGraw himself to a multimillion-dollar four-book world rights deal with editor Dominick Anfuso, who also worked with Miller's clients Robbins and Covey. At the same time, Simon & Schuster boasted that it had signed Jay to three more books.

■ ■ ■

Simon & Schuster's first book with Phil McGraw, *Self Matters,* was released on November 13, 2001. That book spent 48 weeks on the bestseller charts, 13 at number one. Having become a sort of signature book for McGraw, *Self Matters* was ranked as number one in sales of nonfiction books of 2002 by *Publishers Weekly,* selling some 1.3 million copies that year. Today, more than 2 million hardcover editions are in print.

Self Matters is McGraw's take on self-discovery and healthy self-interest. Once again, he steers his readers by the numbers. "Here's a shocker," he writes. "Social scientists tell us that the entire origin of your self-concept, and therefore the determination of who you ultimately become in your life, can be traced to the events of a precious few days and the actions of an amazingly few key people involved in those happenings." In *Self Matters*, McGraw introduces his soon-to-be familiar advice to boil our lives down to "Ten Defining Moments," "Seven Critical Choices," and "Five Pivotal People."

As with his other books, McGraw issued a companion guide to this book, although this time, somewhat audaciously, as a hardcover. *The Self Matters Companion: Helping You Create Your Life from the Inside Out* also sold briskly, though not nearly as well as the original title. It got a skeptical review from *Publishers Weekly.* "Disappointingly—and despite its fairly high price [$22]—this book is half empty (it leaves space for the readers to scribble answers to its questions) and needlessly repetitive," the trade magazine said. "McGraw's many avid fans may want to consider making a smaller investment by purchasing a plain notebook and doing the exercises in *Self Matters* on their own."

■ ■ ■

Paperback versions of McGraw's books sold as fast as the original hardcover releases. To date, more than 10 million copies of McGraw's books have been put into print. They have been published in close to 30 different languages and maintain a presence on bestseller lists in the United States and beyond. Simon & Schuster did particularly well internationally with *Self Matters,* selling translation rights for several foreign languages including Chinese, Danish, Dutch, French, Japanese, Korean, Romanian, Swedish, and Thai.

The McGraw brand now includes not only his books and journals, but also calendars, CDs, and gewgaws sold on the *Dr. Phil* show web site. "If you look at what goes on in self-help books, the author brand really seems to trump everything," says Karen Holt of *Book Publishing Report*. "Once you've got that really great brand name, you can cross subjects and your readers will come with you."

In late 2003, that's exactly what McGraw did, turning his attention to weight loss. It's a subject dear to the hearts of much of the audience he shares with *Oprah,* especially those who have watched and joined the queen of daytime in her struggles with weight. Reportedly, when Miller started discussing the book idea with Simon & Schuster, she told them McGraw would accept nothing less than a $10 million advance—$2 million more than Hillary Clinton got from the same publisher for her heavily-hyped autobiography, *Living History.* Simon & Schuster countered with an $8 million offer but, as he usually does, McGraw won the negotiation and got the eight-figure check he wanted, along with a first printing of 1.5 million copies.

It appears that big check will pay off for the publisher. Even before its release, pre-orders for *The Ultimate Weight Solution: The 7 Keys to Weight Loss Freedom* beat Clinton's record-breaking bestseller. (Incidentally, McGraw credits Winfrey for coming up with the book's title.) He launched the book with a two-hour *Dateline NBC* special, which the network billed as "an unprecedented two-hour live event." The morning of the special, McGraw paid a visit to *Today,* where he proudly told Katie Couric, "I don't *think* I have the answers to solve the [nation's weight] crisis. I [know I] have the answers." McGraw told Couric he knew exactly why Americans were overweight and added, "Somebody's got to lead the charge. Why not me?" And even though it's hard to tell this from examining his life and areas of expertise over the years, McGraw began heavily promoting the claim that he had spent the past three decades studying the issue of weight. Whatever the case, he was about to make big bucks off the topic, and obesity promised to become a major focus of his television show for the upcoming season.

Predictably, son Jay's book on the same subject but targeted at teens was slated to follow close behind.

"I wouldn't be surprised to eventually see a Phil McGraw personal finance book," says Holt. "Why not? If he's gonna do weight loss, why not personal finance? He and Suze Orman can go on *Oprah* together to promote it."

A book by McGraw's wife Robin seems almost inevitable as the next extension of the brand. "I think it would be a huge bestseller," Holt observes. "It would probably rival her husband's book. After hearing his side of the story, how could you resist? I think people would love to know what the woman who's married to this guy has to say."

■ ■ ■

McGraw's books have become fixtures on bestseller lists, bookstore shelves, and in pop culture. One of his titles even took McGraw back into the courtroom, making an appearance during a lurid trial in early 2003.

Clara Harris, an elegant and attractive 45-year-old Houston dentist, sobbed on the stand as she tried to defend herself against a murder charge. She was on trial for running over her philandering orthodontist husband with her silver Mercedes-Benz in a hotel parking lot where she caught him and his paramour leaving hand in hand. As part of her defense, Harris tearfully described all the ways she had tried to save their 10-year marriage, including quitting her job, cooking her husband's favorite meals, promising sexual favors, and reading self-help books. The defense entered two books into evidence to prove this point, one of which was McGraw's *Relationship Rescue*.

Apparently, the book didn't work for Harris's relationship. It didn't help her defense, either. She was convicted and sentenced to 20 years in prison.

McGraw, meanwhile, continued his journey from the courtroom to pop culture ubiquity.

11

Ready for the Spotlight

Obviously this isn't something I sat in the sandbox when I was five years old and said one of these days I'm going to have my own show.

Less than six years after his first meeting with Oprah Winfrey, McGraw's ability to draw an audience as big as hers was becoming clear. His ratings on *Oprah* were high, his books were firmly planted on bestseller lists, and his live seminars consistently sold out. At this point, getting his own television show seemed inevitable. The gamble Winfrey took by bringing McGraw on her show, and then defying her producers by bringing him back when they balked, was about to pay off again. This would be Winfrey's first attempt at developing another talk show, although the opportunity had presented itself many times before. "You can imagine, 17 years of *Oprah*—the experts, the theories. I've had lots of opportunities to produce," Winfrey says. "Phil is better than anybody I've ever seen."

Other Winfrey-anointed hopefuls, such as her best friend Gayle King and author Iyanla Vanzant, tried launching their own shows without Winfrey's official imprimatur, and both failed.

But few observers were surprised when Winfrey started talking about giving McGraw his own show in 2002. "I don't think there was any doubt that he was being groomed and cultivated," says John Nogawski, president of Paramount Domestic Television. "You couldn't ask for a better workshop than what Dr. Phil was afforded."

McGraw credits Winfrey with laying the idea for the program on the table. "Oprah came to me one day and said, 'It's time to do your own show,'" he says. "[She said] 'We don't have enough time, an hour a week, to talk about all the things that people want to talk about.'"

McGraw did some research before committing to anything. "I really had two questions I had to think about . . . Number one, did I really have enough to say for an hour a day, five days a week? And number two, did I really have something to add to the mix of daytime television, because I'm not a big television watcher."

He also considered the difference between riding the *Oprah*-mobile and steering his own talk show. "Think about it," he says. "You're going to do your own show, but the only difference is we're going to subtract the most clarion voice in the history of television."

Ultimately, McGraw says, his experience on *Oprah* convinced him that he was a perfect candidate to tap into the higher power of television. "I got firsthand experience that you can really influence the way people think, feel, live, and behave through the television medium, and that was intriguing to me. I thought it was my highest and best use, and I think that's the platform's highest and best use."

Winfrey's company, Harpo Productions, concluded that producing both her show and McGraw's would spread Harpo's resources too thin. "While we briefly considered producing this new show ourselves, we decided we needed to partner with a company that shared our attention to detail and our values," says Tim Bennett, president of Harpo Productions. Word started getting out that the most powerful woman in television and her formidable friend had an idea on the marketplace.

■ ■ ■

McGraw already had a following at Paramount Studios. Terry Wood, executive vice president for programming at the company, was in a development meeting when she heard that a show starring Dr. Phil was up for grabs. Wood, who was among the women at Paramount who regularly tuned in to *Oprah* for their dose of McGraw, recognized the potential immediately. But she wasn't sure the men on her team would feel the same way. "Guys knew who he was but didn't really watch it [*Oprah*]," Wood says.

In addition, Paramount executives weren't convinced that McGraw could do as well without Winfrey by his side to smooth out his rough edges. McGraw made it clear he was not available to be molded into anything different from who he was, and he was not interested in being the testosterone version of Winfrey. "I'm not doing makeovers and I'm sure as hell not doing fashion shows. I have every intention of being faithful to that phrase: Make sure you dance with who brung ya," he said.

He also wasn't interested in celebrity chitchat, unless it was about personal problems such as substance abuse or divorce. "I won't have a celebrity on unless they're willing to get real," he declared.

Any production company that wanted the *Dr. Phil* show was going to have to accept the show exactly as McGraw envisioned it. "I knew who I was," McGraw maintains. "If they can bend television around that, OK. If not, I'll go somewhere else. If people don't like (what I say), they can get that remote control and keep on sailing."

Paramount's executives remained unconvinced until they witnessed McGraw holding thousands of people in his thrall during one of his live "Get Real" seminars in Nashville, on January 26, 2002. Wood and her team, including Greg Meidel, president of programming for Paramount Domestic Television, saw McGraw's power up close in the sold-out show.

"For two hours, it was just himself and a crowd of 6,500, standing room only, with scalpers getting $130 a seat," Meidel remembers. "He was so at ease, he had people dancing in the aisles, laughing, crying . . . Nothing was scripted, and he talked nonstop for two hours."

That was enough to convince Paramount that McGraw could carry his own small-screen show. "I drank the Dr. Phil Kool-Aid," Meidel testifies. "I believe in his passion, I believe in his ability to make change, and I believe in his ability to cut through the clutter on television."

A contract was signed for the *Dr. Phil* show for the 2002 to 2003 season. King World, distributor of *The Oprah Winfrey Show,* put a price tag of more than $1 million a week on licensing fees. The licensing contract included a noncompete clause for stations carrying *Dr. Phil,* stipulating that McGraw's show would never run in the same time slot as Winfrey's in a given market. At the time, all involved apparently assumed that this would be protection for McGraw, to ensure that *Oprah* didn't siphon off the audience they once shared.

"We did make an agreement with all of our affiliates," McGraw confirms. "Of course, we sat down and talked about it and said there's no reason we should fracture the audience, where they have to choose between the two. She [Oprah] did that. She agreed to it because she's gracious. I agreed to it because I'm not a fool. I don't want to go head-to-head with Oprah. So we've made it where . . . usually if she's on at 3 P.M., I'm on at 4 P.M. And that way, people don't have to choose."

Harpo retained an ownership interest in the show, giving the company creative input, while Paramount handled the actual production. After the contracts were signed, Paramount took another year and nine months to develop the show. "[We wanted] to get to know him, to get a staff in place, and to start doing test shows," says Paramount's Nogawski. "So the question for us really was how big could we make him before he went on the air."

A staff was hired to come up with topics and investigate both potential guests and subjects, while producers compiled notebooks full of information on each guest, which McGraw would study for background before the shows. These notebooks would become familiar props to his television audience. As at CSI, the staff ultimately hired to work on the show was predominantly female.

■ ■ ■

Sources say Paramount built McGraw a lavish office and dressing room, but skimped on crew salaries and amenities. "From the very top, they were very cheap with the crew. They tried to low-ball us on our rates and there was no crafts services [aka food—a common amenity on sets]," complains a former show employee. "Our call time was 6 A.M., and there'd be maybe a box of donuts and a box of bagels and some coffee and that was it for the day, basically. I was so busy, most of the time I didn't get a lunch break." In addition, the ex-employee says, workdays were frequently 15 or 16 hours long.

As at CSI, McGraw's perfectionism, demands, and controlling ways made the job "a living hell" for some of his experienced staff and crew, which probably had 100 Emmys among them, says the former employee, who worked on the show start-up for a few months. "I will say without hesitation, in my 25 years of being in this business, that was the worst show I'd ever worked on. It was just a very negative vibe, a very unhealthy atmosphere. Just horrible.

"All of us went into that show anticipating great things," this employee continues. "We were all excited to be working full-time and steady, but we kind of got an inkling of it after the first couple of days" that life on the *Dr. Phil* set would be difficult.

While start-ups are bound to hit bumps, the staff and crew at Paramount were all generally pleased with the quality of the first week of test shows. "Paramount was ecstatic with what we had done with a brand-new set, brand-new control room, new equipment, everything," the former staffer recalls. So when everyone, from technicians to writers, was called on stage for a meeting with McGraw, "We were expecting a little pat on the back.

"We walk in, and Phil's on stage. He has his arms crossed and he's pacing and he's waiting for everybody to sit down and settle down and everything. He says, point-blank, *'This show looks like an f-ing train wreck.'* We all sat there in shock," the staffer claims. (While preferring not to say the actual word, the employee adds that McGraw used the full profanity when addressing his stunned team.)

Not everything had gone perfectly in those first test shows, the former employee concedes, but that was to be expected for a start-up. The dismayed staff didn't believe McGraw understood the challenges of building a show from the stage up. "This guy came from doing one hour a week on an established show—*Oprah*. We were thinking we were doing pretty good for a start-up, especially the first week. But no, not according to him."

Nor according to wife Robin, who was making her opinions known and taking liberties with her status as the boss's wife. By second-guessing staff, she was also causing trouble, the ex-staffer maintains. Robin's continual complaints about the lighting, which was tweaked, changed, and redesigned several times, finally pushed the multiple Emmy-award winning lighting director to lose his temper. "Essentially, she was insulting our lighting director, and he'd had it," the former employee recalls. "I don't know his exact words, but he said something like, 'Lady, you really don't know what you're talking about, you're not in the business,' and that was pretty much the straw that broke the camel's back. You don't talk back to her [Robin]." The lighting designer was fired.

McGraw's boyhood home in Vinita, Oklahoma, where he and his family lived for a couple of years in the 1950s. (*Photo credit:* Gary Dunn.)

McGraw's senior year photo from the 1968 Shawnee Mission North High School yearbook.

McGraw's father, Joe, in a photo from the 1951 Vinita High School yearbook, where he was a teacher, counselor, and football coach.

McGraw in full dress gear as the senior tackle on his high school football team at Shawnee Mission North High School in Overland Park, Kansas, in 1967.

McGraw and Debbie Higgins at the Shawnee Mission North High School homecoming dance in 1967. The two married after graduation, although their union lasted just a few short years.

McGraw and friend Delores Emmett Jones at the wedding of a mutual acquaintance in 1985. McGraw was the groom's best man, while Jones was the matron of honor. (*Photo credit:* Delores Emmett Jones.)

Brenda Ray and Sheila Lorene (who died in 1994) get a hug from McGraw at a seminar the two attended as college students in 1985. Jay McGraw is in the foreground. (*Photo credit:* Delores Emmett Jones.)

Thelma Box, McGraw's former Pathways partner, stands on a table making announcements after a seminar in the early 1990s. McGraw's father, Joe, is to the left, wearing a suit and holding on to the back of a chair. (*Photo credit:* Thelma Box.)

McGraw talking on the phone in the living room of his former Pathways business partner, Thelma Box, in 1983 (*Photo credit:* Thelma Box.)

A happy Thelma Box (left) with Darla Randolph at a Dallas Christmas party in 1992, minutes after announcing to McGraw, his dad, and about 400 seminar attendees that she intended to leave Pathways. (*Photo credit:* Thelma Box.)

McGraw leans against his black Mercedes in front of his Irving, Texas, mansion in 1999. He has since moved to an even larger home in Beverly Hills. (*Photo credit*: David Woo/Dallas Morning News.)

Fresh off the success of his appearances on *Oprah* and shortly after the release of his first book, *Life Strategies*, a beaming McGraw poses for the media in his hometown. (*Photo credit*: David Woo/ Dallas Morning News.)

McGraw signs books for his adoring fans, including some who cry tears of joy upon meeting him. (*Photo credit:* David Woo/Dallas Morning News.)

McGraw at a Dallas open house, signing books for friends and fans in 2002. (*Photo credit:* Juan Garcia/Dallas Morning News.)

Newsweek was the first major magazine to put McGraw on its cover. The September 2, 2002, issue featured the headline "TV's Hottest Self-Help Guru Has Some Advice for You: 'Get Real!'" (*Photo credit:* PR Newswire Photo Service.)

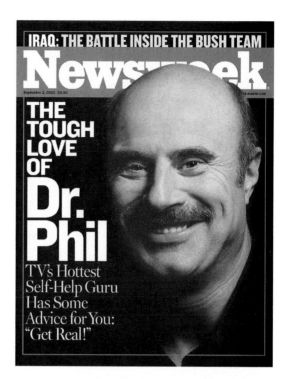

IRAQ: THE BATTLE INSIDE THE BUSH TEAM

Newsweek

September 2, 2002: $3.95

THE TOUGH LOVE OF

Dr. Phil

TV's Hottest Self-Help Guru Has Some Advice for You: "Get Real!"

McGraw played himself on an episode of the hit NBC sitcom *Frasier* titled "The Devil and Dr. Phil." Pictured from left are Kelsey Grammer, Peri Gilpin, Harriet Sansom Harris, and McGraw. (*Photo credit:* PR Newswire Photo Service.)

McGraw made his long-awaited visit to the *Late Show with David Letterman* on Monday, February 17, 2003. Although this was his first time as a guest, he had been a regular *Late Show* presence in "Dr. Phil's Words of Wisdom," a popular feature that made fun of clips from McGraw's own TV show. (*Photo credit:* CBS Photo Archive.)

The McGraw family. Pictured clockwise from top are Robin, Phil, Jordan, and Jay McGraw. (*Photo credit:* David Woo/Dallas Morning News.)

Son Jay reportedly caused similar problems for the crew. "We had a nickname for him—'El Diablo,'" the former employee says. "He causes trouble wherever he goes." (However, this person recalls, "Phil's other son [Jordan] was nice and quiet. We liked him.")

Some say Jay, like Robin, at times overstepped boundaries. In one case, the employee alleges, Jay's input into the editing of footage of his interviews with a group of teenagers caused the interviews to be so manipulated, the teens threatened to sue the show when they saw themselves. That show never aired.

■ ■ ■

Although, as at *Oprah*, employees of the *Dr. Phil* show are required to sign confidentiality agreements barring them from ever publicly discussing their experiences with McGraw and his show, reports about the tense set soon started appearing in the press.

"In one staff meeting, he went ballistic at some ideas," a show employee complained to a tabloid magazine. "He yelled: 'Didn't you people read my work? Didn't you see me on *Oprah*?'" Another staffer told *TV Guide*, "He has unforgiving standards and runs the show like a boot camp. He needs to treat people a little better and come down a notch."

"People on the set were intrigued when the first tabloid story appeared. We were all wondering, 'Okay, who leaked this?' because it was all dead-on true," says another former employee, who was interviewed exclusively for this book.

Among the tabloid's allegations that the *Dr. Phil* show refugee concurs with is that people were leaving the set in tears and were having to work all night. In one instance, according to the former employee, producers and editors had worked for weeks on footage for a particular show. The night before the show was scheduled to tape, McGraw saw the pieces. "He said, 'I hate it. Change everything. I don't care if you have to work all night, I don't care if you eat or sleep. Get it done and do it right.' They [the people working on the tapes] were literally up all night."

The woman who operated the teleprompter also had particular problems with her demanding boss. A prompter and a host need to learn to work together, to find the proper pace that's comfortable. "He [McGraw] never gave her that chance," the former employee says. "He would say things in front of the audience, really putting her down, [such as] 'Honey, you gotta keep up with me,' and worse than that. It was a constant badgering. I call it harassment. She tried at the beginning talking to him, asking, 'How do you want it done, let's work together,' but he refused to rehearse with her." The prompter operator was one of the first crew people to quit.

McGraw answers such complaints about his being difficult on the set with his customary self-confidence, spinning his reputation for being difficult into a point of pride. "Am I hard on people? Have I raised the bar of expectancy?" he asks. "Yes . . . [and I] make no apology for it whatsoever. None whatsoever. We do have high expectancies here. I do expect that research [on guests who appear on the show] to be done. I do expect those guests to be screened. I do expect for everything to be on time and professionally and properly done, and everyone here takes tremendous pride in achieving that."

Besides, Paramount was too enamored (and scared, the former employee suggests) of their new star to interfere or refuse any of his demands. "Paramount wanted *Dr. Phil*," says the former staffer, who was also eventually fired. "They wanted the show so bad, they were bending over backwards for him. They would do anything."

■ ■ ■

At one point, perhaps fearful that too much of McGraw would grow tiresome to viewers, producers discussed bringing a co-host or guest experts on the show, but that concept quickly evaporated, according to self-proclaimed Beverly Hills media psychiatrist Carole Lieberman, who got wind of the opportunity through the Hollywood grapevine and jumped on it. "I sent a letter, a demo reel, and a resume," she says. "They were trying to figure out ways to save the show. They thought maybe they would have some experts on various topics. But his [McGraw's] ego was too big for that. What it came down to is he didn't want anybody else. He wanted to be the big cheese—the only cheese—except for his son [Jay]."

In July 2002, two months before the show was set to premiere, McGraw gathered workers for a dressing-down. Shortly thereafter, a reportedly infuriated Winfrey flew into town to see what was going on. "Oprah got here in the nick of time," an unhappy staffer said. "She was just seething. Everybody refocused when she showed up. But she still saw that the show just doesn't jell." Winfrey's appearance on the set was "inspirational" according to another person, who said the problems on the set were just standard growing pains.

Winfrey's visit was a salve, the former employee confirms, in part because of the talk show diva's warmth. Although McGraw didn't bother to learn the names of his staff and crew, Winfrey made a point of introducing herself to everyone. "She was a really lovely person," the ex-staffer recalls, adding that McGraw and Robin were both on their best behavior when Winfrey was around. "He threw a party at his house, and they brought muffins and extra stuff that morning. We wanted to beg, 'Oprah, could you stay?'"

Meanwhile, Paramount, King World, and Harpo soldiered on. The studio's marketing engine kicked into high gear, placing *Dr. Phil* billboards in Miami, Los Angeles, New York, and other major U.S. markets. Promotional spots featuring McGraw talking with real people soon hit the national airways. The reported price tag for developing the first year of shows climbed to about $30 million.

■ ■ ■

*D*r. *Phil* premiered on September 16, 2002. "It's got everything, 'cept for Oprah," McGraw said in his opening remarks. The topic of the day was "Families under Stress." The show included gripping, troubling footage of Cathy haranguing her 10-year-old son. "Shut up, Vincent!" she snapped. "I'm so sick and tired of you saying stuff. I'm not even listening to you now."

"I'm tired of crying because I've been crying a lot. That's why I want my mom to get help," the child said in a taped interview.

"This is gonna be a changing day in your life," McGraw told Cathy. "It isn't gonna be an easy ride, but this is gonna be a day that changes things for you and your family. I'm not just barking at you. We're headed somewhere with this. We're talking about stress in people's life today. We're talking about how it affects your children."

That first show pulled in ratings that were beyond the producers' wildest dreams. Ranking number one in its time slot in 35 of the top Nielsen-metered markets, its 5.2 rating from Nielsen Media Research was the highest rating for a first-run syndicated show debut since Winfrey took the national stage in 1986. Even King World executives were amazed. "Considering we were optimistically looking for a rating in the mid-3 range for *Dr. Phil*, I would say we have a new major player in syndication," said Roger King, CEO of CBS Enterprises and King World Productions.

Success came quickly. After its dazzling debut, *Dr. Phil* continued to pull in high numbers, settling securely at the top of the daytime talk show ratings, right behind *Oprah*. *Dr. Phil*'s 5-plus national rating set the bar considerably higher for other syndicated shows, which average a national rating between 1 and 2. "The success of *Dr. Phil* has been important for everyone in the business because it makes everyone believe again," says Joel Berman, chairman of Paramount Worldwide Television Distribution.

Advertising rates rose with the show's star. A 30-second spot sold for $20,000 before the show hit the air. Two months later, the price jumped to $35,000.

■ ■ ■

Not only is *Dr. Phil*'s audience large, it is high quality. "He's tied with *Judge Judy*, who ties with *Oprah* in some markets [in terms of ratings]," says Paige Albiniak, Los Angeles bureau chief for *Broadcasting & Cable* magazine. "But *Judge Judy* skews much poorer than *Oprah*. He [McGraw] has a good daytime demographic, which usually tends to be unemployed people, old people, and stay-at-home moms. McGraw's audience is mostly women, but they are more affluent."

Television stations that purchased *Dr. Phil* have been unilaterally elated by the show's performance. In Los Angeles, KNBC-TV dropped its 4 P.M. newscast and inserted *Dr. Phil* into the time slot, which helped pump up numbers for the station's 5 P.M. newscast. In Cleveland, with *Dr. Phil* leading in, WKYC-TV's 6 P.M. languishing newscast saw its rating rise to the point where it was no longer limping far behind the competition and had claimed a solid position in the race. Even more dramatically, San Francisco station KRON-TV—once an NBC affiliate, then a struggling independent—nabbed *Dr. Phil* and scheduled it for 8 P.M. *Dr. Phil* now regularly beats much of its prime time network competition in northern California in ratings, households, and important adult demographics—a feat virtually unheard of for syndicated fare. *Dr. Phil* has also significantly bolstered ratings for KRON's 9 P.M. newscast. Not surprisingly, when the show came up for renewal, KRON gleefully re-signed. "*Dr. Phil* continues to provide our station with prime time ratings growth across the board while out-drawing many of network television's most powerful shows," says Dino Dinovitz, the station's president and general manager. "*Dr. Phil* has by far exceeded our expectations."

■ ■ ■

The success did not ride entirely on McGraw's formidable shoulders. Industry experts agree that Winfrey's grooming and Paramount and King World's positioning gave *Dr. Phil* a boost even before it hit the airwaves.

"King World did a really smart thing launching this show," says Marc Berman, columnist for *MediaWeek*. "They introduced him slowly, on *Oprah*. Viewers were familiar with him and they knew what he did. Plus, he created a show that was really informative, entertaining, and addictive. I give him credit for that."

Not surprisingly, as the 2003 Daytime Emmy Awards ceremony approached, the betting was that *Dr. Phil* would emerge as the evening's big winner, given the show's enormous freshman year success. McGraw was nominated in two categories: Outstanding talk show host and outstanding talk show. A confident McGraw made appearances on numerous talk shows during the week of the awards show and blushed as interviewers made it clear they felt he would emerge victorious.

When asked how he felt about the nominations by a gushing Larry King, McGraw responded, "Well, you know, I'm proud of it, I really am, because . . . I think we've done some quality television this year. You probably don't remember this, but starting out is a different challenge."

It was a challenge McGraw met with astonishing results. During the 2002 to 2003 season, more people watched *Dr. Phil* on a daily basis than all of the other daytime talk shows that premiered during the season combined. McGraw was clearly pumped up and secure with his success. When Berman called to interview McGraw for an article about daytime television for *Emmy* magazine, a publicist responded that McGraw would not talk unless he was guaranteed to be on the cover of the magazine.

Although McGraw and his show didn't win any Emmys this first time out of the gate (he lost to Wayne Brady and *The View*), the show will most likely get at least two more opportunities to grab one. On target to make a profit of about $52 million its first year for King World—not to mention a hefty take for both Paramount and Harpo—*Dr. Phil* was renewed in 60 percent of the country through the 2005 to 2006 season. Its success inspired bidding wars among stations around the world clamoring to air it. By mid-2003, *Dr. Phil* was aired on 200 domestic affiliates and in about 40 foreign countries. McGraw's paycheck for the show? A reported $10 million a year.

■ ■ ■

But whether McGraw's audience will stick with his "all me, all-the-time" formula for the long haul remains to be seen. The show doesn't offer the same kind of variety as *Oprah,* with its mix of serious topics, makeovers, and celebrity interviews. In addition, says *MediaWeek*'s Berman, "The thing about *Oprah* is that Oprah is everybody's best friend. She's the girl next door. She's warm and fuzzy and feel-good. That's not Dr. Phil. He's so out-spoken, so in your face. I think that gets tiresome. *Oprah* could continue for another 10 years. I don't know if *Dr. Phil* can."

Dr. Phil's licensing fees, which doubled in the second cycle, also have some industry executives grumbling about the possible damage to other syndicated programming. "As good as the show is, the license-fee increases are so exorbitant that they will cause people to start looking for cheaper alternatives throughout the rest of their schedule," predicts Alan Frank, president of the Post-Newsweek station group.

Some wonder whether McGraw will be able to maintain enthu-siasm for the work. "Honestly, I think it's beneath him," says one former CSI employee. "Phil will be successful at whatever he does. He works like a horse. He never sits on his butt. He's very, very smart and he's very, very driven. I think his show is beneath his intellect. It's not nearly as intellectually stimulating as what he was doing at CSI."

McGraw has an inarguable gift. "I have an ability to analyze things real fast," is how he describes it. This is evident in his show and the way he cuts through complex problems, pulls out the nut of the issue, and prescribes a seemingly obvious solution. But demonstrating this skill over and over, season after season, may seem increasingly like performing a parlor trick. Time and ratings will reveal if audiences ultimately "get it" and decide to move on.

McGraw isn't worried. In fact, he thinks that as good as the numbers are on his show, the show itself is even better. That's why the big ratings alone are not quite enough to satisfy his ambition. "I hate that [there are still] some people [who] missed the show," he says.

The *Dr. Phil* Show

*The fact that you're on television regularly should not lend to
your credibility, but I think it probably does in people's minds.*

B y 6 A.M. on a chilly spring day, a few ticket holders are already waiting outside a nondescript door on the Paramount
Studios lot for the morning taping of the *Dr. Phil* show. By
6:15, the line is about 10 people long. By 6:30, it is close to half a
block. By 7 A.M., it stretches for a full block. No sign marks the
rust-colored door, but instructions from the show say to line up
by the large Wyland whale mural—clearly visible overhead—
for first-come, first-serve seating. The genial and well-dressed
McGraw fans are primarily female and of various ages and eth-
nicities, but they are mostly middle-aged and white. A few have
reluctant men in tow.

A couple of 50-something friends and their mothers have driven
three hours from Tulare, California, which is half-way between
Fresno and Bakersfield, to treat themselves to the show. They have
made a girl-bonding excursion out of it, spending the previous
night at the Hollywood Renaissance ("Where the *Dr. Phil* show puts
its guests up," one of the women boasts), taking themselves out to

a nice dinner the night before, and nabbing their places in line shortly after 6 A.M. They snack on trail mix and sunflower seeds, shivering a little in the crisp air, as they wait for the studio doors to open.

"I absolutely love him," says one of the mothers with a happy giggle. "He's so honest, it's refreshing. I watch him every afternoon at 3. *Oprah* is on at 4. Sometimes I don't even watch her anymore."

The metal door outside Stage 29 finally swings open around 7:30 A.M. A young male guard admonishes everyone to have photo IDs ready, and the crowd starts filing in. Just inside the door, IDs are checked, release forms are distributed, handbags are searched, and those who didn't follow the list of rules for attending the show have their cell phones, pagers, and books confiscated. Everyone is then escorted through a metal detector and told to walk single file to a cold metal bench outside the studio.

There, audience members have plenty of time to read through a blue release form—eight paragraphs of small print advising them that the show owns all images taped that day and can use them in any way it pleases—which they must sign to get inside the studio doors. The release further states that by signing you agree that any airing of dirty laundry is being done voluntarily; that you won't sue if you don't like what you see on the air; and that you promise not to use McGraw's name, photo, or quotes to market any product. Paragraph five reads: "I represent that I do not suffer from a mental illness and am not currently under psychiatric care. I further acknowledge that Dr. Phil McGraw, the host of the series, does not and will not administer individual, group, or medical therapy; and his advice, opinions, or statements should not be considered individual, group, or medical therapy or a substitute or replacement for those therapies."

The form includes space for one's name, phone number, and Social Security number. When an audience member questions why they need a Social Security number, an usher responds,

"That's just the way it is." When asked for a copy of the release form to take home—it is a binding contract, after all—another young usher seems startled. "Blue sheets can't leave the building," she recites, without further explanation.

Guests on the show receive a similar consent form, which also specifies that they may not appear on any other talk program for 90 days. And those who want an appointment with Dr. Phil can't be too sick: Guests are required to state that they have never been institutionalized or on psychotropic drugs, among other things.

■ ■ ■

About 30 minutes after making their way to the bench, the crowd of about 250 people is ushered inside, but not into the actual studio just yet. Instead, they enter a large, meat-locker-cold room draped with black curtains. Everyone is herded into folding metal chairs, companionably set up with rows facing each other. A small table with coffee urns at the side of the room draws a crowd clamoring for a warming cup. Many people hold the cups up to their cheeks or wrap their frigid hands around them.

One woman, attending her second taping, has come prepared in a full-length winter coat. She pulls up her hood and burrows her head into it. A member of the group from Tulare wonders aloud if the trip was worth all the effort and waiting. "I wouldn't do it again," she sighs. Three hours have passed since she staked out her place in line, and there's still no sign of her television hero. When McGraw's voice finally emanates from behind the curtain, in discussion with someone in the studio, a buzz of excitement moves through the crowd.

At long last, a young woman dressed in black with matching hair stands in the middle of the room and identifies herself as an audience coordinator. She bellows out a list of caveats, such as "No gum chewing because you'll look like a cow with your lips flapping. I'm saying this for your sake—you won't like what you see on TV." The audience is then instructed to take off hats so the cameras can see their faces, to remove glasses from the tops of heads, and not to open the bag of goodies they would find under their chair until after the show. Cards soliciting ideas for future *Dr. Phil* shows are distributed. If your topic is chosen, everyone is told, you will be flown back in to sit in the audience of that show.

A few minutes later, video screens suspended from the ceiling flicker to life with a promotional video for the *Dr. Phil* show. The crowd, faces turned up and glowing blue in the overhead monitors, is rapt. They watch Oprah rave about her protégé and laugh appreciatively at McGraw's one-liners. "I don't want this show to be successful," McGraw boasts. "I want it to be an addiction." The tape ends with a reel of McGraw's bloopers. "I don't say crap like this," he complains, before the monitors go dark again.

Finally, an audience wrangler calls the names of about 15 parties and has them line up at the entrance to the studio. This first group turns in its release forms and is ushered inside the studio. The remainder of the crowd follows behind.

■ ■ ■

Television studios are often surprisingly small compared with how they appear on television, but this one is quite large. Black-clad techs mill around the stage, which is bare except for large plasma screens with the *Dr. Phil* show logo and two high mustard-colored chairs that are to be occupied by the doctor and his guest. Front-row audience seats hold reserved signs, awaiting the guests who will sit there before and after they take the stage with McGraw.

As they wait, audience members fluff and puff for their moment in the spotlight, refreshing lipstick and checking their hair. A woman in the second row offers rice papers to the ladies around her so they can blot oil from their shiny faces.

More waiting, then another audience coordinator takes the stage.

"Are you glad to be here at the number one show on television?" she asks. The audience cheers, though not loud enough, in her opinion. "Let's try that again. Are you GLAD TO BE HERE AT THE NUMBER ONE SHOW ON TELEVISION?" The applause is obligingly louder this time around.

After the audience is permitted to stop their thunderous cheers, more stern instructions follow, including what to do if you want to ask McGraw a question on the air (raise your hand), and why you shouldn't read along with McGraw's teleprompter (more about flapping lips). The coordinator's tone is patronizing and testy. Her response to one audience member's wisecrack is to invite the joker up on stage to do the talking, like a teacher chastising an unruly student.

Next, *Dr. Phil* show publicist and showbiz hopeful Chandler Hayes takes the stage to pump up the crowd. Hayes claps, shouts, and skips. He gives away McGraw's books to the person in the audience who traveled farthest to come to the show (Colombia, South America, in this case) and the one who got the least shut-eye the night before (an insomnia sufferer who claims not to have slept a wink). Hayes then invites a bald-headed audience member to come up and rehearse McGraw's entrance, to make sure the crowd reaction is properly enthusiastic.

"How'd they do?" Hayes asks the man following his entrance.

"I've heard better," replies McGraw's stand-in, prompting Hayes to order a second run-through with better results.

After the pseudo-Phil returns to his seat, Hayes instructs the audience to stand and do "The Twist," to the blaring strains of Chubby Checker. He brings a few people on stage for a twist contest. Then, Shania Twain's "Man! I Feel Like A Woman!" video starts playing on the plasma screens around the stage. The audience, still on its feet, is urged to clap along. Immediately following the video, the *Dr. Phil* show opening—"Let's do it"—starts playing.

At this moment, McGraw is standing backstage, out of audience view. While waiting, he perhaps glances occasionally at the old black-and-white picture of basketball legend Kareem Abdul-Jabbar hanging in the back of the studio. This photo has a special significance. No show taped in Stage 29 has ever made it past the first month except for one: *The Arsenio Hall Show.* Hall kept this same picture of Abdul-Jabbar up in the studio from the day he started taping to the day he left. McGraw's staffers found the picture and put it up for him, hoping that the magic would rub off on *Dr. Phil.*

Seconds before his cue, McGraw might sway back and forth and do a quick exercise routine of squats and stretches, perhaps to soothe his nerves. Just before McGraw's big entrance, wife Robin walks into the studio and takes her seat in the front row of the second tier of seats. Then, up flies the center scrim and out steps the man everyone has awaited for hours.

McGraw emerges looking somehow smaller than he does on TV. He walks onto the set, waving mechanically as the crowd frantically claps and hollers. It is finally show time.

■ ■ ■

McGraw's pale blue eyes fasten on the teleprompter as he begins reading his opening comments. During videotaped background segments, his eyes flicker over the audience, gauging its reaction. While guests talk, McGraw often appears distant and unfocused. He occasionally thumbs through the white binder of background information on his guests. His responses frequently match his guests' comments, and sometimes seem only marginally relevant.

During commercial breaks, McGraw says little to the audience, other than the occasional, "How ya'll doing?" Likewise, McGraw rarely talks to the guests who sit a foot away from him. He saves that interaction for when the cameras are rolling. In between, quick makeup touch-ups keep McGraw's bald head from glowing under the lights. The host doesn't like long commercial breaks and encourages his staff to keep the show going.

Contact between McGraw and his guests is pretty much limited to the time spent on stage. For one former guest, this was a particular disappointment. Paula Reinhardt, an avid McGraw fan from Fresno, California, decided that the best way to meet him was to get on the *Dr. Phil* show. She responded via e-mail to a call from the show for wives whose husbands had trouble buying them gifts. (Reinhardt's husband, Matt, qualified by presenting her with a leaf blower one Christmas.) The Reinhardts were immediately contacted by *Dr. Phil* show staff. The couple was told on December 5 that they would be flown to Los Angeles on December 9 for a taping on December 10. In this short time, they had to e-mail photos for the show to use on the program, scramble to find babysitters for their two sons, and host a film crew in their home on December 7, which came to shoot background video.

Once in Hollywood, Reinhardt's dream of a tête-à-tête with McGraw barely came true. "The one thing I wanted to do was get to meet Dr. Phil. He greets you when you come on stage but you don't talk to him before or after the show," she complains. The guest experience manages to be both intimate and impersonal, a close encounter with a closed man.

In the audience, however, everyone fully understands the job at hand. The crowd gasps at the shocking, nods sagely at the sensible, laughs at the humorous, and shakes their heads at the ludicrous. Applause is sometimes prompted by loud clapping from a stagehand, but is just as often spontaneous and heartfelt. On this day, McGraw is good for some clever sound bites, a couple of small laughs, and a few one-liners. Although the audience doesn't know it, each time McGraw spouts one of these so-called Phil-isms, producers in the control booth ring a bell to signify the moment.

■ ■ ■

Among other things that the audience never sees are the weeks of work that go into making each show happen. McGraw has close to 150 staffers, 90 percent of whom are women. They are divided into nine teams led by four producers. Each team spends about a week preparing the show it is responsible for, often fine-tuning it right up to the taping date. Team duties include finding and booking guests, arranging and editing field shoots (video segments that are prerecorded for the program), conducting research, and reading through the viewer mail that pours in daily.

"The most challenging thing about working here is booking the guests," says executive producer Carla Pennington Stewart. "That is where, you know, the heart attacks come . . . the cancellations and booking people at the last minute."

According to Stewart, staffers continually worry about what guests will do once they're on the air. "Are they gonna back-pedal on their story or are they really gonna get real and tell him the real deal?"

Adds producer David Goldman, "Once you get the people on board, you then have to keep 'em on board because once they start to think about it [they begin to fret], 'Oh my God. I'm coming on TV to talk about, you know, my sex life.' "

Each program is produced with the show's primary audience in mind: women—especially stay-at-home moms who watch *Dr. Phil* with an eye toward a take-home message. McGraw's staff says they rely on him to make sure each show carries this message.

"Any time we're picking a topic, choosing guests, and deciding what all we're going to go through, our number one question is what's the takeaway?" McGraw explains. "What can someone take away from that show that they can use today or tomorrow in their lives."

The taping, tightly choreographed and quickly accomplished, with only the briefest breaks where commercials will be inserted, is an experience that differs only slightly from watching the show on television. After hours of waiting, the audience is treated to an experience that takes about 60 minutes, the length of an actual program.

Then, it's all over. McGraw says goodbye to his TV fans, walks into the audience, takes wife Robin's hand, and the two walk out together. This hand-holding ritual began at the first taping. "I walked down the runway and my wife was sitting there, and it seemed totally unnatural for me to walk past my wife like I didn't know her," McGraw explains. "So, spontaneously, I just reached down and got her hand and she ran off the stage with me behind her. We've done that ever since." Robin, who arrives at the studio every morning before show time, barely comes up to her husband's shoulders even in skyscraper heels. A few moments after their hand-in-hand departure, McGraw returns alone to the front of the stage to talk with his guests a bit longer while the cameras roll, offering a little extra footage for producers to use in the final edit.

■ ■ ■

After each taping, producers and the host gather in a conference room for the postmortem, a quick meeting to discuss how well the guests and the taping worked. Staffers speak of taking pride in following up with guests and in ensuring that they all have a good experience with the show.

Attorney Richard Hitt of Jackson, Michigan, who appeared on the show twice with his client Amanda Redman, can testify to the amount of time producers put in to each guest. He spent many hours with the *Dr. Phil* show staff, on the phone and in person, before getting on a plane for the taping in Los Angeles. The show he and Redman appeared on was about mothers with overweight children. Redman's children were taken away from her by the state after she allowed her firstborn to reach 120 pounds by the age of three. "Considerable telephone interviews went on back and forth among producers and myself and my client Amanda," Hitt says. "Then they sent a camera crew out and conducted an interview with both of us to air during the segment. I imagine we spent a good five or six hours in total with them, including the initial telephone interview and the actual in-studio taping."

Hitt was pleased with the overall experience. "They were sensitive to the nature of what was going on. I was impressed with the producer from Hollywood, and I was most impressed with the interviewer who was sent out here to do the preliminary TV work. The high caliber and high character with the way everything was handled was most impressive."

Redman also has good things to say about the show, though she admits to having a case of nerves during the taping, especially when she saw how McGraw dealt with the guest who was on right before her. "The first lady that was on there, she was kind of in denial and he really got on her," Redman recalls. "I was like, 'Oh my gosh, please don't let me go next.' "

"I kind of winced when I saw the way he handled that first client as far as putting her feet to the fire," Hitt adds. "But he definitely was able to shift gears and be appropriate for what he was actually facing."

The production kept in touch with Hitt and Redman and brought them back for a follow-up show two months later, after Redman's second child was taken from her by the state.

Hitt and Redman admittedly came to the show with an agenda. They hoped to get the message out about how unforgiving the Michigan court system is, given that it took Redman's second child even though she successfully and willingly completed all court-ordered classes. Still, the attention they got from being on *Dr. Phil* was a mixed blessing.

"It's been helpful in that it centered the attention of the community and the people in Jackson on what was actually happening. We had a lot of letters to the editor and so forth," Hitt says. "The downside was that I definitely had the impression that putting the light of scrutiny on the Michigan court system was held against Amanda."

Nevertheless, Hitt has nothing but praise for McGraw. "I was very impressed with Dr. Phil. His toughness, and at the same time fairness and kindness, showed through. I can understand why he's so well received and widely acclaimed."

■ ■ ■

L ike Hitt, many of the guests brought back on the *Dr. Phil* show for follow-ups express gratitude to McGraw for the changes he inspired. After an appearance on a show about teens who dress inappropriately, Sally DeWitt from Sarasota, Florida, told the local news media that the advice she got from McGraw was helpful and that her daughter was dressing and behaving differently. Her daughter Victoria said she was shocked to see her style on television, and it changed her ways.

But not all guests are so impressed. Tabetha Yang found being on the show to be an underwhelming experience. Yang is the owner of Mystique Model Management, an adult-industry talent agency in Beverly Hills. "They [McGraw's producers] contacted us because they were doing a show about the adult industry," she explains. "They wanted to know if I had any talent who had bad experiences in the industry. I did, because I deal with several ladies that are leaving the adult industry for various reasons, going into legitimate modeling or acting." Yang accompanied one of these models, named Friday, on the show.

The *Dr. Phil* staff sent a limo to bring Yang and Friday to the studio. Unlike other programs on which Yang has appeared, however, she says staffers offered no allowance for expenses, lost time on the job, or child care. The producers were professional and polite, Yang admits, but she found the host to be chilly and the environment to be sterile. "I've been on *Ricki Lake,* Friday's been on *Jenny Jones* before. *Dr. Phil* was much more cut and dried," Yang says. "Dr. Phil himself was not very personable at all. There was no interaction with him except for the questions he asked. We didn't even get to shake his hand. We felt like he wanted to have nothing to do with us because of the industry we're from. We were a prop for his show, because he's the moralistic character and we're all the poor demons. Just like so many of these shows where they try to get you to believe it's going to be two sided, it very rarely is. It didn't do any harm, but it certainly didn't do us any good."

Yang adds that the show never contacted her or Friday to follow up on whether Friday left the adult industry, as Friday told McGraw she intended to do.

That is the exception, not the rule, McGraw maintains. "We have an after-care program where we follow-up with 100 percent of the people that are on the show," he insists. "Some don't need it at all. They come in with a very isolated situation, we react to it, and move on. But for others we provide them at no expense to them care in their own community to work out the problem."

■ ■ ■

After the day's first taping ends, the audience files out of the chilly studio and into the blissfully warm sunshine, clutching their *Dr. Phil* shopping bags, which on this morning contained hair care products, lipstick, makeup samples, a small box of dry cereal, some nutritional supplements, and the current issue of *O* magazine. Outside, the old audience passes by a new group of *Dr. Phil* fans who are lined up, excited and ready for the afternoon taping. And so it will go, twice a day, throughout the season, for as many years as the show lasts.

Even before his show hit the airwaves, McGraw denied any fear of failure. "There's probably two reasons for that," he said "One is complete ignorance . . . And the second reason is I believe that what needs to happen will. If there is a need for what I intend to do, it will be successful."

Judging by the ratings, the crowds lining up outside the studio, the letters that pour in, and the acclaim that has gathered around McGraw, that need appears to be there.

Mass-Marketing Tough Talk

It's really nice to be there live with the people and to take some questions sometimes [and] sometimes not.

While McGraw is on television five days a week and has several bestselling books, do his fans really ever get their fill of Dr. Phil? Apparently not, judging by the thousands of excited women streaming into the Greater Columbus Convention Center's Battelle Hall to see their idol live at his "Get Real" seminar.

The hall has a capacity of nearly 7,000 people, and a thrilled female Phil fan will fill almost every seat on this spring evening. Some already clutch copies of McGraw's books as they enter the building; others stop to buy books, videos, and other "Dr. Phil" products from merchants at folding tables inside. The few men who are here no doubt hope to gain valuable relationship points with their significant others by being present at this female-centric Phil-fest.

The greater Columbus area is the number one morning market for the *Dr. Phil* show in the country. A healthy percentage of the 87,000 local viewers who watch the show each month are trying to see their hero in the flesh. The escalators and lobbies are clogged with happy fans making their way to the auditorium.

"He has such good things to say. He helps me analyze myself better," says Char Knowles, a teacher from Sugar Creek, Ohio, as she settles excitedly into her seat and waves energetically at her husband, sitting halfway across the crowded venue.

Knowles, who has taped *Dr. Phil* daily since its debut and now has a library of episodes, decided at the last minute that she simply had to get real with McGraw. Getting a "sold out" message from Ticketmaster, she logged onto the online auction site eBay for the first time, got into a bidding war for a pair of seats for her and her husband, then bailed out when the price topped $200. But instead of giving up, the couple hopped into their car and drove 2½ hours to Columbus on the chance that they might be able to negotiate with a scalper—another first for Knowles—for a couple of seats. They succeeded, although the seats weren't together—hardly a thrilling turn of events for Knowles's husband, she admits. But, she says, "I figure if he picks up something good here, that's cool."

No doubt about it, McGraw is one hot ticket.

■ ■ ■

McGraw began to pack them in at large auditoriums shortly after hitting it big on *Oprah*. It is a far cry from McGraw's Pathways days. By mid-2003, McGraw was at the top of the motivational speaking circuit. "He certainly has a following. People are excited because of his popularity," says Salim Khoja, vice president of Power Within, which produces all-day multispeaker motivational seminars for which McGraw is a frequent speaker. "It's no different than if it were a major rock band on top of the charts." Khoja also points out that women are typically the audience for motivational events, so the estrogen-heavy demographic of the "Get Real" tour isn't unusual or necessarily unique to McGraw.

Top of the charts also means top dollar, and hiring McGraw to speak at an event now costs more than, for example, hiring motivational stalwart Deepak Chopra. McGraw reportedly commands $100,000 to $125,000 per speech (about the same as former New York mayor Rudy Giuliani and former president Bill Clinton), plus a private jet. "He's not going to get on a commercial flight," Khoja says, and he requires more security than your run-of-the-mill motivational speaker. For the public, tickets for "Power Within" events (which include several motivational speakers) are $100 to $200. Tickets for McGraw's solo Columbus event ranged from $55 to $135.

Khoja, who says he books McGraw about six months in advance for his events, immediately learned that McGraw was a formidable negotiating opponent. That is to say, negotiation was not really part of the equation. Rather, McGraw calls the shots. "He says, 'This is what I am and this is what it is,'" Khoja explains. "In fairness to him, he sets the rules and if you stick to them, he's very accommodating. It's not that he's difficult to deal with, he lets you know up front how it is. If you adhere to those parameters, you get what you expect. If you deviate, then you've got to let him know in advance, and then he's accommodating."

To meeting planner Beth Katsinas, the huge price tag is worth it. She hired McGraw to address the University of Illinois' Biennial Conference for women in 2002 and saw attendance double on the day he spoke. "Women love him," Katsinas says. "It was like having a rock star there."

The AARP hired McGraw to be a keynote speaker at its annual member convention in Chicago in 2003. He headlined a list of celebrity guests that also included Debbie Reynolds, Louis Gossett Jr., sex therapist Dr. Ruth Westheimer, film critic Leonard Maltin, Republican political consultant Mary Matalin, and former *Golden Girls* star Rue McClanahan.

■ ■ ■

The Columbus live seminar was McGraw's idea, according to Frank Willson, director of operations for WBNS-10TV, promotional partner for the event. Willson got a call from Scott

Madsen, McGraw's chief of staff. After that, "Scott and I were on the phone a minimum of once a week."

The day after local promotions launched in January, Willson says, Madsen phoned him to report they had seen their highest first-day ticket sales ever. Ultimately, the venue decided to pack away some of the equipment taking up floor space to add 1,000 seats, which fans quickly snapped up.

McGraw may be a tough negotiator, but Khoja says he is also generous about providing promotional support for shows and has gladly done interviews with the local media to support upcoming seminars. In Columbus, McGraw delighted WBNS by turning up the afternoon before the show at a station-sponsored food drive, toting shopping bags of food. "He spent a solid 45 minutes out here, not only doing interviews on air, but also collecting food from people," Willson says. "He didn't have to do that. He had a little relaxation time scheduled which he cut into."

■ ■ ■

The Columbus seminar is late getting started as people continue streaming into the hall. Finally, after an ebullient introduction from a WBNS personality, McGraw's publicist Chandler Hayes takes the stage to kick things off, as he does at *Dr. Phil* show tapings. Black curtains surround the stage, which is decorated only with potted plants and a massive video screen on either side, so fans in the nosebleed sections can see McGraw's face up close. Hayes holds a drawing for books and a vacation, plays a video of McGraw being adored by his fans, and urges the audience to rise to its feet while three bedazzled women drawn from the crowd join him in a rousing chorus of "Shout," the feel-good song made famous by the Isley Brothers. Out in the audience, the risers shake as fans sing along, lifting their hands with each "shout." Then Shania Twain's "Man! I Feel Like a Woman!" video starts playing, just like at the TV studio. Finally, when the air is thoroughly electric, McGraw steps out from behind the curtains. The audience cheers and stomps.

"What the hell am I doing in Ohio?" he asks, and the audience laughs and cheers some more. He has them at the first hello.

■ ■ ■

Shy in small groups, remote and sometimes chilly in the false intimacy of the television studio, McGraw is clearly in his comfort zone on stage in front of thousands. "If I have something structured to do, you put me in front of 10 million people with an agenda, a job to do, that doesn't bother me at all. You put me in a cocktail party making small talk, and I'd rather get a root canal," he says.

Standing alone on an empty stage in front of thousands of fans, with just a headset microphone, a trove of well-worn anecdotes to back up his Life Laws, and his own quick mind, McGraw is sensational. Dressed in all black against a black backdrop, he appears as just hands and a bald head on the video screens. He comes across warmer in person than on television, and his self-deprecation is more appealing if no less believable. He tells stories with rich visual imagery and exhibits a natural sense of physical comedy. When he relays his oft-told tale—you can read it in *Life Strategies*—about being stopped by a policeman for drag racing when he was a teenager, he describes himself and three friends lining up "like crows on a fence," clamping his arms to his sides, and taking three sideways steps, turning himself into a row of four tense teens facing the law.

The audience is spellbound, soaking up his every word, laughing loud and hard at his jokes. When he wraps up the teens and cop story with the Life Law it inspired—"Either you get it or you don't"—a woman in the audience suddenly scrambles through her purse, pulls out a little notepad, and writes, "Either you get it or you don't." Throughout the program, a parade of women crouch in front of the stage to take snapshots, then scamper back to their seats.

Still, even in his favorite setting, McGraw is not entirely without his trademark impatience and arrogance. Before launching into his program in earnest, he asks the audience how many have read his books. The cheer is less than robust. He asks how many watch him on television. This time, the applause is loud and prolonged. He shakes his head disgustedly at the TV-centric response. "Geeze," he says. "No wonder the Japanese are kicking our butts."

He talks about his "Debate Dr. Phil" shows and complains about people misunderstanding him. "They will misquote me. They do it all the time," he says. When a woman in the front row gets up to go to the bathroom, he hassles her about leaving. "Now where do you think you're going?" he asks. When she finally slinks off, he turns back to the audience with a grin. "She ain't gonna come back," he says.

"I'm watching you all," McGraw warns the crowd.

That's the way he works even a big crowd, and it is part of his genius. McGraw pays attention. "You have to feel the audience and feel the country to know what needs to be said and done. I really do it that way—it's intuitive. I've got a very skinny script, and I go with what feels right at the time . . . You look into the audience and see how many mothers and fathers, husbands and wives are there, and you speak to them. You have to meet them where they are.

"If they're leaning forward, or they laugh when they should, or they cheer when they ought to—then you know you're connecting," he explains. Anyone McGraw spots who appears to be resisting gets a good dose of his tough talk. A man in Battelle Hall who is sitting near the front with his arms and legs crossed defensively gets the video cameras turned on him. The audience laughs delightedly at his ornery image on the giant screens. Any contradiction, implied or literal, gets a McGraw raspberry. He tells the crowd, "Just for tonight, I want you to move your position and say, 'You know what? I'd rather be happy than right.'" It seems McGraw can—and must—be happy and right simultaneously.

But the love just keeps on coming. The audience even cheers his digs. This is the Dr. Phil they came to see. They also relish the personal anecdotes he shares—that he once had a cat named Catface, that he was freaked out in the delivery room and didn't want to watch his first son make his entrance, that Robin took up tennis because of the clothes, and that he was a failure as a marriage counselor. "I quit because everybody I talked to got a divorce because I'd been teaching them what I was taught in the ivory tower," he says.

The audience loves his embarrassment over a Freudian slip he makes while discussing Monica Lewinsky's gig hosting a TV reality show. "Everybody's gotta eat," he says, and the audience whoops while he blushes and adds—"Oh God, there's another tabloid."

Here, nobody worries about the line between psychology and entertainment, therapy versus motivation, because this is pure motivational speaking. Even when McGraw trots out research to back his points, it is sometimes the urban legend research used by other motivational speakers. Near the end of the program, McGraw cites a study by Yale University about successful people and life plans. "The five percent of people studied who had a life plan had more success than the other 95 percent *combined*," he says. This is certainly a powerful statistic to make his point—but it's also bogus. "This has been widely quoted but it is based on no fact whatsoever. Such a study never took place," according to a spokeswoman from the Yale Office of Public Affairs, anxious to set the record straight.

But in this venue, with McGraw's adoring fans gobbling up his every word, how much does it matter whether the facts are exactly right? This is McGraw the entertainer, motivator, and showman—not the shrink. This audience isn't seeking credentials, facts, and statistics. They're here for the buzz, for the performance, and they aren't disappointed. By the time McGraw leaves the stage, to the strains of Springsteen's "Born in the U.S.A.," his fans are glassy-eyed with pleasure and, one assumes, hope for the future. One young woman wraps her arms around her boyfriend and kisses him emphatically. "You're all energized, aren't you?" he says delightedly.

McGraw has the power to do that to a crowd. But he is only one man. Given his far-reaching ambitions, if his empire is to continue to grow, he must continually find new ways to spread himself even further than is physically possible for one human being. And he's finding myriad opportunities to do just that.

■ ■ ■

McGraw continues to reach deeper into the print medium. Not satisfied with only his monthly column in *O* magazine, Winfrey's blockbuster glossy, McGraw joined forces with American Express Publishing's custom publishing group to launch a monthly newsletter in October 2003 called *The Next Level*. Charter subscriptions are $34.95, more than double the $15 annual cost of *O*. One reason for the higher price: The publication doesn't include any advertising.

McGraw's presence in cyberspace remains strong. His web site, DrPhil.com, receives about 14 million hits every month and is treated as an extension of the show. The web site team sits in the control room with producers during tapings to figure out what show content should be carried from the show to cyberspace each day.

Producers use the online site to solicit guests for future shows by inviting visitors to tell their stories about such topics as. "Are you living beyond your means?" and "America's most talented mom." Here, too, visitors can obtain free tickets to attend a show taping; and they can buy all kinds of "Dr. Phil" merchandise—books, videos, transcripts, coffee mugs graced with McGraw's mug, boxer shorts, T-shirts, key chains emblazoned with an "I Love Dr. Phil" logo, and logo-adorned spiral-bound notebooks to "jot down your notes during your favorite *Dr. Phil.*"

Web site message boards allow *Dr. Phil* fans to meet and discuss shows. Some notes are directed at other posters, but many are written directly to McGraw or the producers. Some sign on to comment about particular shows. "Sorry Dr. Phil, but I thought today's show was a major snoozefest," one post reads. Others want to confide and commiserate over subjects inspired by the shows. "Am I really as crazy as people think when they find out I am on anti-depressants? Help!!" one participant pleads. "I am on Zoloft [an antidepressant] and everyone I know is very understanding," another person writes in a consoling response. Many fans send adoring messages to Robin. "Robin, you are the best. I love how you call Dr. Phil, 'Philip,'" one post reads.

Occasionally, former guests chime in to talk about the experience of being on the show—sometimes complaining about a lack of contact with McGraw except during the taping. "I don't like the idea of meeting someone face to face for the first time with a camera showing it to the world," wrote one former guest. "I think he should make an effort to at least just walk into the 'green room' (which is actually beige . . . with dark green furniture and a bar and a bunch of plants . . . lol) and just say 'HI' and shake the guests hands before they all go out there."

Any single message thread can pull in dozens of responses in a week. "When the show ends on the East Coast, we begin to see the messages arriving, and a lot of them start out, 'I have never responded to a television show before,'" says Carla Pennington Stewart, executive producer of the *Dr. Phil* show.

Show executives say McGraw reads e-mails, including those that disagree with him. "Especially from experts who disagree with him," emphasizes Terry Wood, executive vice president of programming for Paramount Domestic Television.

"His viewers are very opinionated. That's the way they interact with him," Stewart adds. "That's how we keep our core audience, which listens and responds. We don't ignore negatives."

■ ■ ■

McGraw's marketing machine has found a way to reach further still, by assembling an army to increase the level of cultural saturation for which he apparently strives. In the McGraw style of sharing the wealth with his chosen friends and family members, Dr. G. Frank Lawlis—McGraw's old friend and advisor at North Texas State University—has launched seminars with the Dr. Phil imprimatur on LearnDrPhilFromLawlis.com.

In the live and online seminars, Lawlis, who is identified as "the principal content advisor for the *Dr. Phil* show," teaches McGraw's philosophy as a brand-name psychological treatment to psychologists, social workers, and therapists. In the field of psychology, a "therapist" can be anyone who hangs up a shingle. The only requirement to sign up for a workshop is a four-year college degree. Live workshops qualify for continuing education credits under the guidelines of the National Board of Certified Counselors.

Lawlis has stellar credentials to offer help to both the distressed, psychological professionals, and wannabes. He has a Ph.D. in clinical psychology and a master's degree in counseling. Lawlis has been awarded a Diplomate (ABPP) in both counseling and clinical psychology. He has been on the medical school faculty of New York Medical Center, Stanford Medical School, Texas Tech Medical School, and the University of Texas Health Center at San Antonio and Dallas, and is the supervisory psychologist for American Mensa. He is also a member of McGraw's inner circle and is one of the few psychologists McGraw speaks well of.

Texts for the 10-hour classes, which cost $295, include the McGraw canon: *Self Matters, Life Strategies,* and *Relationship Rescue.* Modules are available through both live and online training sessions. "Self Matters" launched in February 2003; the rest are scheduled to begin by April 2004.

Even though the project is still a work in progress, the content for the "Life Strategies" module, for example, promises to include the following (as outlined in the summer of 2003 on the LearnDrPhilFromLawlis.com website):

- Understand and appreciate the integration of the major counseling theories behind the approach designed by Dr. Phil.
- Learn how to assess the level of authenticity for a person in his or her personal terms and develop a plan toward that goal.
- Recognize why a person has chosen the lifestyle he or she has in light of his or her experience.
- Become aware of the internal dialogue that individuals have at least 100 times a minute 24/7. This dialogue serves as the primary filter to one's personal, daily experience and creates depression and adjustment problems.
- Learn Dr. Phil's five-step action program that brings the client back to the path of authenticity.

To market Dr. Phil as a brand of therapy is diabolically clever. But there's more: The LearnDrPhil Therapist Network, as it's called, is a recruiting station for the McGraw army. With the LearnDrPhil Therapist Network, counselors not only can get training for McGraw's methods, but also can become part of a network to which the *Dr. Phil* show refers guests who need further attention, or viewers who contact the show for help. Each *Dr. Phil* show generates thousands of phone calls and e-mail queries for information. LearnDrPhil is poised to capitalize on that while spreading McGraw's message. Network therapists are expected—and coached—to perform counseling online as well as face-to-face.

Members of the network must complete the LearnDrPhil training program, be licensed and insured for malpractice, and present the network with a bio, list of specialties, available session times, and a fee structure. Therapists are encouraged to set fees at $1.60 per minute for online counseling, from which the network takes a 25 percent cut. The limited-time offer, one-time processing fee for joining the network in the summer of 2003 was $45, which bought 10 days of "Provisional Credentials." For longer lasting credentials, you have to sign up for two more classes.

Gary Lewis, Ph.D., heard about the LearnDrPhil program through mytherapynet.com, the online counseling service that supports the LearnDrPhil network, and through which Lewis was already providing online counseling. Lewis was intrigued both because he likes what he's seen of McGraw on television—Lewis says his approach to counseling is similar to McGraw's—and because he wanted to be part of the LearnDrPhil network of therapists. Lewis was impressed that McGraw decided to train those therapists to which he'll offer referrals.

"A lot of talk show therapists that I've known of or encountered in the past, when they make referrals, they just make referrals," Lewis says. "They'll give people three or four names, but they really haven't checked these therapists out. At least with Phil, he is making an attempt to make sure people [therapists] understand his approach and they've had a rather lengthy workshop."

The seminar Lewis attended stretched over two days, the first from 9 A.M. through the evening, with lunch provided, and a dinner break. Participants then returned for another half-day session. Lawlis taught the seminar himself, coming off as "a good ol' Texas guy who likes to talk, likes to tell stories, likes to ramble on," Lewis says.

As a marketing plan, LearnDrPhil is genius. It increases awareness of McGraw's teachings, pulls in money, and widens the market for his books, assuming that the counselors who take the course refer their patients to McGraw's books. But how helpful the LearnDrPhil information is to trained therapists is open to debate.

Allison Conner, Psy.D. has a private practice in behavioral-cognitive therapy. She is a fan of McGraw and recommends his books to her clients. But she's skeptical that LearnDrPhil has much more value than as another income stream for McGraw. "Either you practice that way or you don't. I read all the books, so what more would I actually learn from the seminar? I really don't know what else I could get—especially if you know cognitive-behavioral theory. I guess the actual value in taking the seminars is in the referrals and being part of the network."

In addition, while therapists who join the network must be properly licensed, licensing is not necessary to take the seminars, which means that anyone with a four-year college degree—be it in marketing, mathematics, or botany—apparently could take the series of seminars and promote themselves as a LearnDrPhil therapist.

"That would potentially blur the lines for the public if people who become certified are presenting themselves as LearnDrPhil therapists," Conner says. "This may confuse people, misleading them to believe they are licensed professionals."

Although she decided to enroll in LearnDrPhil's online courses, Conner is somewhat wary of the program's emphasis on online counseling. "If you'll notice, there are many disclaimers regarding the online counseling service, and that is for a good reason. The inherent limitations of assessing and advising people online could be problematic," she cautions.

These disclaimers warn users of network therapists: "Neither Dr. Phil McGraw, The Dr. Phil Show, LearnDrPhil, mytherapynet.com, or any of these organizations' parent companies, partners, subsidiaries, affiliates, officers, employees, or associates make any guarantees or warranties regarding the services that you receive by using this service." The same parties also disclaim liability for "any decision made, or action taken, that is made by any user who relies upon information contained in this site." And McGraw himself gets the following disclaimer: "Dr. Phil disclaims any liability for counseling opinions or recommendations that may be rendered, or may have been rendered by any person relying on training or information delivered via personal presentations, Internet-delivered online courses, or training or information that has been delivered in any form by LearnDrPhil, its personnel, or its Internet activities."

After taking a couple of the online courses, Conner found them to be what she expected. "Decent," she says. "They're certainly no substitute for reading the books and watching Phil at work. They're a good refresher for those already familiar with the approach and theoretical bases, but not a substitute for those who don't have a solid foundation."

As of mid-2003, the network had signed up more than 1,000 licensed therapists, although it had not yet officially launched. Still, the website continues its recruiting efforts and the project appears to be moving forward. Not surprisingly, a weight loss unit was added to the curriculum when McGraw's weight loss book was released.

Perhaps McGraw simply became distracted by yet another marketing endeavor, plunging into what has been a lucrative field for others: diet products. As *The Ultimate Weight Loss Solution* hit bookstores in September 2003—which DrPhil.com touted as not only a book, but also "the beginning of a movement that will revolutionize America"—McGraw launched a line of nutritional products called "Shape Up!" These products sit on drugstore and supermarket shelves next to already established brands such as Atkins and Slim Fast.

The meal replacement bars and drinks—coded to different body shapes such as apples and pears—have McGraw's photo on the packaging and are manufactured by CSA Nutraceuticals, LP, a company located in McGraw's old stomping ground of Irving, Texas. Also involved in the venture is Alticor, the parent company of Amway. Alticor's Access Business Group subsidiary manufactures the products. The company also manufactures shampoos, cosmetics, and other food supplements, including the Nutrilite line of vitamins and minerals.

To promote the new products, McGraw launched yet another website, Shapeup.com. But he first had to obtain the web address from Louisiana-based fitness and beauty pageant consultant Sharon Turrentine, who turned out to be a negotiator that might make the hard-driving McGraw proud. Turrentine, who has had several Miss Americas among her clientele in the past, used Shapeup.com for 12 years to promote her web-based fitness consulting business. After the shapely grandmother finally retired from the business, she held onto the website for sentimental reasons—until she got a call from a Wisconsin attorney offering her money for it. Initially, Turrentine refused to sell. A couple of weeks later, the attorney called back and offered her four times as much as he first suggested. "I said if you quadrupled what you [first] offered in two weeks, it [the address] clearly has some value," Turrentine countered. She then told the attorney that she planned to put the name up for auction on the online auction site eBay for twice his last offer to see what happened. "He laughed at me," she remembers.

The attorney would not disclose who he was representing and Turrentine still doesn't know if he was acting as an agent for McGraw, or whether he was buying the address to then sell to McGraw. Whatever the case, he finally called back with an offer halfway between his number and the doubled amount that Turrentine was threatening to auction the address for. Turrentine accepted. It was, she says with a happy laugh, "A five-figure amount. Five good figures." Still, when she learned that McGraw would be using the address to sell nutritional products, the fitness pro—who earned her Physical Fitness Specialist Certification at the prestigious Cooper Research Center in Dallas, Texas—was disgusted. "I don't believe in that at all," she says. "True physical fitness has three parts: proper nutrition, aerobics, and weight training. All the pills and books and products in the world aren't going to make you physically fit."

That may be, but the Shape Up! Products are sure to make McGraw even richer than he already is.

A Perfect Marriage

I don't know anybody with a better marriage than I have, and that's because of Robin.

As first impressions go, it wasn't the greatest. She was 19. He was 22, but could easily have passed for being at least a decade older. The look on his face the first time they met—that don't-mess-with-me look that so many people have come to know—said to her, "I am here, and I am going to kill anyone that gets in my way," remembers Robin McGraw. "I thought, 'What is wrong with him? He's so mean."

"I was sick," Phil McGraw protests when he hears his wife tell the tale.

"I don't think you were sick, I think you were just being you," she counters.

"Well, if I was so scary, why did you fall head over heels in love with me?" he demands.

"Because I knew I could change everything about you, and make you just the sweetest, dearest, most precious man in the world," she responds.

Sweet, dear, and precious are hardly the first words most people reach for to describe McGraw. Even Robin's own family was unsure of him when she first brought him into their lives. "He was very intimidating and I would have family members and friends for years just be so afraid of him," Robin says. "And I would go 'Oh, you just don't understand . . . He is not intimidating at all.' He used to be so big and so sweet to me and so gentle and like a little puppy."

At home, she sees the gentle side of the aggressive, tell-it-like-it-is doc that the public rarely gets a glimpse of. Who knew, for instance, that the former middle linebacker with a mean competitive streak writes poetry? For their 20th wedding anniversary, McGraw wrote his wife a book of poems, one for each year of their marriage. He composed them for the mother of his two sons, the woman about whom he gushes to his seminar audiences, "If I was not married to my wife right now, I would find her and ask her [to marry me]."

McGraw followed up the debacle of his first marriage with a long-term relationship that he often references when advising other couples. He is not the perfect husband, his wife says of him, but in matters of the heart, McGraw seems to have met his perfect match. "My wife is an amazing woman," he says. "We have a great marriage because she won't have it any other way."

■ ■ ■

The world calls him Dr. Phil, but she calls him Phillip. He was not a celebrity when they married, and for Robin, McGraw's ascent into stardom has brought both the perks and perils of being a celebrity's wife. Her husband's growing wealth affords her and their sons a comfortable lifestyle—beautiful homes, private schools for the boys, country club memberships, tropical vacations. But being married to Dr. Phil means she can no longer trust the people around her. In 2001, for example, a former personal trainer pleaded guilty to attempted extortion. Federal prosecutors said that he called Robin and threatened that unless she loaned him $7,500 he would falsely tell a tabloid that he had given her speed and methamphetamine while he was training her.

Authorities noted that the trainer knew the tabloids would jump on the story since it involved the wife of Dr. Phil. Though she may not have asked for the limelight, Robin hasn't shunned it either. As her husband launched one of television's most successful talk shows, the spotlight spilled onto Robin, who quickly moved out of her role as the quiet, anonymous Texas mother and homemaker that McGraw had once ascribed to her. "I live with a world-class champion. Robin . . . lives her life quietly, anonymously, but meaningfully, with the very same qualities and commitment of heart that you would expect to find in a Michael Jordan or a Cheryl Swopes," McGraw has boasted of his wife.

When McGraw began taping his syndicated television program in the fall of 2002, there was Robin—loyal Robin—the dutiful wife, sitting in the audience at every show. "When we were deciding about making this huge change in our lives," Robin says of moving from Dallas to Los Angeles, "Phillip said he wanted me there every step of the way. 'I can't do this without your support,' he said. 'I want you there. I want you by my side.' "

After each of the first shows, Robin would walk out of the studio with her husband, a ritual they still observe. But she didn't stay in the audience long. From her start as an infrequent guest—sharing ideas for Valentine's Day gifts, helping to redecorate guests' homes, and speaking openly about her struggles with perimenopause—Robin has become a minor celebrity in her own right. She is now an official FOO (Friend of Oprah), presenting her gal pal with gifts that have included an alligator embossed-leather notepad. As a sure sign of celebrity status, she even has her own detractors at the web site www.amiannoying.com, where people have cast votes calling her one of the country's most annoying public figures.

Despite her insistence that she does not like to be on camera, the petite, dark-haired Robin seems more affable on stage than her husband, a soft yin to his harsh yang. Self-described as shy, yet talkative, she has spoken publicly about such very private matters as her menopausal hot flashes and night sweats to help other women. "I would love for women to think, 'I'm going to embrace this and not panic or run from it,' because we all have to admit there's nothing you can do to stop it," she says.

As the public gets to know her better, it learns the somewhat odd lengths she will go to for her husband, beyond serving as his wardrobe advisor, right down to choosing the ties and socks for his suits. Revealing each other's pet peeves on one show, Robin divulged how much McGraw hates little noises, especially in his beloved car.

Once he made her lie down on a towel in the garage while he drove back and forth over her, she said, hoping she could figure out where the rattle was coming from. But that wasn't how he remembered the incident and he sternly corrected his wife in front of his audience after she told the story. "That is such a crock," he insisted. "You did not lay under that car. You wouldn't fit under the car. I put you in the trunk."

"Oh, my gosh," Robin said. "That's right! You put me in the trunk and drove real slow."

■ ■ ■

Robin now spends her days on Paramount Studio's Stage 29, arriving every morning before each show taping. Her growing involvement behind the scenes didn't sit well with all staff members. Some considered her input to be wifely meddling.

"She never interrupted rehearsals, but she didn't need to. Phil stopped it quite a bit himself. She would interject her thoughts and feelings to him," says a former show employee. "There wouldn't be a problem, and all of a sudden she'd create one by putting this bug in Phil's ear and he would be, 'Yeah, you're right.'"

It didn't seem like even one month went by before Robin was a guest on the show, the former staff member says. "It was the show where they traded places. 'And now we go play tennis . . .' The crew was cringing."

The ever-emerging picture of the previously private Robin is not always flattering, sometimes portraying her as the pampered wife. She keeps a "favorite robe" made of 100 percent Egyptian cotton, treats herself every day to at least one of the expensive chocolate truffles she so adores, and sprays the bed sheets and the bathroom with $100-a-bottle perfume.

McGraw perpetuates the perception by telling stories about how much attention his wife pays to her looks. He is the one who revealed that she insisted on wearing makeup in the delivery room. He joked that during mixed-doubles tennis she wouldn't run after the ball unless it came right to her because she didn't want to mess up her hair.

He makes her at-home beauty routine sound like a freakish, high-tech procedure. If they need to be somewhere by 9 in the morning, he says, he gets up at the last minute. "Robin, on the other hand, slithers out of bed about 4:30, and it starts," he says. "Strange lights glow from under the bathroom door, and then these gaseous clouds of powdery stuff appear. It looks like the Twilight Zone in there."

McGraw also likes to tell people that Robin, who has a twin brother, talked of marriage the very first time they were together. Though she protests that it didn't happen, he repeats the story often of how she chased him. "She was on me like a duck on a June bug," he says. "From day one, she was picking out a wedding dress, I guarantee you! I think it was our first date, we were walking down the street and she says, 'How do you feel about marriage?'

"Boy, that was my warning sign, but I kept walking—and the rest is history. I knew what was coming and I volunteered for it."

In truth, he was quickly taken by her. His first impression of his younger sister's friend, Robin Jameson, in the summer of 1972 was "Wow!" But it wasn't just her looks that turned his head. After being around her for a few days, McGraw "figured out how spunky," she was. He was attracted to her irreverent attitude: "That the whole world was just a playhouse and I really liked that energy. It was good because I was pretty serious. I thought, 'This is a balance for me. This is good.'"

Robin, who is from Wichita Falls, was also instantly smitten. "Phil's sister and I knew each other from high school," she explains. "We hadn't been close friends, but she was about to move away, so we got together at her house. When Phil walked in, I said, 'Who is that?' And she said, 'That's my brother.' He and I went out the next night, and we've been together since."

■ ■ ■

From their first date, McGraw struck Robin as a very kind, nice man. Within six months of meeting him, she knew she wanted to marry him. McGraw won her over with the promise of lifelong security. "He told me one time when we were dating that what would bring him the greatest peace in his heart was knowing that his wife and his mother and his children would never want a thing."

Both were small-town children of alcoholic fathers who had decided not to repeat mistakes they had seen in their own young lives. In the aftermath of a sour first marriage, McGraw was clearly searching for the secrets to a successful relationship and apparently began finding them when he and Robin married in 1976 after four years of dating. He used to tell her that he wanted to make a worthwhile living if she made the living worthwhile. She told him that's exactly what she wanted to do.

Three years after they married, McGraw went back to school, taking graduate school courses at the North Texas State University where he finished his master's degree and doctorate in psychology in 3½ years. His singular focus on school, and hours spent studying and completing internship work, stole attention from his new marriage. Robin describes her husband as single-mindedly driven to succeed during those days, to the point where he demanded dinner within a particular 20-minute window or he would refuse to eat. "I was like a machine," McGraw admits of those years, "way over the top." His first wife had made similar complaints about his demanding ways.

McGraw says he's made just about every mistake there is to make in life, acknowledging that his workaholic habits nearly crippled his family life over the years. Though she worries about him not getting enough rest, Robin has had to accept that he is not "Mr. 9 to 5," and that faxes will come to the house at 2 in the morning and he will read them. As she advises other husbands and wives to do, she has accepted her partner as he is.

In one of those life-defining moments he puts so much stock in, McGraw began paying closer attention to his wife's needs when her parents died, one right after the other, early in their marriage. Robin's mother was the first to pass away. The young and vibrant woman unexpectedly had a heart attack not long after Phil and Robin's marriage. Robin's dad called Robin asking for help. She and McGraw jumped in the car and drove over to her parents' home. "Her [Robin's] mother was lying across the bed and I began doing CPR," McGraw reflects. "After the paramedics came, we went to the hospital and I was in the ER with the doctors. But Robin's mother died." McGraw had to deliver the bad news to Robin. "When I opened the door, she looked at me with so much hope—and I knew that she thought I could handle anything," he says. "Yet I couldn't fix the first thing that really mattered to her. That was the longest walk I've ever taken."

A short time later, Robin's dad died. A devastated Robin told her husband, "I feel like an orphan."

"I remember that day with great clarity," he says. "I looked at her and said, 'I will never leave you. I feel that's the day I got married. Once I said that, it changed my life."

McGraw admits he didn't completely buy into his marriage with Robin until that moment. Yes, he accepted Robin as his wife, but ironically, what really bonded them was the loss of her parents. "And at that point, I knew she was my life partner forever," McGraw says. "That was the day my love matured into a committed one. And you know what? That love didn't have anything to do with mini-skirts or how much we'd giggled on a date . . . It had to do with, 'Girl, it's you and me. We're right here in this room, in this life, and we're going to do this one together.'"

McGraw adds that his marriage changed at that moment. "A peace settled over our home, our hearts, and our relationship," he shares.

Fatherhood transformed him, too. Although it wasn't planned, Robin became pregnant with their first son, Jay, in 1979. McGraw wasn't immediately excited about the prospect of having his own bundle of joy. He feared that the baby would take center stage, causing Robin to pay less attention to him. "I said to her, 'I'll make you a deal: If you promise to continue being the fun, sexy, energetic girl that I married, and if you don't turn into some Campbell's soup mom, then I can get really happy about this pregnancy,'" McGraw remembers. "But I'm not willing to trade you for a baby right now." Robin agreed to comply.

Three weeks after Jay was born, the McGraws almost lost him when the valve leading to his stomach squeezed shut. The baby needed surgery or he would starve to death, doctors told the new parents. Ignoring hospital rules, McGraw insisted on carrying Jay into the operating room and even monitoring his anesthesia because he was so afraid of what could happen.

"Being a father all of a sudden, you say, 'Okay, it's not just about you anymore,'" McGraw says. "I've never been reckless or cavalier as a pilot, but I did fly on the edge . . . flying in weather, thunderstorms all around. All of a sudden I had an image of lying in a cornfield and my son getting a call and thought 'You don't have a right to do that.'"

McGraw had a vasectomy after Jay's birth, because he had no interest in having more children. But when Jay was 5, McGraw overheard Robin telling a friend how much she regretted agreeing to the surgery. She loved being a mother. "During a relationship seminar I was teaching, I overheard Robin say from across the room, 'I regret that I ever agreed to have only one child.' And I thought, Oh my God," McGraw says. So, he secretly underwent microsurgery to reverse the vasectomy. He sprung the news on Robin by arriving home after the procedure, still walking unsteadily, with a baby gift under each arm. In 1986, Jordan—their second son—was born.

■ ■ ■

For 12 years, the family made its home in Irving, Texas, where they moved in 1989 after McGraw left private practice with his father in Wichita Falls. He remembers in vivid detail the day he decided to unshackle himself from the counseling work he hated, the day Robin helped him stop whining.

It was a crisp fall day in October. He and Robin had just stepped off a client's private jet at Love Field in Dallas and McGraw was lost in thought. He was not excited about his life anymore. As he pondered this life with no dreams, his wife's voice broke in.

"Where were you just now?" she asked. "You have to tell me what you're thinking! Tell me where you go when you are lost in that hundred-yard stare. More and more each day, I feel like I'm losing a part of you. When it's just the two of us, or when we are alone with our boys, it's like the real you, the way you used to be before all of *this* we call our life. But as soon as the world creeps in, you glaze over. The phone rings, or something breaks the spell, and you become totally different—like a robotic machine."

He told her that he was going "jack-ass batty" in a career and town he hated. "A huge part of my life sucks," he whined. "I screwed up big time and now I'm stuck, trapped in a life I hate."

Having finally spilled his thoughts, Robin helped him decide that they couldn't afford to waste any more time on a life that wasn't working for him. They decided that he needed to stop whining and do something to change things. Robin told her husband, "Don't you realize that my passion is my family and as long as my husband and sons are with me, I can bloom wherever I am planted?"

"We made a decision, pulled the trigger and in less than ninety days that long and heavy chain was broken and a new one begun," McGraw says.

In their new life in Dallas, as her husband became successful with his legal consulting business, Robin's world revolved around her family, home, and community activities. All she wanted to do, she told her husband when they married, was to take care of him and their children, so it's not surprising that McGraw describes her as the heart and soul of the family.

Over the years, she's had to hold her own in a home where she is outnumbered by testosterone, three to one. She is the family's self-appointed arbiter of taste, the one who trained all her men to have good manners, something she is a stickler about. "I can't stand vulgar language and you'd never find things like a burping contest going on under my roof," she says.

"She is a very family oriented person," says Karen Tingle, who met Robin through her volunteer work in Irving. "In the interviews I have seen her do, I think her warmth has come through. She's very down-to-earth and easy to meet."

Robin opened the family's home to host thank-you luncheons for volunteers who helped raise money for the Irving Healthcare Foundation. "Of course, that was awesome. People were thrilled to get to go to her home," says Tingle. "The McGraws have always been very willing to help us out when they could. I think they feel like they want to give back to their community."

Family, though, always comes first. From the time they first met, Robin says, she and Phil wanted the same thing in life—happy, healthy children in a happy, healthy home. "It's always been that important to us," she says. "And I think that we've worked very hard to achieve that."

McGraw remembers the 90-hour vigil his wife kept at Jay's hospital beside when he was deathly ill. The same loyalty and hardiness shone through when Robin nursed her father through months of a painful bout with the cancer that eventually killed him.

"Yet she was still there every single day for our sons and me," says McGraw. "She is a mother and wife and she fills those roles with passion and vision. Although she's only five foot two and 115 pounds, mess with one of her children and you have a serious problem. She would fight a bear if he had a buzz saw."

■ ■ ■

This love of family was evident in their Irving home. "Family photos [filled] nearly every nook in their sitting area and the table in their bathroom," observes friend Oprah Winfrey. "The whole place [was] somewhat rococo: greenery atop baroque pillars, chandeliers descending from what must be at least 20-foot-high ceilings, the sweet smell of potpourri and candle wax."

Strong family allegiances extend to in-laws, too. In 2001, McGraw flew to the aid of Robin's sister in Oklahoma after she became the victim of a random act of violence. On June 5, 2001, Cindi Broaddus and a male companion were driving under an overpass when a container filled with sulfuric acid shattered the windshield of their car. Broaddus underwent several skin graft operations to repair burns on her face, arms, and chest.

To help catch those responsible, McGraw went to Oklahoma, gave interviews to the local media to bring attention to the case, and offered a reward. In a gesture that brought tears to the eyes of those who watched, McGraw presented his sister-in-law with a new car donated by Dallas car dealers. The attention and Broaddus's own campaigning prodded Oklahoma to tighten penalties for people who throw objects off overpasses and bridges.

Being related to Dr. Phil does not come with the luxury of a low profile. Being married to a man who gives advice to other husbands and wives means that the world sometimes hears what goes on behind the closed doors of his own marriage. McGraw once revealed that he spent many years secretly, and not so secretly, believing that his wife was nuts, an odd declaration he used to illustrate how frustrating it can be for the sexes to understand each other.

"I would listen to her talk and say to myself, 'That's just not possible (because it didn't agree with my logical thinking). How could someone so brilliant and capable be so screwed up in her thinking?'" he said of his wife. "I believed a great relationship existed only when both partners fully understood each other. As a result, I was sometimes overwhelmed with frustration by what was happening between Robin and myself. I was trying to understand Robin through the use of my male logic, and she was trying to understand me from her point of view."

Robin has not always appreciated that her husband pulls back the curtain on their life. McGraw recalls that writing his bestseller about self-esteem, *Self Matters,* affected his relationship with everyone in the family.

"I could see that it was a very different project than the other books, that it was very personal," says Robin. "I could see him reflecting [on] our marriage and our life together. When I was reading it, I would think back about many things that happened in our lives [that he mentions in the book]. And I have to say, there a few times that I got a little mad at him."

McGraw says his wife got more than just a little mad. When she came to parts she didn't like, "she'd come in and slam that book down."

"I will say," Robin says, "that by the end of the book I realized that I am happy. I often think, life is wonderful but am I missing something? Am I supposed to be doing something different? It gave me a real peace to know that I'm supposed to be here and it's supposed to be this way. I've worked hard and I've created this life."

She often speaks of her marriage being something the two of them have "created," an assessment that borders on the clinical. "We love each other and we've got what we want," she says. "We've created a life that works for us. We're each other's number one fans, and we'd never do anything to hurt each other on purpose. There's no one better than him for me."

Robin did not marry a man who says I love you easily, a personality trait that helped bring down his first marriage. "I'm not real emotionally expressive with my wife—I don't come home and tell her I love her," McGraw says. "But I almost always have physical contact with her in some way. She says, 'I always feel acknowledged by you.'"

McGraw wasn't about to change his ways for his second wife and she wouldn't want him any other way. As he wrote in *Relationship Rescue*, "Years ago she was grouching about how I can be occasionally rude and crude, and I said, 'If you could change how I acted, how I talked, how I thought and how I expressed my feelings, what would you change?' She got all starry-eyed and described this caring, sensitive, emotional, tearful man who liked to get a blanket and go out in the woods and talk about our feelings.

"I said, 'What you're telling me is you want a middle linebacker who fought for everything I ever got to become some kind of ballet dancer who writes poetry. But I guarantee you that's not what you want. You weren't attracted to me because of my sensitivities. You were attracted to me because, among other things, I made you feel safe and secure, I protected you and protected our cave.' She later confessed that if she had changed me to what she said she wanted, I wouldn't have still been the person she chose to spend the rest of her life with."

■ ■ ■

Tough as McGraw may be on TV, Robin has no trouble standing up to her towering husband, a fact that appears to awe him. "I remember once arguing with my wife, and I thought I was doing just great. I was making terrific points and resisting her points, and I knew I was about to win and emerge victorious. Hooray for me! Then all of a sudden she just stopped, the emotion drained from her voice, and with cold and scary eyes, she looked at me and said, 'You're right. You're always right. How could I have been so foolish?'" he says.

"Now, I'm not all dumb, so I recognized this was not a good development. I quickly said, 'No, I want to hear what you have to say; tell me what you think.' To which she said, 'No, it's okay, you're right, really. I don't know what I was thinking.' As she walked out of the room, head held high, hair tossed back, I knew that I had won the battle, but I wasn't even close to happy . . . In my mind I was thinking, 'Boy, am I gonna pay for this one.' "

Robin is the family engine, the one responsible for many of the decisions that have dramatically changed her family's life. When the chance came for her husband to launch his own talk show, to begin a new career in Hollywood, a thrilled Robin was the one who said, "Get me some boxes!"

They packed up everything for the cross-country move, even the sidewalk. Sentimental Robin hired workers to dig up the sidewalk in front of their Texas home where the boys had left their handprints years before. She wrapped up the chunks of concrete and gave them to McGraw when they got to their new home in California.

They also took with them a green easy chair that Robin had bought McGraw more than 20 years ago. It is the comfy chair he settles into at the end of every workday, the seen-its-better-days chair that Robin once tried to sneak off to the dump. The chair had become a decorating bone of contention between the two.

But showing yet again that she will do anything for her man, Robin McGraw has given in. "I'm just going to give up the battle," she told him recently. "Phillip, it's yours."

McGraw maintains that his marriage to Robin is now stronger than ever. "When I married her, it was because she was cute and fun and sexy and entertaining," he says. "Since then I have watched her go through the deaths of her parents. I have watched her when I have been under attack, and I have learned that this is a woman of depth and strength, which is humbling to me."

The Son Also Rises

Jay can get in their world and deal with them and talk to them. And yes, he's a great kid.

If fans think that McGraw's I'll-take-no-excuses-from-you style is harsh on TV, they have never played basketball under his watchful eye at home. But his son, Jay, has. From the time Jay was old enough to dribble a basketball until he started playing on his teams at school, McGraw coached his firstborn in the ways of round ball. And no one was a harsher critic of Jay's skills on the court than his father.

"But I always knew it was because he just wanted me to be the best player I could be," Jay says today. "So, he was very critical, but you know we've always done things together."

Now he can add getting famous to that list of father-son activities. Jay is the son who nearly died after his birth, the firstborn son, just as McGraw had been in his family. In this handsome, articulate, athletic-built, not-quite-6-foot offspring, who obviously inherited his thatch of dark hair from his mother, McGraw history is repeating itself. At 23, Jay is making a name for himself in the advice-giving field, following in the path cleared by his father. Only this McGraw is more hip, and some say more likable, than dad.

Jay is less "Texas" than his father, though he was born and raised there. His voice sounds more generic, even somewhat northeastern at times with its fast clip and clear, short syllables. He doesn't spout the "Jed Clampett" sayings, one observer notes, that his father is famous for and he makes points quickly, which prompts others to venture that perhaps he inherited more of his mother's genes than his father's.

But like his dad, Jay has a *New York Times* bestseller to his credit. His *Life Strategies for Teens,* an advice book for teenagers published in 2000, builds on the Life Laws his dad set forth in his own *Life Strategies* guide a year earlier. Jay wrote his version in teen talk, with quotes by philosophers ranging from Aristotle to Ziggy, the balloon-headed comic strip character. By the time his second book, *Closing the Gap: A Strategy for Reconnecting Parents and Teens*, came out in 2001, Jay was a celebrity, and his photo graced the front cover.

Like his father, Jay is a sought-after public speaker, touring the country spreading his own brand of life principles. But unlike his dad, Jay has been named one of *People* magazine's most eligible bachelors. He also still has his hair and can add squiring a fashion model around town to his social resume. While juggling all the activities associated with fame, he is studying law at Southern Methodist University in Dallas.

■ ■ ■

Those who have seen Jay in action say he plays well to crowds. He comes across as sincere and earnest when assuring teens that despite all their feelings of hopelessness, they do have control over their lives and can change them. On one episode of his father's TV show, Jay spent a day with runaway teens on the streets of Las Vegas to help bring their plight to light.

"I'm proudest when I see how Jay treats other people," his dad says. "He's tenderhearted like his mother, but the boy can't sing or dance. He gets that from me."

How far the slacker has come. McGraw says his relationship with his eldest son crashed on the rocks during Jay's teen years, as even the best parent-child connection is prone to do during that tumultuous life transition. In his books, Jay offers a guiding hand to other teens negotiating those painful years and reveals how tough they were for him. He also discusses how McGraw played psychologist even at home and how he hassled him about having poor grades and such little direction in his life.

"I think his parents knew when to turn up the heat on him, and that sort of comes through in how Jay writes to his audience," says Chris DeBello, a New Jersey talk radio host who has interviewed both McGraws several times. "And he is communicating that— that there is a right time and a wrong time, and right way and a wrong way."

Now father and son stand shoulder to shoulder on stages across the country, a franchise in the making, riling up workshop audiences hungry for that trademark McGraw slap in the face of common sense. The Baby Boomer dad is playing off his MTV son. "I love the opportunity to support him in doing it by saying 'I'm going to come out with a younger perspective' because it's a bunch of parents that are out there and I'm going to tell them, 'This is how you sit down and talk to your teenagers,'" Jay says. "'This is what you've got to do to plug into their lives, and it's a great time.'"

They work well together, say those who have witnessed their sharp repartee. "These days, we get along better than you would believe," Jay says. "People say, 'Yeah, right.' But it's true."

Helen Anders, a journalist based in Austin, Texas, arranged Jay's press tour in Austin for his first book. During the tour, Jay and his father appeared together at BookPeople, an Austin bookstore. "He came across as this very nice but unbelievably smooth and polished young man, above his years," she says of Jay. "He came across with all the right quotes, said all the right things. When they were talking . . . both of them, the father and son, it was almost like it was scripted. The back and forth was just electric. Everybody was loving it. You couldn't help but be happy for the kid."

■ ■ ■

The harshest criticism anyone levels against the newest McGraw star is that sometimes Jay comes across, personality-wise, as privileged. But he is. His parents made sure of it. Growing up in Wichita Falls and the Dallas area, Jay enjoyed the comfortable lifestyle that his father and mother never had, part of their marriage pact to create a good life for their children. Jay and younger brother, Jordan, attended Greenhill School in Dallas, a private day school attended by students from pre-kindergarten through grade 12. Jay graduated from Greenhill in 1998.

When Jay was in high school, the family moved into a custombuilt, two-story, 8,000-square-foot mansion with two dozen rooms overlooking the Las Colinas Golf and Sports Club in Irving. The house had its own exercise room and a game room with a pool table, pinball machine, and a wall lined with pictures from family scuba-diving vacations. Not only is Jay an avid golfer, certified scuba diver, and a black belt in tae kwon do, but, like his father, he can fly a plane.

Because his father's TV fame didn't come until after he was in college, Jay did most of his growing up outside the public eye. He got to know the ways of his dad long before there was a "Dr. Phil," when he was simply the "Old Man."

Out on his own now, Jay seems to be milking his childhood for all it's worth, using it as fodder for the advice he gives and even sometimes for soliciting sympathy. Imagine, he says, what it was like to grow up with Dr. Phil. "My dad is a psychologist who has spent his whole life studying human behavior. He is fascinated at figuring out why people do what they do and don't do. He really analyzes things top, side, and bottom," he says. "I'm hoping you'll join in a chorus of sympathy moans for me and my little brother. He really knew how to chap my ass sometimes, but I have to admit, all in all, it hasn't been that bad of a deal."

Jay's little brother, 16-year-old Jordan, is the son born after McGraw had his vasectomy reversed. The birth order of the McGraw boys, and the fact that Jay has grabbed so much of the public spotlight, calls to mind the similar relationship of Princes William and Harry of England, known as "the heir and the spare." Jordan, who attends high school in California where his parents now live, doesn't appear in public as often as his big brother.

■ ■ ■

Testosterone is in high supply among the McGraw males. Whenever he can, Jay seems to grab the chance to note how much better he is than his dad at even the simplest things, like playing video games. Jay says he enjoys suckering his dad into playing because his dad is so video-game-impaired, most of the time he holds the controller upside down. Dad doesn't know where the trap doors are and doesn't know how to score extra points, Jay adds, reveling in how he can slaughter his dad at video games every time. Using McGraw's own famous catch phrase, when it comes to video games, Jay says, his dad just "doesn't get it."

Much of the time in school Jay didn't get it either, having inherited from his father an aversion to schoolbooks. Both make a big deal out of their mediocre high school grades, as if that makes their current accomplishments all that more awe-inspiring. "I was a horrible student," says Jay. "I loved playing basketball, and I focused on that—religiously."

McGraw concurs, now that he is able to laugh about his son's youthful obsessions. "If he couldn't eat it, date it, or bounce it, he wasn't interested," he says.

Jay, on the other hand, received help that his father probably never did. A former employee at McGraw's Courtroom Sciences, Inc., claims that Robin McGraw used to ask CSI employees to work on school projects with her two sons. If they weren't done correctly, the employees heard about it.

English obviously wasn't one of Jay's favorite topics, as evidenced by the sly remark he makes about his advice book not being "like an English class lecture, where you can doze off and not miss anything." He makes similar snide comments about math teachers who drone on and on. He doesn't hide his lack of enthusiasm about school as a teenager and is unashamed to divulge that he brought home "dirtbag" report cards to mom and dad.

Those grades earned him a lot of lectures that he rolled his eyes at. When you bring home these bad grades, his father challenged him, what's in it for you? Maybe the payoff for not doing well in school is that you don't have to admit to yourself what kind of potential you have, Dr. Phil, the father, told him. As long you stay a C student, you don't have to live up to the responsibility of being a top performer, McGraw challenged his young underachiever.

Though angry, Jay knew his father was right. "When I was cruising (or so I thought) through my teens, I hopelessly did not 'get it' about grades," he says. "Whenever the report card came out every six weeks my dad would sit me down for the big talk. He'd say, over and over, 'How can you not want to study? How do you not have a thirst for knowledge?'

"I think I heard the 'thirst-for-knowledge' speech a thousand times. I'd tell my dad that I would really do better and study harder the next six weeks. But as soon as I was back in my room, I'd go back to staring at the ceiling. Apparently, I just didn't want to work the system. I'd rather have fun with my friends, concentrate on things like basketball."

■ ■ ■

Like his dad, Jay was a jock in high school, allowing him to craft this definition for his first book from personal experience: "For these people, class is just a time to rest up for the next game. Jocks don't have friends, they only have teammates. If you see them carrying books, I'll bet you they are just playbooks."

Playing basketball was his defining passion in life, just as football had been his father's. Jay had been perfecting his game since fifth grade. He attended summer basketball camps and YMCA leagues, and he worked for hours on the fundamentals with his dad in the driveway.

When he was 16, Jay was the starting point guard for his high school team, the Greenhill Hornets. That year, the Hornets seemed assured of a winning season. But at a midseason tournament, Jay tore all the ligaments in one of his knees. McGraw and his coach helped him off the court and into the locker room. Later, at the emergency room, Jay heard a doctor tell his dad, "It's bad, he may not play again."

"I was faced with the realization that I had created my experience thus far as an athlete and that was now gone," he says. "And if I didn't do anything about it, no one was going to do anything for me. No one else's life was going to stop just because a phase of my life had ended, so I had to make a decision."

His father didn't let him wallow in self-pity for very long, snapping him out of it with the same tough love he gives strangers on TV. Less than a year later, after hours of riding a stationery bike, then graduating to jogging and running, Jay was back on the court.

When he and his brother were growing up, Jay says, their parents "always let us know they were supporting what we did and they always let us know that they loved us. And, if you don't feel loved at home, you're not going to feel love out in the world, and it just puts a value that you put on yourself that says, 'You know I'm not going to settle.'"

■ ■ ■

Like a spark suddenly flashing into a full-blown flame, Jay somehow found his focus in life when he moved away from home to the University of Texas in Austin, where he earned a degree in psychology—with honors—in three years. Finally, it had sunk in: You screw up college, you screw up your life.

"He turned it on at UT," says Skip Hollandsworth, a Dallas-based writer for *Texas Monthly* magazine who edited *Relationship Rescue* with Phil McGraw. "I came across him right as he was starting law school and I just thought 'He's got it.' He was smart, he had a gift of saying stuff. Here comes McGraw junior getting groomed."

Jay's big life-defining moment, as his father would call it, came when his dad's publisher suggested that McGraw write a *Life Strategies* book for teens. Jay sat in on the brainstorming session with the publisher and, according to him, not too politely pointed out that his father hadn't seen hair in 30 years. Jay then talked his way into writing the book himself.

"I grew up with my dad, so I definitely took a lot of what he said for granted," says Jay. "As with most teens, I dismissed what he said. I knew his book had great advice in it, but I also knew that when a parent or an authority figure writes something, kids kind of become resistant to the idea regardless of whether it's right or wrong. That's why I wanted to write a book for teens."

He had no true writing experience, with the exception of class papers. While he wasn't shy about giving advice to his own friends, when they asked, writing a book for the masses was a lot more complicated. He had no idea what he'd gotten himself into, but decided to base the book on his own experiences in high school and college, something he could speak knowledgeably about. "I thought it would be like writing a really long English or psychology paper, but it wasn't," he says. "It took a lot of time and organization, but it was actually a lot of fun to do . . . I got together panels of teenagers and asked them 'What's bothering you? What are you going through? What do you wish you had an answer to?'" he said. "Based on their answers I angled the book to address a lot of those issues."

He began writing the book over the summer of 2000 while at home in Dallas from his first year in college. "I spent a lot of time sitting in a room with just a pen and a blank sheet of paper," he says. "Sometimes I would dictate stuff into a tape recorder and get it typed up. For too long, just scattered thoughts and ideas came out, but slowly they turned themselves into chapters. It was really exciting to see that."

Jay didn't just concern himself with the words, though. As one of those students who flip through their textbooks to see how many pictures they have, he knew he wanted the book's graphics to be attractive to teens. "If one class's book is just solid text and the other's is text with charts, pictures and tables, then I'm far more likely to read the one with charts, pictures, and tables because it's not just huge blocks of text."

The book's text-only cover—Jay's picture is on the back— didn't get rave reviews all around. When the *Edmonton Journal* in Calgary, Alberta, Canada, asked three teenagers to judge the book by its cover, one panelist sniffed: "Looks like something an adult wrote and teens are supposed to read. You know what I mean?" The adult leading the panel who actually read the book, on the other hand, recommended it for parents. "Young McGraw has all Daddy Phil's dissertation in easier-to-understand jargon. It's the stuff you wish your kids would read and memorize. It's the stuff we wish we knew and used more often."

Jay's own review of the book is blunt. The ideas are not "rocket science," he admits. "We're not trying to kid anyone here. It's all commonsense stuff."

Anders is amazed that Jay could write a book while also taking college courses, marveling that he "managed to write a book while he was acing everything he was taking—taking a course overload at UT and getting ready to graduate.

"The book's very formulaic. Granted, it wouldn't take forever to write that sort of thing. But at the same time, you know, it's got to be done. He certainly seems sharp enough. I think there's probably some really bright genes in that family."

■ ■ ■

C ritics, though, charge that Jay simply rides his famous father's coattails—a ride that is his own to complete or end. Dan Coughlin, a corporate advisor and coach in St. Louis, Missouri, likens the McGraw franchise to that of advice columnists and twin sisters Ann Landers and Abigail Van Buren, who became the United States' greatest advice givers.

"The dad got in and now the son's gotten in," says Coughlin. "There are probably 150 million others who would have a bachelor's degree and were once teenagers. Are they experts, too? If he can get a book contract, more power to him. It's only one step less ludicrous than the dad solving people's problems in 20 minutes. I think it's mainly about the American obsession with silver bullets."

But maybe Jay is just different enough from his father to be the "variety" in the McGraw message that Coughlin believes is desperately needed. "At this point, basically what Dr. Phil does is the exact same thing, over and over and over again. I don't know how long the audience can believe that one guy can be the expert on every single thing," says Coughlin. "I thought he'd be over in three months."

From the start Jay has made it publicly clear that whatever he achieves, he achieves on his own. Others, like Hollandsworth, concur. "Phil has always said this is completely Jay's deal. He didn't help, he was not involved in the writing of that book. He read it once it was getting in the final stages. He let the kid make it on his own, and he says he stays out of his business entirely."

Hollandsworth recalls that McGraw told his son something to the effect that, "I got you into the big pond, but it's up to you to sink or swim."

Sure, Jay got his shot at fame through dad, "but what family member would not do that for a family member?" asks radio show host DeBello.

Jay recognizes that his dad opened the door for him to walk through, DeBello says. "But he also knew dad was not going to keep pushing the baby carriage for him. He is driving himself along. It's his to lose, basically. And if it starts happening, I almost think Phil would let him get to the edge of losing it all."

It's tough to measure the marketing of Jay with the making of McGraw, since Dr. Phil's break through Oprah is one of those lightning strikes that happen once in a lifetime. Now Jay, determined to make it on his own, "is the one who stands the chance of having his flame flicker," says DeBello. "I get the sense that Jay is not" one to just ride on Phil's coattails.

DeBello, who interviewed the father and son duo in December 2000, was struck more by the differences between the two than their similarities. "As far as Jay versus Phil," he observes, "they both have locked up the franchise to say with a smile 'Hey, wake up, you're being an idiot.' Where Jay differs is that he used his life or events more as examples, where Phil tends to shy away from that.

"I think it's the way that Jay establishes contact with his audience—teens and adolescents—as 'Hey, I'm one of you.' Whereas with Phil, they're realizing that something's not working here and that's when Phil throws in with his Texas drawl, 'Hey wake up, you moron.'"

Jay may not have the same breadth of life experiences to draw on, but he is just as deft as his dad at slipping references from his books into conversations, DeBello says. "I think the two of them share the common ground of they don't believe in self-victimization, 'It can't possibly be my fault.'"

McGraw couldn't hide his fatherly pride when DeBello spoke to him shortly after Jay's first book debuted. "I asked Phil, 'The kid's doing pretty good, isn't he?'" DeBello shares. "And Phil said, 'I'm starting to think someone replaced my son with a robot.'"

Robot, perhaps. Clone? Not hardly. "There is no way to say that Jay is a carbon copy of dad," says DeBello.

He might be a seedling from the family tree with the same genetic makeup. But he's definitely not the same tree.

Quick-Draw McGraw

I mean, what is this "inner child"? You know what that is?
That's a word that's designed so people can sell books.

auri is a sturdy-looking, conservatively dressed blonde
with sadness etched in her face. She and her beefy, musta-
chioed husband Nick have been married for 11 years.
Today they're appearing as guests on *Dr. Phil.* The topic for the
show is "Cheaters." Lauri and Nick have come to McGraw for
help because Nick had a two-year affair four years earlier,
which resulted in a child. To make matters worse, Lauri has had
three miscarriages and fears she'll never be a mother.

Lauri nervously dabs her red-rimmed eyes with a handkerchief
as she explains her anguish over the affair and the guilt she feels
over her inability to accept Nick's child. "I tell myself that I know
it's not his [the child's] fault," she says quietly. "But I—it's hard
when I see him—Nick with him, because I know I couldn't give
him what he wanted." She momentarily loses her struggle against
tears, then composes herself.

"Because you—you couldn't successfully carry a child, at least
thus far?" McGraw confirms.

"Yes," Lauri says.

"Because you've had the miscarriages?"

"Yes."

"And that's been a painful thing for you?"

"Yes."

"And you knew that?" McGraw asks the stone-faced Nick.

"Oh, yes," Nick responds.

The couple doesn't look at each other. They don't touch each other. McGraw dominates the discussion. Nick's face registers nothing when McGraw scolds him for appearing cold toward Lauri's fear that when Nick goes to visit his son, he might take the opportunity to revive the affair.

"What part of that is confusing to you?" McGraw demands of Nick. "What part of that do you not get? You—you've gone and had an affair, you're continuing to go to that woman's house. You had a child. And you—you're there with the mother and the child."

Nick remains impassive.

Lauri's eyes are fixed on McGraw's face as he urges her to accept her feelings on the matter. He lays out his solution.

"Can you give yourself permission to say, 'I do own this?'" he asks sternly. "'I have the right to my feelings here and I'm not going to feel guilty about the way I feel?'"

"Yes, I—I see—I think," Lauri responds, without conviction.

"You've got to make a decision that you're either going to work to get over this or get out of it," McGraw continues. "Don't live in limbo the rest of your life. And so far as the child is concerned, you either need to get that right or you need to get out of the child's life. But do not continue to fail to accept that child."

McGraw wraps up the segment with firm words advising Lauri that the message she needs to send to the boy is, "I'm not going to make you pay for the sins of your father." Lauri looks pained and dabs away tears.

And then, time is up. After roughly seven minutes of McGraw-style therapy, the two have exhausted their appointment with the good doctor and the show goes to commercial. When *Dr. Phil* returns, another couple is there in the hot seat with another heartbreaking tale that McGraw stands ready to resolve in short order. It is a scene repeated, with some variation, each weekday on his popular syndicated talk show.

■ ■ ■

While the general public might eat it up, many professionals in the field of psychology are less enchanted. McGraw's mantra is that everyone has 10 defining moments, 7 critical choices, and 5 pivotal people in life. If you can identify those, you're on your way to the life you want. But is life really that easily quantifiable? The problem, his critics point out, is that no matter how dazzling McGraw's ideas for changing your life might seem under the bright lights of the TV studio with an audience cheering you on, the stretch between deciding to change and accomplishing change can be long, bleak, and lonely. If change were possible with a snap of the fingers, wouldn't we all be loved, rich, famous, happy, and, what the heck, beautiful, too?

"It's the psychological version of *Who Wants to Be a Millionaire?*" says Ellen McGrath, Ph.D., a psychologist and consultant to national news shows. "It's the quintessential cultural product. Get some quick advice and change your life. You, too, can hit the psychological jackpot."

"No one changes by themselves," McGrath argues. "You need to work through the problem, talk through your struggles with somebody, figure out why you do what you do. Only then can you consolidate the change by making it a habit. That takes time. Not 15 minutes of fame."

McGraw is quick to deny that he presents himself as a therapist. "I think about myself as an educator," he says. "I think about myself as an alarm clock. I think about myself as an emotional compass for people."

But he also professes little patience for the techniques of his fellow psychologists, although much of his seemingly homespun wisdom comes directly from psychology textbooks. Still, while other psychologists might urge people seeking help to nurture their "inner child," McGraw advises them to set up appointments with their inner "life manager." In McGraw's version of therapy, gentle nurturing and navel gazing are out. McGraw has no time for such indulgences, and as with everything else, he's free with his views. "You know, you go into psychoanalysis four days a week for five years or something like that. I'm thinking, you know, 'If you can't figure this out by Thursday, one of us is a fool,' " he says.

McGraw admits that it's generally not possible to solve complex problems in a fast-paced TV segment. "I don't look at what I'm doing as practicing clinically on the air," he says. "Look, we don't think we're doing eight-minute cures here. We know we're not doing eight-minute cures here."

But McGraw rarely gives a positive nod to the sort of in-depth work that can help people move from "wake-up call" to change. He is also outspoken with his opinion of psychotherapy as being out of touch, full of meaningless lingo and buzzwords, and lacking clear goals.

"Let me tell you, I know all the big words," he boasts. "I can sit down here with you and tell you I think there's a repressed problem due to a schizophrenogenic mood that puts you in a double bind and so you're developmentally arrested. Now what are you going to do with that? So instead I say, 'Look, your mother was mean. Get over it! You got to give yourself what you couldn't get from her.' That's the same thing I just said [earlier] in simple language."

On rare occasions, you can catch McGraw admitting that what he does is rooted in pretty standard stuff to the study of psychology. "Let me tell you, there ain't nothing new under the sun in human functioning or psychology, and I'm damn sure not reinventing the wheel," he says. On the day his talk show premiered, in a rare concession, he told Phil Donahue, "I don't mean to minimize or trivialize complex therapy, because we have some fabulous people out there that are doing this. They're very dedicated, they're very knowledgeable. And they save a lot of lives and they present a lot of quality."

But McGraw took direct aim at the field of psychology in *Life Strategies,* writing, "In my view, it's too fuzzy, it's too intangible, it exists in a world of opinion and subjectivity. Maybe that's okay if you live in some ivory tower and can afford to pontificate about ambiguous and abstract elements of life. But I don't think that's what you want and I don't think that's what you need."

■ ■ ■

Not that the ivory tower crowd is losing sleep over McGraw's opinions. In response to an interview for this book that perhaps confirms McGraw's contention that professionals are out of touch with Joe TV-watcher, a few prominent educators made it clear that the TV therapist is barely a blip on the radars of many psychologists.

"Alas, I don't even know who Dr. Phil is, other than there is a guy on television called 'Dr. Phil' and that he was once on *Oprah,*" wrote one highly placed academic.

"I've only seen a few minutes of McGraw's show. I know nothing about him so I have no comment," wrote another, whose specialties include research in family television watching. "As long as I can remember, back to pre-TV days on radio, there were always advice-givers."

"I really do not have any information about him, have never seen him 'at work,'" replied yet a third psychology professor.

"Have they been living in a cave?" wonders Allison Conner, Psy.D., a cognitive-behavioral therapist whose private practice in Manhattan puts her on the front lines of psychotherapy. Conner uses TiVo to get her daily dose of McGraw, and sometimes uses modified Dr. Phil-isms in her practice, such as, "How's that workin' for you?"

"I won't say it with a Texas accent but I will say, 'That doesn't seem to be working for you,'" Conner explains. "I'm the feminine Dr. Phil. My husband calls me Dr. Phyllis."

Conner says McGraw's approach is similar to her own style of psychotherapy. "He's very practical, very direct. He doesn't use fancy jargon that I find to be essentially meaningless. And he gets results." She sees these results in his follow-up shows, and she also measures what she assumes to be McGraw's results by comparing her own results with similar techniques in her practice—though she stresses that she spends more time with her patients than McGraw does.

Nevertheless, Conner bristles at the way McGraw throws a negative blanket over all psychology without differentiating between analysis—which is the Woody Allen style, decades-on-the-couch, tell-me-about-your-childhood approach—and the more active cognitive-behavioral approach, which emphasizes thinking patterns and behavioral changes. Conner, who is among the psychologists using the cognitive-behavioral approach, even wrote a letter to McGraw complaining about this, though she never heard back.

"Sometimes Phil doesn't admit to the idea that he does what other therapists do," Conner frets. "He presents himself as a life strategist. I don't even know what that means. He presents himself as an antidote to therapy. But when he's bashing therapy, he is bashing a particular sector of therapists. He's targeting the open-ended, meandering type of ineffective psychotherapy that's commonly ridiculed these days. For political reasons, he wouldn't want to name the analytic camp. He says he doesn't like how therapy is practiced today. But if he were paying attention to cognitive people, I don't think he would disagree with how it's being practiced. He just won't acknowledge us."

Nancy Levin, Ph.D., a psychologist with a private practice outside of Detroit, Michigan, also admires McGraw's straight-to-the-point style. "I view his program as free continuing education units. I find his program absolutely stimulating and challenging.

I think he is having an impact on the public's view of therapy and, in a deeper way, he's impacting people's notions of accountability. He also is normalizing the whole process of therapy, change, and 'problems.' He's making people feel that therapy is part of life, and this information has an opportunity embedded in it.

"I'm a regular watcher and find my own style has been affected by the show," she adds. "I'm more direct in a sense. In today's world, you don't know how long you're going to have a client anyway, so you have to speak what you think. We may have more than just eight minutes, but we don't have the luxury to see a client on and on."

Another front-line therapist, Denise Hayes, Ph.D., director of counseling and health services at Depauw University in Indiana, is more troubled by McGraw. She believes that because he is a trained psychologist and markets himself as such, his harsh, quick-fix advice is all the more ethically troubling. The power and authority conferred by the title "doctor" carries a weight of responsibility that Hayes does not feel McGraw respects.

"I just wonder what it's like for these people to get on and talk about their most personal fears and things and have him just slam them," Hayes says. "Of course these are adults capable of making their own decisions, but there's a power difference with a professional and a client. The therapist has a responsibility for informed consent so people understand that there is some risk involved, that there's a possibility that problems won't be solved, and that, in fact, they could even get worse. McGraw doesn't seem to be following American Psychological Association guidelines. Just because guests are adults who say 'Yes I want to do that' doesn't abdicate him from his responsibility as a mental health professional. That seems unethical to me."

■ ■ ■

McGraw emphasizes that he doesn't let just anyone on his show, and the deeply troubled need not apply. All potential guests are carefully screened and told what to expect, he says, adding that not everyone who would like to be a guest is accepted to appear on the program. "We have exclusionary criteria that are very rigid," McGraw insists. "I won't book any guest that is on major psychotropic medications or anti-psychotics. We won't book any guest that's ever had institutionalization for a mental or emotional disorder. We don't book any guests that are currently in therapy unless and until we contact the therapist, give them a full briefing on what the show is, make sure they know who I am, and then get their written permission before they come on the show. And no one with any suicidal history or suicidal ideation is on the show."

With such self-imposed restrictions, he's a therapist only for the worried well. And although he has the educational training, McGraw is no longer licensed. Does that make him a psychologist or showman? Considering that McGraw's license to practice in Texas is inactive and he is no longer allowed to see patients there, Beverly Hills "media psychiatrist" Carole Lieberman, says, "He is practicing psychology without a license. He's just being an entertainer."

Certainly the product McGraw delivers is more theater than therapy. "It's not unlike the old tent revivals. When you're there and you get caught up in the spirit, you get saved. But when you get home . . . ," says Robert Simmermon, Ph.D., an Atlanta psychologist in private practice who also works extensively with the media. Simmermon maintains that it must be show biz because, as a model for psychotherapy, *Dr. Phil* has the whole thing backward.

"Do you remember the Harlem Globetrotters?" Simmermon asks. "The Harlem Globetrotters always traveled with the other team. Nobody ever thought much about the other team—they just made it possible for the Globetrotters to play the game. I think Phil's kind of like that. Traditionally in psychology, and particularly psychotherapy, the focus is on the patient. Here, the focus is on Dr. Phil. People tune in to the show not to hear the patient, but to hear Phil."

McGraw doesn't deny that what he's doing is showbiz. "There is some theater to it," he says. "Look, if you don't make it entertaining, if people don't find it interesting, if you don't have compelling stories, then they're not going to watch it. I mean if you just put on there we're going to have Psychology 304 today, just tune in, you're not going to get people doing it."

And McGraw argues, convincingly, that presenting the general public with ideas they might not otherwise seek out is a service, even if there is an element of theater to it. "I know this about people in America: I know that most people in America won't go pick up a book on human functioning. I know most people in America won't ever be in therapy. I know most people in America don't have any idea where to turn to get information if they're being really angry and they're afraid they're going to do something with their children, or if they are fighting in their marriage and the wheels are coming off . . . here is someone that's going to deliver it to their home so they can listen to it in the privacy of their own home, and it's going to be direct and it's going to be straightforward. And that's worth doing."

■ ■ ■

People who have experience with psychotherapy can recognize the differences between psychotherapy in the real world and Dr. Phil's style. But critics worry that others are likely to come away with a distorted view of the field of psychology and a warped notion of how therapy works in the real world.

"It's real easy to exploit the problems these people have, the drama," Simmermon says. "Sometimes it's Jerry Springer dressed up in a tuxedo. We in the field of psychology have worked long and hard to build a trust with the public that they won't be used, that what they say will be confidential, and that there's a legitimacy to the field that transcends the theater component. But this show is all done in public, it's all done with an audience. You couldn't get more opposite from the privacy and the sanctity of the therapy room. That's where we do people a disservice."

This theater of exploitation is among the reasons psychologist Ellen McGrath condemns the show. "I've watched a number of times where I think people actually felt humiliated and ashamed and embarrassed listening to his take on whatever problems they have," she says. "People feeling bad about themselves will not lead to change."

"I'm not for everybody," McGraw concedes. "There are some people that respond very well to my straightforward, cut-to-the-chase approach, and there are some people who don't."

Without naming names, McGraw bristles at comparisons between his program and others, such as Jerry Springer, Maury Povich, and Montel Williams. "You see a lot of these shows where it's just like circus come to town; look at these weird people; thanks for tuning in; good day," McGraw counters. "My commitment is not to do that."

While McGraw's television show—and even his books and live seminars—may or may not be effective, Simmermon does not go so far as to call them dangerous, especially compared with some of the other tell-all talk shows. He finds many of the hosts of such shows to be considerably more exploitive, because they lack psychological training, ask bad questions, give unhealthy advice, and scold people. McGraw, however, is "a pretty reasonable, regular guy," Simmermon concedes. His cures might not be deep, but they can be sensible. "You know, it's 'doctor it hurts when I hold my arm like this;' 'So don't hold your arm like that' kind of advice. It's a solution, but not a resolution, a short-term fix that may or may not facilitate a long-term change."

Still, McGraw insists, reaching some of the people some of the time with his message is better than never broadcasting the message at all. "Now, there will be some people who get a wake-up call and then go right back to sleep. No question about it," he admits.

"But let's say you wake up 10 million people and you keep a million of 'em. If you've saved a million kids from getting screamed at today, that's a good thing."

Admittedly, that is an honorable goal. Beverly Hills psychiatrist Lieberman has no problem with the quick-fix concept of the *Dr. Phil* show. She has appeared as an expert on numerous other television and radio programs and wouldn't mind hosting one of her own. But she is skeptical of McGraw's take on matters psychological. "He addresses problems from a very superficial, simplistic point of view," she contends. "He pretends to be helping people at a deeper level when actually he's just like a medicine man dispensing placebo-type elixirs. The emperor is wearing no clothes."

Lieberman claims she's seen many instances on *Dr. Phil* in which a guest was trying to get a message across that McGraw missed entirely. "It just kept going over his [McGraw's] head," she says. "Patients will do that. If you [the doctor] are not getting it, they keep presenting it. There are clues you have to look for. Some of Dr. Phil's shows got boring because he didn't know where to go with it."

Lieberman also points to an incident when convicted murderer Laurie Bembeneck, who had spent seven months in solitary confinement, arrived to appear on *Dr. Phil*. The show, which was paying for DNA testing that she hoped would clear her, placed her under surveillance in a hotel room. Bembeneck, according to her attorney, suffered a bout of claustrophobia and tried to escape out a window in the room, about 12 feet from the ground, by climbing down a rope of sheets. She fell, seriously injuring her foot in the process.

This escape attempt was predictable, Lieberman says. "Obviously Dr. Phil didn't understand that by imprisoning this woman while she waited to go on his show, he recreated for her the traumatic experience of being in prison," she points out. "He couldn't anticipate that this would cause her to have a strong psychological reaction? The show producer was instructed to take away her cell phone because they didn't want information to leak out before it aired. If he [McGraw] was educated enough in psychological issues, he would have realized that imprisoning her in this way would have disastrous psychological results."

Lieberman concedes it's likely that McGraw wasn't very involved with decisions about housing this guest, but suggests that when dealing with such a delicate situation, his leadership as a trained psychologist would have been advisable.

McGraw, however, is so confident of his own insights and advice, he invites people who disagree with him to take the stage with him in the occasional "Debate Dr. Phil" shows. In these programs, he allows viewers with the temerity to engage in public debate with him to try their skills against his courtroom manner. Predictably, he often emerges from these debates victorious. He ended one such debate with a guest simply by chanting, "Na-na-na-na. Na-na-na-na. Na-na-na-na."

Implied translation: I was right, you were wrong. Debate over.

■ ■ ■

Whatever others think of McGraw's advice, he says he has never regretted any advice he's given on television, only the things he hasn't said.

"There are millions of people listening to everything I say, and I have a real spontaneous delivery style," he says. "But the truth is I weigh very carefully what I say to people before I say it. I weigh it very carefully. This is a powerful platform, and I think I need to be a good steward of that platform. So I know I have kind of a shoot-from-the-hip sort of delivery, but I can tell you there's a lot of deliberation that goes into what I say before I say it. The only time I ever have any anxiety is if I feel like there was something I should have said that I didn't."

Enjoying Celebrity

I get underwear mailed to me all the time.

From the moment Phil McGraw stepped on stage with Oprah Winfrey, he quickly climbed the stairway to stardom. McGraw made the transition with ease, establishing the same level of control over his image that he exhibits in all factors of his life. With Winfrey's help, he devised the mythological character of "Dr. Phil," painting his background with colorful tales and staunchly protecting his creation by making sure the press heard and reported only what he wanted them to.

The media initially came calling shortly after McGraw became a regular on *Oprah*. Interest in him intensified after his first book was released. The Dallas press was among the first to feature McGraw in full-page spreads, and the national media weren't far behind. In all these early interviews—and most of the current ones as well—you find McGraw repeating the same stories, phrases, and jokes over and over, further establishing the character he has become so famous for.

Never at a loss for a quick turn of phrase and telling anecdote, McGraw fast became a darling of prestigious print publications and network television talk shows. While some people have a hard time making the transition from Regular Joe to superstar, McGraw seemed right at home in the spotlight. He was comfortable on camera and basked in the attention. "Honestly, I've never seen him nervous," said wife Robin moments before McGraw was to step on *The Tonight Show* stage.

With his gleaming pate, goggle eyes, and mouthfuls of folksy aphorisms, Dr. Phil begged to be satirized. The first shot was fired by *Saturday Night Live,* which ushered McGraw into the realm of mega-celebrity in November 2000. Wearing a bald wig and twanging emphatically, Will Ferrell played McGraw while Maya Rudolph, dressed as Winfrey, cheered him on as he honked out such meaningless advice as, "It's like this: You cannot eat at the Chinese buffet if there's no duck sauce." Cast member Jeff Richard later donned the Dr. Phil wig, spewing more incomprehensible maxims in another *SNL* skit. "I mean, a rooster only crows so many times before the mama knows the henhouse fulla graham crackers!" he hollered at a befuddled Santa Claus.

McGraw's fame only grew from there. Although not especially known for his looks, in 2001 *People* named McGraw the "sexiest self-help guru" in its annual issue of sexy celebrities. "Dr. Phil McGraw is the rock star of TV therapists," the magazine gushed, next to a photo of McGraw casually dressed and untucked in loose shirttails, striking an approximate beefcake pose on a garden bench.

While McGraw is an unlikely sex symbol, his female fans are devoted, determined, and legion. McGraw is a pop star for the mature woman, as son Jay realized one day when the two arrived at a hotel together. "*NSYNC happened to be staying at the hotel, so all the mothers had brought their kids and their daughters to see *NSYNC arrive. And then my dad shows up, and all the mothers start pushing their daughters out of the way and asking him for pictures," Jay recalls.

Not all of this attention is necessarily welcome, and some of it is downright bizarre. One fan, who walked into an elevator with McGraw, thought she'd get some free advice from the good doctor. "I want to know if you think my husband's whatsit is too big," the woman said. "Show the man, Henry!" After her husband obligingly unzipped his pants, the woman asked McGraw, "Now, doesn't that look like it belongs on a gas pump?" McGraw stammered his agreement and fled the elevator on the next floor. As McGraw might (and probably did) say, "What was she thinking?"

■ ■ ■

As *Dr. Phil* prepared to launch in the fall of 2002, McGraw polished his image by making the rounds on talk shows to promote his new program. He chatted and took calls with Larry King in a two-part interview. He flustered a fussy Phil Donahue, ribbed Katie Couric on *Today* about whether she watched him on *Oprah*, and flirted with Jane Pauley on *Dateline NBC*, telling her he guessed she was shy at cocktail parties. "Fess up here. You can't lie to the doctor," he teased.

In September 2002, McGraw was on the cover of *Newsweek*. That November McGraw made *People* magazine's "most intriguing people" list. In December he was named one of the year's "most fascinating" people by Barbara Walters. By the time McGraw made VH1's list of the 200 greatest pop culture icons in 2003 (squeaking in at 194; mentor Oprah Winfrey topped the list at number one), he was well on his way to pop culture ubiquity.

McGraw seems especially enamored of NBC and appears on the network often. When Couric swapped jobs with Jay Leno for a sweeps stunt in May 2003, McGraw surprised her by dropping in on *The Tonight Show*. "I thought it was Jeffrey Tambor at first, then I realized it was Dr. Phil," Couric later joked with McGraw on *Today*. And when Pauley retired from *Dateline NBC*, McGraw was among those paying tribute on her farewell show. "She could

be vulnerable and professional and ask the incisive question
. . . That's an amazing quality to be able to do all of that at one
time," McGraw said.

Jay Leno and McGraw hit it off beautifully from the start.
McGraw has become a regular on *The Tonight Show,* trading jokes
and jabs with Leno many times. "Jay Leno is one of my favorites,
not just because Jay's a good guy but because his staff takes such
good care of me," McGraw once told his *Dr. Phil* studio audience.

McGraw had a rockier start with Leno's late-night competition, David Letterman. Shortly after McGraw's TV show debuted, Letterman began a nightly segment called "Dr. Phil's
Words of Wisdom" on the *Late Show with David Letterman,* in
which he blew raspberries at the made-for-satire doctor. The
shtick showed McGraw in brief, authentic, but context-free clips
from *Dr. Phil.* "We produced them in a manner to make the man
look ridiculous," is how Letterman has described the feature. "I
don't know what I'm doing," were one night's words of wisdom
from the doctor. "Put some leaves in my mouth and set 'em on
fire," and "You couldn't be any dumber if we cut your head off"
were among "Dr. Phil's Words of Wisdom" that Letterman
served up. For some *Late Show* viewers, this was their first introduction to McGraw. Letterman's poking fun at McGraw only
made him that much more famous.

Letterman also lampooned McGraw in his opening mono-
logues, and included him in his nightly "Top 10" lists. Number
two on the "Top Ten Things a Drill Instructor Would Never Say"
list is "Dr. Phil changed my life." But McGraw, with a tongue as
caustic as that of the dry-witted Letterman, proved that he could
take the talk show host's jokes. He even seemed to like them.

Because of Letterman's relentless ribbing, it was big news
when the *Late Show* announced that McGraw had agreed to appear as a guest. In preparation for the notable day, on Thursday,
February 13, 2003, Letterman aired a clip he received from the
Dr. Phil show. In it, McGraw is seen strolling his television stage

between takes, glass of water in hand. "I'm thinking of going to New York on Monday and dropping in on Letterman," he says to his delighted audience. "I'm thinking of opening up a serious can of whoop-ass on that boy."

True to his threat, McGraw braved a record-breaking blizzard in New York to face down his wise guy tormenter the following Monday. Over the years, Letterman has ridiculed and angered many stars who have held a grudge, refusing to appear on the show. But McGraw took a different tack. "He's man enough, a big enough guy, to actually show up tonight and to be on the show. So that's a big deal," Letterman said. Nevertheless, on this night "Dr. Phil's Words of Wisdom" were, "You don't want to be here, trust me."

■ ■ ■

When McGraw strode onto the *Late Show with David Letterman* set, the two large men—McGraw is slightly taller than Letterman—shook hands at center stage. McGraw waved to the audience, before folding his athletic frame into the guest chair. "So, how are you?" he asked Letterman. Then, leaning forward, he took control of the interview in quintessential McGraw style. "I want my check," he said. "I've been working here six months, I want my check."

McGraw's performance that night was dazzling. He admitted to being a fan of Letterman's, and said he found the comedian's barbs to be funny. "I particularly liked a book that you had me writing: *More Advice Dr. Phil Just Pulled out of His Ass*," he joked as Letterman cringed and blushed. McGraw was quick-witted and droll. The audience was delighted when McGraw pulled out a paper from his breast pocket and read a list of all the names Letterman had called him in the past: "Pothead, magician, hump, I look like the guy who approves your check at the supermarket, evil genius, bonehead, pinhead, complainer, whiner, dopey, loopy, 300-pound fatboy, weasel, half-baked quack, quack, and meddlin' sunovabitch."

"I can't imagine why people don't come on your show," McGraw continued, looking Letterman straight in the eye. "I mean, how did I qualify for all these? I mean, I've known some pinheads, I've known some boneheads . . . but how do you get to be all of those things at one time?"

"Well, we've got an hour to fill every night," Letterman explained, laughing nervously. "You know what that's like. Well, and again, even more the reason why we should thank you for being here. I had no idea that you'd accumulated that level of evidence."

The list really did take Letterman by surprise, according to McGraw. "They [*Late Show* producers] like to do these preinterviews and say, 'Well, what are you going to talk about?' And my answer was: 'Just show up and find out.' I didn't tell them anything I was going to talk about."

The good-natured confrontation complete, the two moved on to pleasant banter and discussion, with McGraw throwing only the occasional barb at the host, calling him neurotic. McGraw even counseled Letterman on some personal problems, advising him to get over his fear that Winfrey—who has refused to appear on Letterman or to invite him on her show—disliked him. "It's like my dad used to say," McGraw advised Letterman. "You wouldn't worry so much about what people thought about you if you knew how seldom they did."

McGraw was Letterman's only guest that night, aside from musical artist Beck. And plenty of people tuned in. Letterman's ratings jumped ahead of rival Jay Leno's for the first time in years. In the show, McGraw established himself as a man who could take the heat of celebrity.

■ ■ ■

But that wasn't as hot as things would get for McGraw. He would soon be forced to accept the downside of being famous. The tabloids jumped right into the dig for McGraw's dark side, with lurid headlines. "He was a boozing, hot-headed bully ex pals say" the *Star* scolded in a four-page spread titled "Dr. Phil Exposed." In another headline, the magazine wrote "McGraw ripped off my idea—and he's a phony, says mentor."

McGraw's personal problems soon became a media treasure hunt. When Dallas-based aviation firm DDH Aviation sued McGraw for allegedly failing to pay a $135,962 aircraft charter bill in 2002, several news outlets picked up the story. The suit was later dropped, but some members of the media reported it with vindictive glee. "When Dr. Phil McGraw left the nurturing bosom of Dallas last September and set to make his fortune (even larger) with his very own television show in LA, there were some of us who wished him failure," wrote *D* magazine's deputy editor Tim Rogers. "There was the matter of his less-than-nuanced advice (Dr. Phil to bulimic woman: 'Stop doing that!') But, more important, the man never returned our calls. It drove us batty seeing just how little Dr. Phil needed us."

When the lawsuit was quickly dropped, according to the *D* article, editors for the Dallas city magazine were crestfallen, but undaunted. "Dr. Phil, if you're out there, watch your step. One day you'll stumble. And we'll be hungry and waiting."

■ ■ ■

McGraw got used to living in luxury shortly after CSI became a success, moving to a high-end nouveau riche Dallas suburb. But the good life got even better when he and his family arrived in Hollywood. McGraw rented his first place—an elegant, six-bedroom, 7,000-square-foot gated mini-estate in Westside Los Angeles—in December 2002. The $20,000 a month French-style home had maple, hardwood, and slate floors, with granite kitchen counters, a master suite with a sitting area, a guesthouse, pool, spa, and gardens. A few months later, he reportedly plunked down $7.75 million in cash for a place of his own—a 12,000-square-foot Beverly Hills mansion with a circular drive, library, five bedrooms, guesthouse, three-car garage, and palm-tree-lined pool. He also bought a $200,000 Ferrari.

To keep roots in his Texas hometown—and because he remains connected with CSI, though he's behind the scenes more often than in the courtroom these days—McGraw also purchased a luxury Dallas condo in a new high rise managed by The Mansion on Turtle Creek, an adjacent hotel-to-the-stars.

But even though he has upgraded the trappings, McGraw insists that much of his life in California is unchanged from the way things were in Texas. Even his favorite old green lounge chair made the move across country.

His day, when he was in Dallas, was to, "get up, go to the office, do what I do, leave there about 5, go to the tennis court and run around like a chicken with its head cut off for two hours," McGraw said. "I come home sweaty, rested and relaxed, go to the green chair and have dinner with the family.

"In California, I get up, go to the office, do what I have to do, go to the tennis court and run around for a couple of hours, get all sweaty, come back home and get in the green chair," he continues. "Our life is very much the same when we're out here as when we're home."

While McGraw might have the same general routine as always, he's now batting the ball around in the Beverly Hills Country Club and waving to neighbors like talk show host Larry King. But he hasn't gone completely Hollywood.

"He'd much prefer to be sitting with his wife and boys watching some old movie at home than hobnobbing with Sylvester Stallone and all the rich and famous people," says brother-in-law Scott Madsen, who moved from Texas to Los Angeles to work as McGraw's personal assistant and business manager.

McGraw finds himself surprisingly nonplussed by his own new status. "I don't feel like a celebrity because I don't feel like celebrities look, if you know what I mean," he says. "You watch some movie star going down the red carpet or you watch somebody—

you know . . . where there's 10,000 flashbulbs going off at one time and everything . . . and I don't feel like that looks. That looks glamorous, but I guess when you're in front of those 10,000 flash-bulbs, it's just 10,000 flashbulbs."

Growing up in a family that counted every penny and barely stayed in one town long enough for anyone to care that they were there, McGraw probably never imagined he'd be living the luxuri-ous life he enjoys today. Nor could he have guessed how much in-terest the world would have in him. Now, each time McGraw steps outside his door, everyone watches. "My lifestyle has not changed at all, really, since I started doing the show," he says. "What's changed is the notoriety. And that's not all good. You do appreci-ate the public and . . . the sincere people that support what you do. And then there's the down side, of the tabloids and photogra-phers hanging out in trees . . . We had a guy the other day in a hedge in camouflage trying to get a picture of me washing the car, or something. I mean, God, come on in, sit down, do the wheels, will you?"

McGraw alternates between complaining about the tabloids and circumspection. "It comes with the territory," he says. "If your name and face sells newspapers, then your name and face are going to be on those newspapers. Frankly, I don't read them."

Paparazzi notwithstanding, McGraw seems to be enjoying his new position and social status, and is happily settling down in his glamorous new neighborhood with exciting new friends, neigh-bors, and colleagues. He was elected to the Board of Governors of the Beverly Hills Country Club, joining a star-studded list that in-cludes Buzz Aldrin, Bjorn Borg, Jimmy Connors, Barbara Eden, Merv Griffin, Sherry Lansing, Tommy Lasorda, Leslie Moonves, Matthew Perry, Wolfgang Puck, and Tom Selleck. He gave back to the community by guest-hosting the Black and White Ball benefit-ing The Beverly Hills Police Officers Association. An avid tennis player, he put his skills on the court to work on the celebrity ben-efit circuit, playing at the Chris Evert Pro-Celebrity Classic in

Delray Beach, Florida, alongside comedian Fran Drescher, newscaster Stone Phillips, and others. He also became a favorite in the pro-celebrity event at the Mercedes-Benz Cup in Los Angeles, a benefit for MusiCares, an affiliate of the Recording Industry of America (the folks behind the Grammys). In 2002, McGraw and his teammates Michael Bolton and Matthew Perry triumphed over the team of Kelsey Grammer, Dennis Miller, and James McDaniel. McGraw won again in 2003, when he doubled with tennis pro Lleyton Hewitt to play against pro Gustavo Kuerton and actor Tom Arnold.

■ ■ ■

Perhaps McGraw's true initiation into Tinseltown's inner circle occurred in May 2003 when the real-life television psychologist was invited to meet fictional radio psychologist Frasier Crane on the hit NBC sitcom *Frasier*. "I really wanted to do this show," McGraw says. "And I haven't confessed this to him, but I have seen every episode [star Kelsey Grammer has] ever done." With the *Frasier* studio just around the corner from *Dr. Phil* on the Paramount lot, the highly promoted guest appearance was easily accomplished.

In the episode titled "The Devil and Dr. Phil," McGraw plays himself. He appears as an old friend of Frasier's, in Seattle to conduct a seminar. Frasier is angry at McGraw for supposedly swindling him out of $200 in a long-ago poker game. Frasier is also surprised to learn that his horny and histrionic former agent, Bebe Glazer (played by Harriet Sansom Harris), now represents McGraw.

"Oh, Phil, darling. That was sensational," Bebe raves to McGraw after his seminar. "That audience simultaneously leapt to its feet and fell to its knees." And, she gushes, "He's a cowboy wrapped in a genius wrapped in a dream wrapped in another cowboy."

Frasier is envious, and offers Bebe a raise if she'll drop McGraw and represent him (Frasier) again. He then learns that

Bebe never actually worked for McGraw. Instead, McGraw had her trick Frasier to help him to pay off another gambling debt. The last we see of McGraw—who makes scattered and competent appearances throughout the show—he is grinning wickedly over his deception. It is a surprisingly cynical depiction of the good doctor.

McGraw brought cameras backstage to the taping, to get behind-the-scenes footage for his *Dr. Phil* audience. He immediately made his presence known at his first visit to the set, joking to one *Frasier* staffer, "I've rewritten all my lines. I hope that's okay." The backstage visit reveals a relationship with the close-knit cast that seems awkward, at best. Backstage banter included one show worker telling McGraw that *Frasier* star Grammer had paid him a compliment. "Kelsey tells me you just stroll in, no rehearsal, you know, just do your thing," the man said.

"I bet that broke his jaw to say something nice," McGraw replied. "He'd rather dog on me than eat when he's hungry."

Peri Gilpin, a fellow Texan who plays Roz on the show, was more complimentary, but remained cautious with her comments. "I'd never met him before and we met him over the table read, and he was very prepared and I think he's playing himself very well. And he's got a great funny bone. Got a great sense of humor."

The day before "The Devil and Dr. Phil" aired, Grammer—playing himself—dropped in on the *Dr. Phil* show for a few minutes of strained promotional banter.

■ ■ ■

Indeed, McGraw has come a long way since his first appearance on *Oprah*, when he annoyed her fans and producers alike. The salesman in him has gained more polish, the guru has become more glib, and the possibilities continue to unfold before this master of the media. McGraw is now sampling all that Hollywood has to offer. He's in heady company these days, so who can blame him for enjoying himself? Even McGraw admits he's an unlikely celebrity. "To me a star is Tom Cruise or Julia Roberts," he says. "But to walk up to a newsstand and see your face on the cover of *Newsweek,* or to be sitting there with Jay Leno on *The Tonight Show,* or with Barbara Walters—people you've watched as you've grown up—it's strange."

18

Dr. Phil's Life Laws for Success

How's that workin' for ya?

Phil McGraw has studied success his entire life. As a teenager, he and his dad analyzed his high school football games, looking for those elements that added up to winning results. As a psychologist, he observed and learned from his patients' pursuit of success. And as a trial consultant, he helped formulate the courtroom strategies that would allow his clients to emerge victorious from trial. While the venues may have differed, McGraw's theme over the years has remained the same: Uncover those traits that allowed others to get ahead and that he, in turn, could use to achieve success in his own life.

McGraw's books are filled with formulas for success, starting with the "Life Laws" he lays out in his first book, *Life Strategies*. McGraw started devising these 10 "rules of the game" when he was a young hothead drag racing through the streets of Kansas City. Today, these Life Laws are the cornerstone of the philosophy on which McGraw has built his empire:

Life Law #1: *You either get it, or you don't.*

Life Law #2: *You create your own experience.*

Life Law #3: *People do what works.*

Life Law #4: *You can't change what you don't acknowledge.*

Life Law #5: *Life rewards action.*

Life Law #6: *There is no reality; only perception.*

Life Law #7: *Life is managed, it is not cured.*

Life Law #8: *We teach people how to treat us.*

Life Law #9: *There is power in forgiveness.*

Life Law #10: *You have to name it to claim it.*

McGraw calls these axioms "laws," instead of guidelines or goals, because that term fits better with the philosophy he lays out in *Life Strategies:* "The courtroom is relevant here, because it is indeed a microcosm of life," he writes. "In any trial, somebody is trying to take something away from somebody else. So it is in life . . . In life, as in the courthouse, when the competition starts, or when the world starts coming after you, you'd better have yourself a really good strategy *and* know the rules of the game, or the bad guys will be dividing up what *used to be* yours."

The riches McGraw has accrued in his life—from a devoted family to cold cash—prove that he has long lived by the letter of his laws of success. But, as he explains in *Life Strategies,* applying these Life Laws first requires filling in some blanks. The laws are sufficiently broad to require individual interpretation. "Whether 'winning' for you means healing a relationship or a broken heart, having a new job, a better family life, skinny butt, some inner peace and tranquility, or some other meaningful goal, you need a strategy to get there, and some guidance on how to create one," he writes. Therefore, the Life Laws are the structure, while the particulars are open to individual interpretation.

This goes for McGraw, too. While he has lived his life according to his laws, he has done it *his* way. It is evident that he has customized each law into a jackpot-winning formula. Through observing his life, you can say he follows his own set of rules—

McGraw's Personal Life Laws, if you will. Adhering to the laws has allowed McGraw to become the success he is today.

■ ■ ■

McGraw's Personal Life Law #1: Either I Get It, or Else

In explaining Life Law #1—*You either get it, or you don't*—McGraw writes, "In almost every situation, there are people who get it and there are people who don't—and it's really easy to tell them apart. Those who get it are enjoying the fruits of their knowledge. Those who don't spend a lot of time looking puzzled, frustrated, and doing without." In other words, people who go through life oblivious to the rules are likely to bumble about haplessly, reaching their goals only by accident. The trick is defining *it,* since you can't get *it* until you know what *it* is. And one *it* does not fit all.

McGraw seems to have defined his *it* as "full control over the people and events in his life." According to some, McGraw uses whatever means necessary in his pursuit of *it,* including intimidation—a handy tool for a 6-foot-3 former linebacker with a muscular intellect, a quick tongue, and little patience for hurt feelings.

McGraw's life might have taken some very different turns had he not had *it* over the years. What would have happened if McGraw had asked Thelma Box if he could bring Joe into the Pathways partnership instead of, as she claims, simply telling her that's how it would be? What if he had motivated his employees at CSI through equitable pay and kindness instead of the paycheck games and insults some say were management style? Suppose he had listened to experienced voices in Hollywood instead of grabbing the reins of his television show and flogging his staff into shape?

The answers to these ponderables are unknown, but one possible scenario is that without having *it* in all of these cases, McGraw might have failed to reach his present level of accomplishment.

McGraw continually strives to get *it,* so he can get what he wants—compliance from everyone around him with the laws he lays down, and therefore control of his own success trajectory.

■ ■ ■

McGraw's Personal Life Law #2: You Can Invent Your Own Experience

"Acknowledge and accept accountability for your life. Understand your role in creating the results that are your life. Learn how to choose better so you have better." These are the goals of Life Law #2, *You create your own experience.* This law, McGraw continues, is "absolute truth."

The gist of the law is that you must shun the role of victim and take full responsibility for the situations you find yourself in. "You must be willing to move your position, and, however difficult or unusual it may seem, embrace the fact that you own the problem."

McGraw certainly lives by this law. He learns from every mistake, and never waits for others to make things happen. But McGraw hasn't always been fully accountable for his actions. He sometimes gilds stories, remembers them differently than others, or tries to erase them from the record. He married in haste, divorced quickly, and then pretended it never happened. He filed for bankruptcy after his health club went out of business, then left town in the middle of the night and didn't mention it again. As a psychologist, he bore up under the indignity of a disciplinary action by the Texas Board of Examiners and then denied wrongdoing when pressed to respond.

There is really only one mistake that McGraw seems to keep making: He tries to pretend some things in his life never happened, facing up to the truth only when he gets caught. When the media discovered his first wife, Debbie, McGraw suddenly remembered he'd been married before Robin. When reports of the disciplinary action started leaking out, McGraw moved his position only as much as necessary, claiming the young woman who filed the complaint was just angry at him.

McGraw has created a colorful and wholesome character in "Dr. Phil." He wants to be known as a simple country boy who took the straight and narrow path to success all by his big self, and he's been masterful at crafting his own legend. However, although celebrity fairy tales aren't always true, they give the media a story to tell and the public a hero to worship. McGraw's myth is working for him.

■ ■ ■

McGraw's Personal Life Law #3: Do What Works for You at the Moment

In explaining Life Law #3, *People do what works,* McGraw writes, "The behavior you choose creates the results you get." He emphasizes that no matter how much you claim to hate a particular behavior—smoking, overeating, or (as he unnervingly includes among the illustrative anecdotes) raping women—you must be receiving a payoff or you wouldn't keep doing it. "The truth is, you don't and won't behave in ways that reap only negative, unwanted results," McGraw continues.

The essence of McGraw's beloved behaviorism is this: You learn to repeat actions that reap rewards and to avoid actions that bring punishment. If you are repeating a behavior, it is because you are being rewarded for it. This is another clear and indisputable law with merit. Once again, though, the devil is in the details. Like defining *it,* rewards and punishments are subjective.

The magnitude of McGraw's success and his evident satisfaction with life are indicative of a man who has found a formula that works for him: He calls all the shots, demands perfection at any cost, and shares the wealth with those who toe his line.

But behavior that "works" in one way sometimes fails in others, and it's not always easy to sort out the rewards and punishments. McGraw's bullying works when it comes to getting his way, but leaves him vulnerable to the vindictive urges of those he has bullied. His attempts to hide past mistakes allow him to perpetuate a myth, but fail when his deceptions are revealed. His workaholic tendencies worked to help him blast through school and climb the ladder of success, but they contributed to the end of his first marriage and threatened his second one—a lesson McGraw says he's taken to heart.

McGraw does what works. His life is proof of that. But what works in one respect might be destructive in another. So, like the rest of us, McGraw bumbles along, reaping plaudits and punishments simultaneously, while reaching for the rewards that seem most important at the moment.

■ ■ ■

McGraw's Personal Life Law #4: If You Can't Change It, Ignore or Deny It

Life Law #4 from *Life Strategies* is, *You can't change what you don't acknowledge.* "Be truthful about what isn't working in your life," McGraw urges. "Stop making excuses and start making results." It is here that McGraw deals with the "D" word: Denial—that most stubborn and frustrating of psychological conditions. Denial is the staunch resistance to seeing and accepting things as they are.

McGraw refers back to his psychology textbooks and explains the concept of *perceptual defense.* "Perceptual defense can and does keep you from seeing things you simply don't want to be true," he writes. Illustrating the point with a convincing anecdote from his days of doing expert testimony for airlines, McGraw describes an airplane flight crew who didn't believe what their instruments told them and ended up smashing into a mountain.

McGraw is probably too intelligent to ever smash into a mountain, but he is being tested in the turbulent skies of celebrity. Perhaps the prying eyes of the press are an unfair intrusion, but, as he told Oprah Winfrey during her mad cow trial, "It *is* really happening. You'd better *get over it* and get in the game, or these good ol' boys are going to hand you your ass on a platter."

When things aren't going his way, McGraw shakes his fist, blusters, ridicules, and ignores—techniques that have often worked for him. For example, knowing that he wouldn't have full control over the contents of this book, McGraw met repeated attempts to involve him in the writing process, not with outright refusal, but instead with obstinate silence. He and his associates simply chose not to return calls.

As the curtain is inevitably pulled further back on his past, McGraw must decide to do one of two things: He can own up to his humanity, or he can wall himself in with denials and continue on his course of issuing absolutist advice to his adoring masses.

Fortunately for McGraw, either of the preceding tactics would probably work. That's the flip side of celebrity these days—it can be forgiving, especially for a folk hero like McGraw.

■ ■ ■

McGraw's Personal Life Law #5: The More You Do, the More You Get

Life rewards action, according to Life Law #5. This is among the guiding principles in McGraw's life. "People who win take purposeful, meaningful action; they don't just think about it," McGraw writes. "They don't plan themselves to death; they don't have a meeting to plan a meeting to set up a meeting to decide what to do. There comes a time when you have to pull the trigger. To have what you want, you have to do what it takes."

Who can argue with such timeless wisdom? It is McGraw at his boiled-down best. In *Life Strategies,* he even quotes Benjamin Franklin ("Well done is better than well said") and Plato ("You can learn more about a man in an hour of play than in a year of conversation") to support a point they made first.

McGraw is a man of action and seized opportunities, and he has been amply rewarded for his hard work. One can't help but hope that this ebullient overachiever really does manage to avoid the regrets of later life that he cautions his readers against as he tries to urge them into action.

McGraw is a workaholic who focuses on success in his every endeavor. He is always reaching for more—and usually gets it. He puts the same intensity into being a husband, father, talk show host, celebrity, author, and tennis player. He is an action figure in a suit and tie instead of a cape. McGraw lives by this law with every fiber of his being.

■ ■ ■

McGraw's Personal Life Law #6: Perceptions Can Create Reality

We all see the world through individual filters, McGraw explains in writing about Life Law #6, *There is no reality; only perception.* These filters, he maintains, must be identified for successful living. "The events in your daily life have only the meaning you assign them," he says. "Put another way, there is no good news and there is no bad news; there is only news. You have the power to choose your perception. And you exercise this power of choice in every circumstance, every day of your life"

For beginners in the study of McGraw-think, figuring out what your own filters are is challenging enough. It requires introspection, sometimes with professional guidance. McGraw was originally trained to help people do just that.

But McGraw's ultimate genius is his ability to cut to the chase when it comes to other people's perceptions. McGraw is both insightful and well studied in understanding the motives of others. That's why he helped the patients he counseled more than he admits. That's why he excelled at CSI in jury selection and trial analysis. That's why he wins at negotiation. And that's why he succeeds on his show. His ability to shoot his folksy wisdom straight to the heart of the matter can be dazzling—like a brilliant parlor trick.

McGraw's powers of perception are superheroic. But, as with any superpower, they can be used for good, or not-so-good. This same power helps McGraw find employees who are willing to sacrifice a great deal of themselves for the carrots he holds out as rewards. By seeing and manipulating the ambitions, vanities, and sometimes fears of subordinates, McGraw holds them spellbound even as he browbeats them.

McGraw's power is perfect for television—a snappy medium requiring snappy solutions. On TV, McGraw not only taps into the psyches of his guests, but also the needs of the medium. With his no-bull message and take-no-prisoners style, McGraw has tapped directly into the anxious zeitgeist of the time, creating the perfect character in the down-home doc who stands ready to clean up our act without taking any guff. He is the superhero we felt we always needed to whip us into shape.

■ ■ ■

McGraw's Personal Life Law #7: Manage Your Life for the Bottom Line

Life is managed, it is not cured, states Life Law #7. "This is a long ride and you are the driver every single day," McGraw cautions.

"Understand that success is a moving target, and that in an ever-changing world, your life must be actively managed."

This is where McGraw introduces an important character in his action plan: the life manager. "It will be highly valuable for you, from this point forward, to think about yourself as the manager of your life, in the same way that you might think of and evaluate the manager of a store, or a supervisor in your workplace."

It is in this Life Law that McGraw advises readers to decide, "as a matter of principle, what you will *demand* from yourself, as contrasted with what you are willing to *accept* from yourself." It's time to pull out "project status," he says, meaning "the matter at hand has taken on a special significance and special urgency, lifting it above other concerns."

Among the commitments McGraw advises readers to make with themselves is to honor agreements, "whether with yourself or with others." However, sometimes two different agreements are in conflict. McGraw had to choose between his old contract with Pathways partner Thelma Box, for example, and a potential new deal with Steve Davidson that apparently fulfilled an agreement McGraw had with himself to leave his seminar business behind. In such cases, McGraw might suggest, your life manager needs to consider the bottom line, while always keeping in mind that self matters. In the pursuit of success, expediency and opportunity sometimes appear to trump ethics.

■ ■ ■

McGraw's Personal Life Law #8: Rewards and Punishments Teach People How to Treat You

Life Law #8 cautions, *We teach people how to treat us.* In elaborating further, McGraw states, "Because people learn by results, whether or not you reward, accept, or validate their behavior impacts their conduct, and will influence their subsequent choices." This is pure Behaviorism 101. To teach people how to treat him, McGraw again uses a system of rewards and punishments.

On the punishment side of the equation is McGraw's wrath, the specter of which is fierce. Most people who have been targets of this wrath are reluctant to induce it. McGraw's power is an equal deterrent. After all, he holds many jobs and careers in his massive mitts. When he can, McGraw codifies loyalty. As at the *Oprah* show, those working for *Dr. Phil* have a nondisclosure clause in their contracts, forbidding them from ever speaking to the press about the show or its star.

This fear was made evident while we were researching this book. Many people contacted for interviews were reluctant or outright unwilling to discuss McGraw. Voices trembled, phone calls went unreturned, people agreed to tell their stories and then backed out, and a few openly expressed fear that their talking might prompt some sort of indefinable retaliation.

Among the rewards McGraw offers those who learn how to treat him well: time spent in his exhilarating presence, and sometimes a ride on the Dr. Phil money train. Brother-in-law Scott Madsen, business partner Gary Dobbs, and former college professor Frank Lawlis are among those with tickets to ride. His wife and two sons are also along for the ride, though mostly in a private car—the one closest to McGraw's heart. McGraw feels safest surrounded by this posse of intimates who understand the rules of his game.

To gain entrée into McGraw's inner circle involves a sort of trial by fire. You must submit to yelling and insults, be able to accede your will to his, and understand who ultimately calls the shots. That surely contributed to the fact that members of McGraw's inner circle and current employees were uniformly unavailable for interviews for this book. They either knew better, were under contract, or were sternly advised not to talk. To play with McGraw, you must learn and follow his rules. That's the way it is.

■ ■ ■

McGraw's Personal Life Law #9: Forgive, but Don't Forget

There is power in forgiveness, McGraw preaches in Life Law #9. "Take your power back from those who have hurt you. When you harbor hatred, anger and resentment, your body's chemical balance is dramatically disrupted. Your 'fight or flight' responses stay aroused twenty-four hours a day, seven days a week. That means that hatred, anger, and resentment are absolutely incompatible with your peace, joy, and relaxation."

McGraw insists he has outgrown his hotheaded youth, but childhood friends say they can still see the boy who would "fight a buzz saw if I had half a chance," as he has described his younger self. McGraw might not be throwing punches anymore, but he is still tightly wound. It is hard to tell whether he has truly found his own peace, joy, and relaxation.

Perhaps McGraw's most complex relationship was with his father, who kept the family's life in turmoil with his drinking and frequent moves. Today, the younger McGraw is driven to keep all situations firmly in his grip. Could that be a reaction to having so little control in his childhood?

McGraw claims to have no interest in his so-called inner child and apparently has never undergone psychotherapy to uncover his own motivations and past wounds. McGraw also says that he and his father discussed all they needed to resolve before Joe died, leaving him with no regrets. If McGraw bears wounds from his past, they have healed enough not to handicap his climb to the top.

But the scars might be showing, anyway. Although McGraw never whimpers about his own past, he is a firm and outspoken advocate for children and teenagers. His mantra—no matter what complaint parents bring him on his show—is that children come first. McGraw forces angry mothers to watch themselves on videotape, scolds selfish parents, and ridicules the indulgent. The advice he gives anyone on any subject when children are in the picture is always focused on the children's best interests.

Even McGraw's facial expression changes from firm-jawed conviction to dewy-eyed compassion when he looks at kids. When a bubbly young overweight redhead appears on his show insisting that it's time for "chubby cheerleaders" to make the team in high school, McGraw doesn't tease her or tell her where the rubber hits the road in the real world. He just smiles fondly, cautions her to work hard, and gives her his blessings to audition for the squad. A grown woman might have received a different response from the hard-truth doctor. McGraw protects children above all else.

It seems as if McGraw has forgiven his parents, teachers, and anyone else who might have subjected him to a rough childhood. But he has not forgotten what it's like to be a kid in an adult's world, and it shows. Some might call that listening to his own inner child.

■ ■ ■

McGraw's Personal Life Law #10: Name It, Claim It, Succeed at It, and Then Name Something Else

"If you cannot name, and name with great specificity, what it is that you want, then you will never be able to step up and claim it," McGraw writes when discussing Life Law #10: *You have to name it to claim it.*

"Most people do not know how to describe what they want, because they don't have a clue what it really is," he says, before elaborating on the necessity and challenges of goal setting.

McGraw's success actually seems attributable, not to long-term goal setting, but to his ability to recognize opportunities and take full advantage of them. McGraw seems to have personally mapped out few of the directions his life has taken over the years. His schooling was directed, in a manner of speaking, by his father. Pathways came about through his relationship with Thelma Box, who says she dreamed up the idea. CSI was a collaboration with Gary Dobbs, who had the legal background. Oprah Winfrey's lawsuit was unlucky for her, but fortunate for McGraw, because it opened the door to all the media success that followed. But—and this is key—McGraw quickly recognized each opportunity's potential and applied himself to take full advantage of it. McGraw may have never actively pursued getting his own television show, but when that door opened, he stepped through and gave it his full attention—naming it and claiming it simultaneously, to staggering success.

This repeated pattern of identifying and claiming opportunity as it arises is McGraw's surefire formula for success. It is how he manages his life, and it is how he is rewarded. Phil McGraw is less a self-made man than a self-invented one, but his ability and talent make him a celebrity worth watching. It's impossible not to admire all he's accomplished and wonder what pursuits he will name and conquer next.

Significant Events in Dr. Phil's Life

September 1, 1950	Phillip Calvin McGraw is born in Vinita, Oklahoma. He spends his youth moving from town to town in Oklahoma, Colorado, Kansas, and Texas, while his father works both in the oil industry and as a teacher/coach.
1964	McGraw's father, Joe, returns to college to complete his master's degree and Ph.D. in education and psychology. Phil McGraw moves with his dad to the Kansas City area while Joe completes his internship.
1968	McGraw graduates from Shawnee Mission North High School in Overland Park, Kansas.
1968–1969	McGraw attends the University of Tulsa for one year; an injury cuts short his college football career there.
November 1970	McGraw marries high school sweetheart Debbie Higgins in Roeland Park, Kansas.
June 1971	McGraw opens the Grecian Health Spa in Topeka, Kansas. He and wife Debbie make their home in Topeka.
January 1973	Father Joe McGraw is licensed to practice psychology in Texas.

September 1973	Grecian Health Spa files for bankruptcy, and McGraw abruptly returns to Texas. He later has his marriage to Debbie annulled.
1973–1975	McGraw attends Midwestern State University in Wichita Falls, Texas, graduating with a BA in psychology. He then begins graduate studies at North Texas State University.
May 1976	McGraw receives a master's degree from North Texas State University.
1976	McGraw marries his second wife, Robin.
May 1979	McGraw is awarded a Ph.D. in clinical psychology from North Texas State University.
May 1979	McGraw and Robin return to Wichita Falls, where he joins his father's psychology practice.
1979	McGraw's first son, Jay, is born.
March 1983	McGraw, his father, and Thelma Box hold their first "You" personal growth seminar. The company name would eventually be changed to "Pathways."
1986	McGraw's second son, Jordan, is born.
July 1987	Joe McGraw forfeits his license to practice psychology.
October 1988	In response to a complaint filed against Phil McGraw by a female patient, he is disciplined by the Texas Board of Examiners of Psychologists. He leaves Wichita Falls for Dallas.
1990	McGraw and attorney Gary Dobbs found litigation consulting firm Courtroom Sciences, Inc. (CSI). McGraw, in the meantime, sells his shares of Pathways, ending his involvement with the company.
1993	Joe McGraw dies of a heart attack while teaching Sunday school.

April 1996	The Mad Cow episode of *Oprah* airs. Enraged Texas cattlemen sue the talk show host under a "veggie libel" law. Oprah Winfrey's Dallas-based attorney, Chip Babcock, hires McGraw and CSI to assist with the case.
January 1998	Winfrey's trial begins in Amarillo, Texas. It ends six weeks later with the jury finding in favor of Winfrey. Back in Chicago, Winfrey has her entire trial team, including McGraw, on her show.
April 1998	"Dr. Phil" makes his first appearance on *The Oprah Winfrey Show*. He receives a less-than-enthusiastic reception from the show's fans and producers. Winfrey brings him back again, to a much better response.
January 1999	McGraw's first book, *Life Strategies,* is published by Hyperion, debuting at number three on the *Publishers Weekly* bestseller list and soon staking a place on the *New York Times* bestseller list.
November 2000	*Saturday Night Live* does its first parody of McGraw.
December 2000	Jay McGraw's first book, *Life Strategies for Teens,* is published by Simon & Schuster.
February 2000	Phil McGraw's second book, *Relationship Rescue,* is published by Hyperion and quickly climbs the bestseller lists.
November 2001	*Self Matters,* McGraw's third book, is published by Simon & Schuster and spends 13 weeks at number one on the bestseller lists.
September 2002	The *Dr. Phil* show debuts with the highest ratings for a first-run syndicated talk show debut since McGraw's mentor Winfrey took the national stage in 1986.
February 2003	McGraw appears on the *Late Show with David Letterman*.

April 2003	McGraw and the *Dr. Phil* show are nominated for two daytime Emmys, outstanding host and outstanding talk show. [He loses in both categories.]
May 2003	McGraw makes a guest appearance on the NBC sitcom *Frasier*.
September 2003	Simon & Schuster publishes McGraw's fourth book, *The Ultimate Weight Solution: The 7 Keys to Weight Loss Freedom*, for which McGraw reportedly received a $10 million advance. At the same time, he launches his own monthly newsletter and a line of nutritional products.

ACKNOWLEDGMENTS

From Sophia Dembling: I want to thank everyone who took time out of their lives to assist us with our research, especially those gracious enough to be interviewed. Special thanks to Thelma Box, James Cannici, Ph.D., and Delores Jones, who put up with my endless e-mailed questions. Thanks to Richard Himmel, archivist at the University of North Texas, who dug through dusty volumes with me and so efficiently fielded the oddball e-mailed questions I lobbed his way. Thanks to Marion Underwood, Ph.D., and James Bartlett, Ph.D., psychologists who kindly answered sundry questions about their field; and to my friend and colleague Sue Russell, who was generous with her writerly wisdom.

Special thanks to my coauthor, Lisa Gutierrez, whose enthusiasm even when she was running ragged was always uplifting; and to Kirk Kazanjian of Literary Productions, who deftly and with unflagging cheer steered this unwieldy project to port. This book was truly a three-way collaboration.

And, of course, gratitude and love to my husband, Tom, who was such a good sport about having Dr. Phil "move in" with us for six months.

From Lisa Gutierrez: Thank you to everyone who helped bring this project to life. Special thanks to the helpful folks of Vinita, Oklahoma, especially the Clanton family (who run the best café in town) and Gary Dunn, who walked with me door-to-door to meet neighbors on a hot summer day. Many thanks to all the great folks in Topeka, Kansas—including bankruptcy court employees who crawled over boxes in the basement to find old records for us, former businesswoman Billie Talmage, Marsha J. Sheahan at the Greater Topeka Chamber, and my friend and research assistant Lisa Sandmeyer.

There are not enough thanks to offer my intrepid coauthor, Sophia Dembling, and Kirk Kazanjian of Literary Productions, who gave us his best. Thank you also to my cheerleaders— colleagues at the *Kansas City Star,* neighbors and family members, and especially my sister and niece—Lori and Lauren Wickliffe, who "kept tabs" on Dr. Phil for me.

But no one deserves more of my love and thanks than my husband, Michael Houser, who kept the home fires burning while I did the author thing.

Both authors would also like to thank Debra Englander, Joan O'Neil, Peter Knapp, Elke Villa, Michael Onorato, Jessica Church, Helene Godin, and everyone else at John Wiley & Sons for believing in this project and supporting us in our efforts to bring Dr. Phil's story to life.

SOURCE NOTES

Prologue

Page viii "If we are not nominated . . ." Frazier Moore, "*The View* Reveals Daytime Emmy Noms," Associated Press (March 12, 2003).

Page ix "The slam-dunk . . ." Michael Starr, "Dr. Phil Will Thrill in His First Award Year," *New York Post* (May 12, 2003).

Page ix "You got to know . . ." *Larry King Weekend,* CNN (May 17, 2003), interview with Larry King.

Page ix "I hear the ratings . . ." *Today,* NBC-TV (May 16, 2003), interview with Katie Couric.

Page xi "I met her . . ." *Today,* NBC-TV (September 16, 2003), interview with Katie Couric.

Chapter 1

Page 1 "Your life . . ." Phillip C. McGraw, *Self Matters* (New York: Simon & Schuster, 2001), p. 44.

Page 2 "They [my parents] tell the story . . ." David Tarrant, "Phillip McGraw: With a Book and a Boost from Oprah, Trial Psychologist Is Riding High," *Dallas Morning News* (April 4, 1999), p. 1E.

Page 2 "I look at Dr. Phil . . ." Interview with Sue Sumner Secondine.

Page 3 "Times were tough . . ." Interview with Raymond Carden.

Page 4   "They probably didn't . . ." Phillip C. McGraw, *Relationship Rescue* (New York: Hyperion, 2000), p. 68.

Page 6   "This is the heart . . ." Ginnie Graham, "Dr. Phil Fills Reynolds Center," *Tulsa World* (April 13, 2002), p. A17.

Page 7   "Joe struggled academically . . ." Based on a review of Joe McGraw's college transcripts obtained from the Texas State Board of Examiners of Psychology under the Open Records Act.

Page 9   "He had a profound . . ." Interview with Eddie Berry.

Page 9   "He was somebody . . ." Interview with Tom Clanton.

Page 11   ". . . create your own . . ." "The It List," *Entertainment Weekly* (June 29, 2001), p. 60.

Page 11   "We grew up . . ." From the biography *Dr. Phil Getting Real* on the A&E Television Network.

Page 12   "He was the one . . ." From the biography *Dr. Phil Getting Real* on the A&E Television Network.

Page 12   "He couldn't speak . . ." Christina Cheakalos and Chris Coats, "Direct Males," *People* (June 11, 2001), p. 89.

Page 12   "When Phil was little, . . ." From the biography *Dr. Phil Getting Real* on the A&E Television Network.

Page 12   "They suggested the piano, . . ." From the biography *Dr. Phil Getting Real* on the A&E Television Network.

Page 13   "Always aiming for the stars . . ." Based on interview with Troy Linthicum.

Page 13   "Son, if you're not . . ." Phil McGraw, "Dr. Phil's Manual," *O: The Oprah Magazine* (June 2003), p. 46.

Page 13   "As soon as we were . . ." Phillip C. McGraw, *Self Matters* (New York: Simon & Schuster, 2001), p. 37.

Page 14   "I spent a lot of time . . ." David Tarrant, "Phillip McGraw: With a Book and a Boost from Oprah, Trial Psychologist Is Riding High," *Dallas Morning News* (April 4, 1999), p. 1E.

Page 14   ". . . when you are airborne, . . ." Phil McGraw, "Dr. Phil's Manual," *O: The Oprah Magazine* (June 2003), p. 48.

Chapter 2

Page 15   "He's a role model . . ." Phil McGraw, "Dr. Phil's Manual," *O: The Oprah Magazine* (June 2003), p. 47.

Page 15   "The earliest thing . . ." *Pinnacle,* CNN (September 8, 2001), interview with Beverly Schuch.

Page 17 "My approach is . . ." *Pinnacle,* CNN (September 8, 2001), interview with Beverly Schuch.

Page 17 "Oh, you're Mr. Tough . . ." Phillip C. McGraw, *Self Matters* (New York: Simon & Schuster, 2001), p. 100.

Page 18 "In a flash, . . ." Phillip C. McGraw, *Self Matters* (New York: Simon & Schuster, 2001), p. 101.

Page 18 "You're right. . . ." Phillip C. McGraw, *Self Matters* (New York: Simon & Schuster, 2001), p. 101.

Page 19 "He was an alcoholic, . . ." From the biography *Dr. Phil Getting Real* on the A&E Television Network.

Page 19 "He was just a . . ." Interview with Wayne McKamie Jr.

Page 20 "But, you know, . . ." *Pinnacle,* CNN (September 8, 2001), interview with Beverly Schuch.

Page 20 "One of the things . . ." *KRON News at 9,* KRON-TV (November 18, 2002), interview with Henry Tennenbaum.

Page 20 "He can walk . . ." Interview with Wayne McKamie Jr.

Page 21 ". . . everything just stopped, . . ." *Entertainment Tonight* (August 26, 2002), interview with Jann Carl.

Page 21 "My dad said, . . ." Marc Peyser, Vanessa Juarez, and Ana Figueroa, "Paging Dr. Phil," *Newsweek* (September 2, 2002), p. 50.

Page 21 "I'd fold . . ." David Tarrant, "Phillip McGraw: With a Book and a Boost from Oprah, Trial Psychologist Is Riding High," *Dallas Morning News* (April 4, 1999), p. 1E.

Page 21 "I did take a lot . . ." *Pinnacle,* CNN (September 8, 2001), interview with Beverly Schuch.

Page 21 "They moved in . . ." Interview with Troy Linthicum.

Page 22 "He'd go back . . ." Interview with Troy Linthicum.

Page 22 ". . . screaming down the street . . ." David Tarrant, "Phillip McGraw: With a Book and a Boost from Oprah, Trial Psychologist Is Riding High," *Dallas Morning News* (April 4, 1999), p. 1E.

Page 22 "Boy, you better . . ." David Tarrant, "Phillip McGraw: With a Book and a Boost from Oprah, Trial Psychologist Is Riding High," *Dallas Morning News* (April 4, 1999), p. 1E.

Page 23 "That guy . . ." and story about incident with rental car based on interview with Troy Linthicum.

Page 24 "They're just a couple . . ." Interview with Wayne McKamie Jr.

Page 24 "Phil does not . . ." Interview with Thelma Box.

Page 25 "When we argued, . . ." Joseph Hooper, "The Doctor Is On!" *Elle* (August 2002).

Page 25 "Phil was quite a motivator. . . ." Interview with Wayne McKamie Jr.

Page 26 "We were bad-ass. . . ." Marc Peyser, Vanessa Juarez, and Ana Figueroa, "Paging Dr. Phil," *Newsweek* (September 2, 2002), p. 50.

Page 26 "I started getting . . ." From the biography *Dr. Phil Getting Real* on the A&E Television Network.

Page 26 "I thought if I . . ." From the biography *Dr. Phil Getting Real* on the A&E Television Network.

Page 27 "I think he was . . ." Interview with Rocky Hughes.

Chapter 3

Page 28 "Some people are . . ." Joseph Hooper, "The Doctor Is On! Part Texas Lawman, Part Big Daddy, Dr. Phil's a Straight Shooter," *Calgary Herald* (February 27, 2003).

Page 28 "His mature appearance . . ." Interviews with Debbie McCall and several other childhood friends.

Page 29 "He called me . . ." Interview with Rocky Hughes.

Page 31 "The thing I liked . . ." Interview with Ed Dallam.

Page 31 "Some of those guys, . . ." Interview with Donald Alpaugh.

Page 31 "As the trial . . ." Interview with Richard Kenley.

Page 32 "Former friends choose . . ." Interviews with numerous childhood friends.

Page 32 Dialogue with CNN reporter regarding whether he was a wild kid took place between Phil McGraw and Beverly Schuch on the program *Pinnacle,* CNN (September 8, 2001).

Page 33 "During football season . . ." Interview with Larry McCarthy.

Page 34 "On returning to school, . . ." Interview with Larry McCarthy.

Page 34 "My friends . . ." Interview with Robyn Busch.

Page 35 "He has said he was . . ." Interviews with numerous friends and former classmates.

Page 36   "They analyzed everything, . . ." Interview with Rocky Hughes.

Page 37   "We were night owls . . ." Phillip C. McGraw, *Life Strategies* (New York: Hyperion, 1999), p. 26.

Page 38   "Well, his name is . . ." Phillip C. McGraw, *Life Strategies* (New York: Hyperion, 1999), p. 26.

Page 38   "In retrospect, . . ." Phillip C. McGraw, *Life Strategies* (New York: Hyperion, 1999), p. 26.

Page 38   "One guy did not . . ." Phillip C. McGraw, *Life Strategies* (New York: Hyperion, 1999), p. 26.

Chapter 4

Page 40   "I think if . . ." *Larry King Live,* CNN (September 25, 2002), interview with Larry King.

Page 40   "You were married . . ." Taken from aircheck of radio interview with Randy Miller on KCTE-AM (October 18, 2002).

Page 41   "You have to turn . . ." *Larry King Live,* CNN (September 25, 2002), interview with Larry King.

Page 41   "She alleges that . . ." Interview with Debbie McCall.

Page 41   "I was the big . . ." Marc Peyser, Vanessa Juarez, and Ana Figueroa, "Paging Dr. Phil," *Newsweek* (September 2, 2002), p. 50.

Page 43   "If he had mentioned . . ." Lisa Gutierrez, "Phil in the Blanks," *Kansas City Star* (October 10, 2002), p. E1.

Page 43   ". . . a force that you . . ." Interview with Bill Higgins.

Page 44   "At 17, 18, . . ." Interview with Bill Higgins.

Page 44   "Phil showed up . . ." From the biography *Dr. Phil Getting Real* on the A&E Television Network.

Page 45   "Being blind was . . ." From the biography *Dr. Phil Getting Real* on the A&E Television Network.

Page 45   "Joe didn't become . . ." Based on a review of Joe McGraw's records obtained from the Texas State Board of Examiners of Psychology under the Open Records Act.

Page 45   "He had given . . ." Interview with Debbie McCall.

Page 47   "His take-charge . . ." Lisa Gutierrez, "Phil in the Blanks," *Kansas City Star* (October 10, 2002), p. E1.

Page 48   "When I confronted him . . ." Lisa Gutierrez, "Phil in the Blanks," *Kansas City Star* (October 10, 2002), p. E1.

Page 48   "You want to talk . . ." From the biography *Dr. Phil Getting Real* on the A&E Television Network.

Page 49   ". . . the courage to . . ." Cecelia Goodnow, "Phil McGraw Draws Raves for 'No Bull' Approach to Rescuing Relationships," *Seattle Post-Intelligencer* (March 4, 2000), p. C1.

Page 49   "I think they . . ." Interview with former high school classmate.

Page 49   "I think he's been . . ." Interview with former high school classmate.

Chapter 5

Page 52   "The principle . . ." Phillip C. McGraw, *Life Strategies* (New York: Hyperion, 1999), p. 72.

Page 53   "They hadn't finished . . ." Interview with Jim McNeece.

Page 53   "His business practices . . ." Based on interviews with officials of the Kansas State Legislature and investigators who worked on the case.

Page 54   "The bottom line . . ." Celeste Hadrick, "Going Belly Up: Health Clubs Haunted by Failures," *Kansas City Star* (February 18, 1986), p. 1A.

Page 54   "In 1971, McGraw, . . ." Information based on bankruptcy filings with the United States District Court for the District of Kansas obtained by the authors.

Page 55   "I think people are . . ." Interview with Elizabeth Wooster-Petrik.

Page 56   "It didn't take long . . ." Interview with Elizabeth Wooster-Petrik.

Page 56   "The spa was indeed . . ." Information based on bankruptcy filings with the United States District Court for the District of Kansas obtained by the authors.

Page 57   "The bankruptcy court . . ." Information based on bankruptcy filings with the United States District Court for the District of Kansas obtained by the authors.

Page 57   "He left town . . ." Interview with friend of Debbie McCall.

Page 57   "I don't think . . ." Interview with friend of Phil McGraw.

Page 58   "It was a mess . . ." Interview with Billie Talmage.

Page 58   "McGraw and his partners . . . ." Based on a review of bankruptcy filings, interviews with former members, and an interview with Emery Goad, a former investigator for the Kansas attorney general's office who worked on the case.

Page 59   "Obviously he was . . ." Interview with Emery Goad.

Page 61   "The FTC held . . ." Based on newspaper accounts from the time, along with interviews with Emery Goad, an investigator involved with the case.

Page 61   "Three hundred dollars . . ." Information based on bankruptcy filings with the United States District Court for the District of Kansas obtained by the authors.

Page 62   "Check stub . . ." From bankruptcy filings with the United States District Court for the District of Kansas obtained by the authors.

Page 64   "If I'd known . . ." Interview with man who bought Phil McGraw's Topeka, Kansas, home from him.

Chapter 6

Page 66   "I almost quit . . ." Mark Donald, "Analyze This," *Dallas Observer* (April 13, 2000).

Page 66   "College studies did not come . . ." Information about grades based on a review of Joe McGraw's college transcripts obtained from the Texas State Board of Examiners of Psychology under the Open Records Act.

Page 67   "Joe flunked . . ." Based on a review of Joe McGraw's records from the Texas State Board of Psychology, obtained under the Open Records Act.

Page 67   "If you could fill out . . ." Interview with George Diekhoff.

Page 68   "As part of our grad training . . ." Interview with Donald Trahan.

Page 68   "Younger looking, . . ." Interview with Everett Kindig.

Page 69   "If you were on . . ." Interview with Robert Wernick.

Page 71   "There were still . . ." Interview with James Cannici.

Page 71   "As a student, . . ." Interview with Robert Wernick.

Page 71   "He remembered . . ." Phillip C. McGraw, *Self Matters* (New York: Simon & Schuster, 2001), p. 2.

Page 72   "He had very strong . . ." Interview with James Cannici.

Page 73   "I just want you to know, . . ." *Gayle King Can Talk to Anyone: Dr. Phil,* Oxygen (January 21, 2003), interview with Gayle King.

Page 73   "By that time, . . ." Interview with Donald Trahan.

Page 74 "He lived in an apartment . . ." Interview with Kelley Reese in the University of North Texas public information department.

Page 74 "They knew about . . ." Interview with a former colleague of Phil McGraw.

Page 75 "McGraw's thesis . . ." Based on a review of Phil McGraw's thesis and dissertation obtained from UMI ProQuest Digital Dissertations.

Page 76 "Frank and I . . ." "Learn from Dr. Phil's Mentor," PR Newswire (January 23, 2003), press release.

Page 77 "With this ice, . . ." Roy Appleton, "Relaxation, New Attitudes Key to Relieving Pain?" *Dallas Times Herald* (August 20, 1978), p. 1B.

Page 78 "McGraw would later . . ." Mark Donald, "Analyze This," *Dallas Observer* (April 13, 2000).

Page 79 "No less painfully, . . ." Phillip C. McGraw, *Self Matters* (New York: Simon & Schuster, 2001), p. 2.

Page 79 ". . . to be sure . . ." Phillip C. McGraw, *Self Matters* (New York: Simon & Schuster, 2001), p. 2.

Chapter 7

Page 80 "Pathways is one . . ." Pathways web site, available from http://www.pathways-edu.com/dr_phil_mcgraw.htm.

Page 80 "We were very . . ." Interview with Thelma Box.

Page 81 "They led a colorful . . ." Interview with Delores Jones.

Page 82 "People would come in . . ." Mark Donald, "Analyze This," *Dallas Observer* (April 13, 2000).

Page 82 "Oh, my God! . . ." *Dateline,* NBC-TV (September 13, 2002), interview with Jane Pauley.

Page 82 "I'm just not cut . . ." *Donahue,* MSNBC (September 16, 2002), interview with Phil Donahue.

Page 83 "I see him occasionally . . ." Interview with Delores Jones.

Page 84 "I think that he . . ." Interview with former patient of Phil McGraw.

Page 84 "He told my mother . . ." Interview with Liz Brannan.

Page 84 "There were days . . ." Interview with Peggi Anderson.

Page 85 "He is the most . . ." Mark Donald, "Analyze This," *Dallas Observer* (April 13, 2000).

Page 86   "He had already experimented . . ." Mark Donald, "Analyze This," *Dallas Observer* (April 13, 2000).

Page 88   "He walked around . . ." Mark Donald, "Analyze This," *Dallas Observer* (April 13, 2000).

Page 91   ". . . a complaint against Joe . . ." Based on a review of Joe McGraw's records from the Texas State Board of Psychology, obtained under the Open Records Act.

Page 92   "The official complaint . . ." Based on a review of Phil McGraw's records from the Texas State Board of Psychology, obtained under the Open Records Act.

Page 92   "He'd pull me down . . ." "Sex Scandal Nearly Sank His Career," *Star* (May 20, 2003).

Page 92   "I was emotionally . . ." Mark Donald, "Analyze This," *Dallas Observer* (April 13, 2000).

Page 92   "If I was depressed . . ." Mark Donald, "Analyze This," *Dallas Observer* (April 13, 2000).

Page 93   "The patient learned . . ." From the biography *Dr. Phil Getting Real* on the A&E Television Network.

Page 93   "I have never . . ." Michael Starr, "I Did Not Sexually Abuse That Female Patient," *New York Post* (September 12, 2002).

Page 93   "The Board's disciplinary . . ." Based on a review of Phil McGraw's records from the Texas State Board of Psychology, obtained under the Open Records Act.

Page 93   "Some people just . . ." Interview with former patient of Phil McGraw.

Chapter 8

Page 95   "I feel about . . ." Mark Donald, "Analyze This," *Dallas Observer* (April 13, 2000).

Page 95   "I saw the writing . . ." Interview with Thelma Box.

Page 95   "In law, . . ." Lynn Elber, "Psychologist, Oprah Protégé Flying Solo," Associated Press (September 12, 2002).

Page 96   "Though he denies . . ." Mark Donald, "Analyze This," *Dallas Observer* (April 13, 2000).

Page 96   "I hate that . . ." *Pinnacle,* CNN (September 8, 2001), interview with Beverly Schuch.

Page 96   "He's the best . . ." From the biography *Dr. Phil Getting Real* on the A&E Television Network.

Page 96   "Some people look . . ." Joseph Hooper, "The Doctor Is On!" *Elle* (August 2002).

Page 97   "The story always . . ." Interview with former CSI employee.

Page 97   "Many view it . . ." Interview with Richard Gabriel.

Page 97   "We don't coach . . ." *Late Show with David Letterman*, CBS-TV (February 17, 2003), interview with David Letterman.

Page 98   ". . . the bread and butter . . ." Interview with former CSI employee.

Page 98   "If you tell . . ." *Pinnacle*, CNN (September 8, 2001), interview with Beverly Schuch.

Page 98   "It is unrealistic . . ." David Voreacos, "Dr. Phil Surfaces in Lawsuit: Prepared Fraud Witness for Testimony," *Gazette* (February 15, 2003), from Bloomberg News.

Page 98   "If you start . . ." Interview with Richard Gabriel.

Page 99   "He literally would . . ." Interview with Charice Miles.

Page 99   "Phil had fermented . . ." Interview with James Cannici.

Page 99   "We had talked . . ." Interview with Thelma Box.

Page 100   ". . . to minimize the . . ." Mark Donald, "Analyze This," *Dallas Observer* (April 13, 2000).

Page 103   "He came by . . ." From the biography *Dr. Phil Getting Real* on the A&E Television Network.

Page 103   "He and I . . ." From the biography *Dr. Phil Getting Real* on the A&E Television Network.

Page 103   "I love you . . ." Phillip C. McGraw, *Life Strategies* (New York: Hyperion, 1999), p. 136.

Page 104   "CSI had some . . ." Mark Donald, "Analyze This," *Dallas Observer* (April 13, 2000).

Page 104   ". . . a $20 million a year . . ." Joseph Hooper, "The Doctor Is On!" *Elle* (August 2002).

Page 104   "CSI's headquarters . . ." Mark Donald, "Analyze This," *Dallas Observer* (April 13, 2000).

Page 104   "I've never seen . . ." Interview with former CSI employee.

Page 104   "Corporations pay . . ." *Business Unusual*, CNN (September 10, 2000), interview with Beverly Schuch.

Page 104   "In 1996, CSI . . ." *Business Unusual*, CNN (September 10, 2000), interview with Beverly Schuch.

Page 105   "It is a tool . . ." *Business Unusual*, CNN (September 10, 2000), interview with Beverly Schuch.

Page 105 "The fraud verdict . . ." Felicity Barringer, "Appeals Court Rejects Damages against ABC in Food Lion Case," *New York Times* (October 21, 1999), p. 1A.

Page 105 "There are some good . . ." Interview with Charice Miles.

Page 105 "One observer claims . . ." e-mail correspondence with a confidential source.

Page 106 "I used to be . . ." Mark Donald, "Analyze This," *Dallas Observer* (April 13, 2000).

Page 106 "He [McGraw] has exceptional . . ." David Tarrant, "Phillip McGraw: With a Book and a Boost from Oprah, Trial Psychologist Is Riding High," *Dallas Morning News* (April 4, 1999), p. 1E.

Page 106 "I think suing is kind . . ." Lynn Elber, "Psychologist, Oprah Protégé Flying Solo," Associated Press (September 12, 2002).

Page 107 "Well, it depends . . ." *Pinnacle,* CNN (September 8, 2001), interview with Beverly Schuch.

Page 107 "The people at . . ." Interview with Judith Fletcher.

Page 107 "McGraw insisted . . ." Interviews with several former CSI employees.

Page 108 "He [McGraw] wasn't so much . . ." Interview with former CSI employee.

Page 108 "Phil engenders . . ." Interview with former CSI employee.

Page 109 "Interestingly enough, . . ." Interview with former CSI employee.

Page 110 ". . . an abortion. . . ." Interview with Charice Miles.

Page 110 "Could somebody get . . ." Interview with former CSI employee.

Page 110 "He's verbally abusive, . . ." Interview with former CSI employee.

Page 111 "He would pay . . ." Interview with James Cannici.

Page 112 "He's funny, . . ." Interview with former CSI employee.

Page 113 "They constantly infused . . ." Interview with former CSI employee.

Chapter 9

Page 114 "There's something that . . ." *Dateline,* NBC-TV (September 13, 2002), interview with Jane Pauley.

Page 115   "Now see . . ." Dialogue from *The Oprah Winfrey Show* from Thomas Goetz, "After the Oprah Crash—Food Disparagement Laws," *Village Voice* (April 29, 1997), p. 39.

Page 115   "I never see . . ." Thomas Goetz, "After the Oprah Crash—Food Disparagement Laws," *Village Voice* (April 29, 1997), p. 39.

Page 116   "Engler estimated . . ." Thomas Goetz, "After the Oprah Crash—Food Disparagement Laws," *Village Voice* (April 29, 1997), p. 39.

Page 116   "One of the greatest . . ." "The Verdict Is In," *The Oprah Winfrey Show* (February 27, 1998).

Page 116   "Oprah was scared . . ." Mary Alice Robbins, "A Lot at Steak: Comments Heard on Show Spur Legal Wrangling with Panhandle Cattlemen," *Texas Lawyer* (September 10, 2001), p. 9.

Page 117   "The big value . . ." David Tarrant, "Phillip McGraw: With a Book and a Boost from Oprah, Trial Psychologist Is Riding High," *Dallas Morning News* (April 4, 1999), p. 1E.

Page 117   "You can't be . . ." Cheryl Lavin, "On *Oprah* and Off, Dr. Phil Tells It Like It Is," Knight Ridder/Tribune News Service (June 15, 2001).

Page 117   "Phil stayed very close . . ." Interview with former CSI employee.

Page 117   "Excuse me, . . ." Skip Hollandsworth, "Phillip McGraw," *Texas Monthly* (September 1999).

Page 117   ". . . in the first three . . ." Cheryl Lavin, "On *Oprah* and Off, Dr. Phil Tells It Like It Is," Knight Ridder/Tribune News Service (June 15, 2001).

Page 117   "No one gave . . ." Mary Alice Robbins, "A Lot at Steak: Comments Heard on Show Spur Legal Wrangling with Panhandle Cattlemen," *Texas Lawyer* (September 10, 2001), p. 9.

Page 117   "I told her, . . ." Cheryl Lavin, "On *Oprah* and Off, Dr. Phil Tells It Like It Is," Knight Ridder/Tribune News Service (June 15, 2001).

Page 117   "Think about it, . . ." From the biography *Dr. Phil Getting Real* on the A&E Television Network.

Page 118   "Chip Babcock is . . ." Interview with Charice Miles.

Page 118 "One juror said . . ." From the biography *Dr. Phil Getting Real* on the A&E Television Network.

Page 118 "She came across . . ." Skip Hollandsworth, "Phillip McGraw," *Texas Monthly* (September 1999).

Page 118 "Coming in second . . ." Cheryl Lavin, "On *Oprah* and Off, Dr. Phil Tells It Like It Is," Knight Ridder/Tribune News Service (June 15, 2001).

Page 119 "She's here! . . ." Skip Hollandsworth and Pamela Colloff, "How the West Was Won Over," *Texas Monthly* (March 1998).

Page 119 "Seats were tough . . ." Mary Alice Robbins, "A Lot at Steak: Comments Heard on Show Spur Legal Wrangling with Panhandle Cattlemen," *Texas Lawyer* (September 10, 2001).

Page 119 "During voir dire, . . ." Mary Alice Robbins, "A Lot at Steak: Comments Heard on Show Spur Legal Wrangling with Panhandle Cattlemen," *Texas Lawyer* (September 10, 2001).

Page 119 "Well, I'm in Texas. . . ." "Welcome to Texas," *The Oprah Winfrey Show* (January 26, 1998).

Page 120 "We thought . . ." Interview with Skip Hollandsworth.

Page 121 "From my impressions, . . ." Interview with Charice Miles.

Page 121 "Oprah is exactly . . ." Interview with former CSI employee.

Page 121 "We were behind . . ." Joseph Hooper, "The Doctor Is On!" *Elle* (August 2002).

Page 122 "You get really close . . ." Cheryl Lavin, "On *Oprah* and Off, Dr. Phil Tells It Like It Is," Knight Ridder/Tribune News Service (June 15, 2001).

Page 122 "Sitting on the floor . . ." Phillip C. McGraw, *Life Strategies* (New York: Hyperion, 1999), p. 8.

Page 122 "It is Phil . . ." "The Verdict Is In," *The Oprah Winfrey Show* (February 27, 1998).

Page 123 "Without Phil . . ." David Tarrant, "Phillip McGraw: With a Book and a Boost from Oprah, Trial Psychologist Is Riding High," *Dallas Morning News* (April 4, 1999), p. 1E.

Page 123 "Eighty percent . . ." "The Verdict Is In," *The Oprah Winfrey Show* (February 27, 1998).

Page 123 "I knew that Phil . . ." Interview with former CSI employee.

Page 124 "One day she . . ." *Dateline,* NBC-TV (September 13, 2002), interview with Jane Pauley.

Page 124 "My next guest . . ." "Millennium Time Capsule," *The Oprah Winfrey Show* (April 10, 1998).

Page 125 "We had e-mails . . ." From the biography *Dr. Phil Getting Real* on the A&E Television Network.

Page 125 "I think people . . ." From the biography *Dr. Phil Getting Real* on the A&E Television Network.

Page 125 "Right after . . ." From the biography *Dr. Phil Getting Real* on the A&E Television Network.

Page 125 "It's like riding . . ." Bruce R. Miller, "Getting Your Phil," *Sioux City Journal* (January 3, 2003).

Page 125 "I get really . . ." Joseph Hooper, "The Doctor Is On!" *Elle* (August 2002).

Page 126 "Mercy, that is . . ." "All-Time Best Dr. Phil Moments," *The Oprah Winfrey Show* (September 10, 2002).

Page 126 "This is what happens . . ." "Dr. Phil: Women Who Want to Change Their Man," *The Oprah Winfrey Show* (October 17, 2000).

Page 126 "But, you know . . ." "Ask Dr. Phil," *The Oprah Winfrey Show* (December 5, 2000).

Page 127 ". . . an intense, confrontational . . ." "Dr. Phil's Get Real Challenge: Episode 1," *The Oprah Winfrey Show* (October 16, 2001).

Page 127 "May I ask . . ." "Dr. Phil's Get Real Challenge: Episode 1," *The Oprah Winfrey Show* (October 16, 2001).

Page 127 "I just feel free, . . ." "Dr. Phil's Get Real Challenge: Part 10," *The Oprah Winfrey Show* (December 18, 2001).

Page 128 "I don't foresee . . ." Joseph Hooper, "The Doctor Is On!" *Elle* (August 2002).

Page 128 "I respect him, . . ." Interview with Susan Fletcher.

Page 128 "As he got involved . . ." Interview with former CSI employee.

Chapter 10

Page 129 "I'm not the kind . . ." Phillip C. McGraw, *Relationship Rescue* (New York: Hyperion, 2000).

Page 129 "... wound up selling ..." Jill Wendholt Silva, "Rosie Daley Teams with Wellness Expert Andrew Weil to Write New Cookbook," available from kansascity.com (June 25, 2002).

Page 130 "Within two months ..." D. T. Max, "The Oprah Effect," *New York Times Magazine* (December 26, 1999).

Page 131 "After Winfrey ..." Wally Lamb, author of *I Know This Much Is True* selected as Oprah's Book Club Summer selection, Business Wire (June 19, 1998).

Page 131 "It's pretty stunning, ..." Interview with Karen Jenkins Holt.

Page 131 "McGraw negotiated ..." Skip Hollandsworth, "Love Thy Self-Help," *Texas Monthly* (September 2003), p. 206.

Page 132 "I swear to God, ..." Interview with Charice Miles.

Page 132 "... was like talking ..." Interview with Delores Jones.

Page 132 "While McGraw's presentation ..." *Publishers Weekly* (December 14, 1998), p. 67.

Page 132 "The initial ..." Daisy Maryles, "Behind the Bestsellers," *Publishers Weekly* (January 25, 1999).

Page 133 "He was significantly ..." Interview with John Hogan.

Page 133 "McGraw hit ..." Interview with Skip Hollandsworth.

Page 136 "Not surprisingly, ..." Interview with Jodi Walbaum of Hay House.

Page 136 "... catering to a category ..." "In How-To Bestseller Lists, Prayer Sizzled, The Soup Cooled and The Cheese Finally Moved," *Book Publishing Report* (January 21, 2002).

Page 137 "When the subject ..." Waliya Lari, "Helping Teens Help Themselves," *Daily Texan* (February 8, 2001), p. 8.

Page 137 "The people at ..." Waliya Lari, "Helping Teens Help Themselves," *Daily Texan* (February 8, 2001), p. 8.

Page 138 "Here's a shocker ..." Phillip C. McGraw, *Self Matters* (New York: Simon & Schuster, 2001), p. 90.

Page 138 "Disappointingly—and despite ..." *Publishers Weekly* (October 1, 2002), available from amazon.com.

Page 139 "Reportedly, when Miller ..." Skip Hollandsworth, "Love Thy Self-Help," *Texas Monthly* (September 2003), p. 206.

Page 139 "... an unprecedented ..." *Today,* NBC-TV (September 12, 2003), interview with Katie Couric.

Page 139 "I don't *think* ..." *Today,* NBC-TV (September 12, 2003), interview with Katie Couric.

Page 139 "Somebody's got to . . ." *Today,* NBC-TV (September 12, 2003), interview with Katie Couric.

Page 140 "I wouldn't be surprised . . ." Interview with Karen Jenkins Holt.

Page 140 "As part of her defense, . . ." "Anatomy of a Defense: A Behind-the-Scenes Look at Clara Harris' Defense," abcnews.com (March 6, 2003), available from http://abcnews.go.com/sections/primetime/US /defending_clara_030306.html#.

Chapter 11

Page 141 "Obviously this isn't . . ." *Donahue,* MSNBC (September 16, 2002), interview with Phil Donahue.

Page 141 "You can imagine, . . ." Marc Peyser, Vanessa Juarez, and Ana Figueroa, "Paging Dr. Phil," *Newsweek* (September 2, 2002), p. 50.

Page 142 "I don't think . . ." Paige Albiniak, "He's Syndie's Prom King," *Broadcasting & Cable* (January 20, 2003).

Page 142 "Oprah came to me . . ." *Today,* NBC-TV (September 16, 2002), interview with Katie Couric.

Page 142 "I really had two . . ." *Today,* NBC-TV (September 16, 2002), interview with Katie Couric.

Page 142 "Think about it, . . ." David Tarrant, "L.A. Can't Get Fill of Dr Phil," *Dallas Morning News* (February 17, 2003), p. 1A.

Page 142 "I got firsthand . . ." Paige Albiniak, "He's Syndie's Prom King," *Broadcasting & Cable* (January 20, 2003).

Page 142 "While we briefly . . ." Paige Albiniak, "He's Syndie's Prom King," *Broadcasting & Cable* (January 20, 2003).

Page 143 "Guys knew who . . ." Kim Lamb Gregory, "In Mere Months, *Dr. Phil* Has Made Daytime Ratings History," *Ventura County Star* (March 4, 2003).

Page 143 "I'm not doing makeovers . . ." Melissa Grego, "KW, Par Bet Oprah's Followers Find 'Phil,'" *Daily Variety* (September 16, 2002), p. A19.

Page 143 "I won't have a celebrity . . ." Kim Lamb Gregory, "In Mere Months, *Dr. Phil* Has Made Daytime Ratings History," *Ventura County Star* (March 4, 2003).

Page 143   "I knew who I . . ." Kim Lamb Gregory, "In Mere Months, *Dr. Phil* Has Made Daytime Ratings History," *Ventura County Star* (March 4, 2003).

Page 144   "For two hours, . . ." David Tarrant, "L.A. Can't Get Fill of Dr Phil," *Dallas Morning News* (February 17, 2003).

Page 144   "I drank the Dr. Phil Kool-Aid, . . ." From the biography *Dr. Phil Getting Real* on the A&E Television Network.

Page 144   "We did make . . ." *Larry King Live,* CNN (May 17, 2003), interview with Larry King.

Page 144   "Harpo retained . . ," Interview with Paige Albiniak.

Page 145   "From the very top, . . ." Interview with former employee of the *Dr. Phil* show.

Page 147   "In one staff meeting, . . ." "Oprah Gives Dr. Phil a Dose of Tough Medicine," *Star Magazine* (August 1, 2002).

Page 147   "He has unforgiving . . ." Michael Starr, "Dr. Phil: I Did Not Sexually Abuse That Female Patient," *New York Post* (September 12, 2002).

Page 148   "Am I hard on people? . . ." *Gayle King Can Talk to Anyone: Dr. Phil,* Oxygen (January 21, 2003), interview with Gayle King.

Page 148   "Paramount wanted *Dr. Phil,* . . ." Interview with former employee of the *Dr. Phil* show.

Page 149   "Oprah got here . . ." "Oprah Gives Dr. Phil a Dose of Tough Medicine," *Star Magazine* (August 1, 2002).

Page 149   "Winfrey's appearance . . ." "Oprah Gives Dr. Phil a Dose of Tough Medicine," *Star Magazine* (August 1, 2002).

Page 149   "The reported price . . ." Melissa Grego, "KW, Par Bet Oprah's Followers Find 'Phil,'" *Daily Variety* (September 16, 2002), p. A19.

Page 150   "Considering we were . . ." Marc Berman, "Feel-Good *Dr. Phil* Packs Them In; Biggest Talk-Show Debut Since *Oprah* Could Reap Millions in Extra Revenue; Syndication," *Mediaweek* (September 23, 2002).

Page 150   "The success of . . ." Paige Albiniak, "He's Syndie's Prom King," *Broadcasting & Cable* (January 20, 2003).

Page 151   "A 30-second spot . . ." Daisy Whitney, "'Dr. Phil' Says True to Image," *Advertising Age* (November 2, 2002), p. 24.

Page 151   "He's tied with . . ." Interview with Paige Albiniak.

Page 151   "*Dr. Phil* continues . . ." Young Broadcasting, "Highly-Rated Prime Time Series Continues to Best Network Programming in San Francisco Market" (February 10, 2003), press release.

Page 152   "King World did . . ." Interview with Marc Berman.

Page 152   "Well, you know, . . ." *Larry King Live,* CNN (May 14, 2003), interview with Larry King.

Page 152   "During the 2002 to 2003 season . . ." *Gayle King Can Talk to Anyone: Dr. Phil,* Oxygen (January 21, 2003), interview with Gayle King.

Page 152   "When Berman called . . ." Interview with Marc Berman.

Page 153   "On target to make . . ." Paige Albiniak, "He's Syndie's Prom King," *Broadcasting & Cable* (January 20, 2003).

Page 153   "McGraw's pay day . . ." Gail Pennington, "Taking the *Dr. Phil* Cure," *St. Louis Post-Dispatch* (April 6, 2003).

Page 153   ". . . doubled in the second . . ." Paige Albiniak, "More *Oprah* Crowds Out Successors," *Broadcasting & Cable* (May 12, 2003).

Page 153   "As good as the show . . ." Paige Albiniak, "He's Syndie's Prom King," *Broadcasting & Cable* (January 20, 2003).

Page 153   "Honestly, I think it's beneath . . ." Interview with former CSI employee.

Page 154   "I hate that . . ." *Gayle King Can Talk to Anyone: Dr. Phil,* Oxygen (January 21, 2003), interview with Gayle King.

Chapter 12

Page 155   "The fact that . . ." *Larry King Weekend,* CNN (May 17, 2003), interview with Larry King.

Page 156   "I absolutely love . . ." Interview with audience member of the *Dr. Phil* show.

Page 156   "The release further states . . ." Based on personal review of the release form by the author.

Page 157   "Guests on the show . . ." Based on interviews with guests who have appeared on the *Dr. Phil* show.

Page 160   "Hall kept this same picture . . ." *Gayle King Can Talk to Anyone: Dr. Phil,* Oxygen (January 21, 2003), interview with Gayle King.

Page 161 "The one thing . . ." Rick Bentley, "Fresno Couple to Brave *Dr. Phil* Show," *Fresno Bee* (February 4, 2003), E1.

Page 161 "McGraw has close . . ." *KSEE News at 5,* KSEE-TV (May 13, 2003), interview with Lori Hernandez.

Page 162 "The most challenging . . ." *Gayle King Can Talk to Anyone: Dr. Phil,* Oxygen (January 21, 2003), interview with Gayle King.

Page 162 "Are they gonna . . ." *Gayle King Can Talk to Anyone: Dr. Phil,* Oxygen (January 21, 2003), interview with Gayle King.

Page 162 "Once you get . . ." *Gayle King Can Talk to Anyone: Dr. Phil,* Oxygen (January 21, 2003), interview with Gayle King.

Page 162 "Any time we're picking . . ." *KSEE News at 5,* KSEE-TV (May 13, 2003), interview with Lori Hernandez.

Page 163 "I walked down . . ." Gerri Miller, "Common Sense Conquers All," *Satellite Direct* (May 2003), p. 16–17.

Page 163 "Considerable telephone interviews . . ." Interview with Richard Hitt.

Page 164 "The first lady . . ." Interview with Amanda Redman.

Page 165 "After an appearance . . ." De Anna Sheffield, "Sarasota Family Gets Results from Appearing on *Dr. Phil* Show," available from WTSP-TV web site, www.wtsp.com.

Page 165 "They [McGraw's producers] contacted us . . ." Interview with Tabetha Yang.

Page 166 "We have an after-care program . . ." *Today,* NBC-TV (May 16, 2003), interview with Katie Couric.

Page 166 "There's probably two . . ." *Dateline,* NBC-TV (September 13, 2002), interview with Jane Pauley.

Chapter 13

Page 167 "It's really nice . . ." Kirk Baird, "Doctor Phil Good: McGraw's Quick-Draw Approach Resonates with Fawning Public," *Las Vegas Sun* (March 10, 2003).

Page 167 "A healthy percentage . . ." e-mail correspondence with Tim Londergan, research director of 10TV in Columbus, Ohio.

Page 168 "He has such good things . . ." Interview with Char Knowles.

Page 168 "He certainly has . . ." Interview with Salim Khoja.

Page 169   "Women love him, . . ." Michelle Gillan, "Dr. Phil McGraw," *Successful Meetings* (December 2002), p. 40.

Page 169   "The AARP hired . . ." Available from www.aarp.org.

Page 170   "Scott and I . . ." Interview with Frank Willson.

Page 171   "If I have something . . ." Jann Carl, "One-on-One with Feisty Dr. Phil," *ET Online* (August 26, 2002), available from http://www.etonline.com/celebrity/a12001.htm.

Page 172   "You have to feel . . ." "Dr. Phil's Self-Help Tour," *ET Online* (January 29, 2002), available from http://www .etonline.com/television/a8740.htm.

Page 172   "If they're leaning . . ." "Dr. Phil's Self-Help Tour," *ET Online* (January 29, 2002), available from http://www .etonline.com/television/a8740.htm.

Page 173   "This has been widely quoted . . ." Interview with representative from the Yale University Office of Public Affairs.

Page 174   "The publication . . ." Jim Kirk, "Allied Domecq Has Heady Plans for Flavored Rum," *Chicago Tribune* (May 28, 2003).

Page 174   "The web site team . . ." Elliot Tiegel, "Dr. Phil Ties Web to TV; Site Gives Viewers Instant Feedback with Hit Show," *Television Week* (March 10, 2003), p. 19.

Page 175   "When the show ends . . ." Elliot Tiegel, "Dr. Phil Ties Web to TV; Site Gives Viewers Instant Feedback with Hit Show," *Television Week* (March 10, 2003), p. 19.

Page 175   "Especially from experts . . ." Elliot Tiegel, "Dr. Phil Ties Web to TV; Site Gives Viewers Instant Feedback with Hit Show," *Television Week* (March 10, 2003), p. 19.

Page 176   "His viewers . . ." Elliot Tiegel, "Dr. Phil Ties Web to TV; Site Gives Viewers Instant Feedback with Hit Show," *Television Week* (March 10, 2003), p. 19.

Page 177   Information regarding course content for the "Life Strategies" module was accessed from www.learndrphil.com in April 2003.

Page 178   "Therapists are encouraged . . ." Interview with Allison Conner.

Page 178   "A lot of talk show . . ." Interview with Gary Lewis.

Page 179   "Either you practice . . ." Interview with Allison Conner.

Page 179   "Neither Dr. Phil . . ." Disclaimer information obtained from www.learndrphil.com.

Page 181   "I said if you . . ." Interview with Sharon Turrentine.

Page 181   "A five-figure amount . . ." Interview with Sharon Turrentine.

Chapter 14

Page 183   "I don't know anybody . . ." Oprah Winfrey, "Oprah Talks to Dr. Phil," *O: The Oprah Magazine* (February 2001).

Page 183   "I am here, . . ." *Entertainment Tonight* (November 4, 2002), Robin McGraw interviews Phil McGraw.

Page 184   "He was very intimidating . . ." *Pinnacle,* CNN (September 8, 2001), interview with Beverly Schuch.

Page 184   "My wife is . . ." Nancy Bilyeau, "Dr. Phil's Love Formula," *Good Housekeeping* (October 2002).

Page 185   "I live with a world-class . . ." Phillip C. McGraw, *Life Strategies* (New York: Hyperion, 1999), p. 278.

Page 185   "When we were deciding . . ." As reported on www .drphil.com.

Page 186   "I would love for women . . ." "Hormones from Hell," *Dr. Phil* (May 20, 2003), syndicated by King World Productions.

Page 186   "That is such . . ." *Gayle King Can Talk to Anyone: Dr. Phil,* Oxygen (January 21, 2003), interview with Gayle King.

Page 186   "She never interrupted . . ." Interview with former employee of the *Dr. Phil* show.

Page 187   "Robin, on the other hand, . . ." Phillip C. McGraw, *Relationship Rescue* (New York: Hyperion, 2000), pp. 260–261.

Page 187   "She was on me . . ." *Entertainment Tonight* (January 22, 2002), interview with Dr. Phil McGraw.

Page 187   "That the whole world . . ." *Entertainment Tonight* (November 4, 2002), Robin McGraw interviews Phil McGraw.

Page 188   "He told me . . ." From the biography *Dr. Phil Getting Real* on the A&E Television Network.

Page 188   "I was like a machine, . . ." Joseph Hooper, "The Doctor is On!" *Elle* (August 2002).

Page 189   "Her [Robin's] mother was . . ." Oprah Winfrey, "Oprah Talks to Dr. Phil," *O: The Oprah Magazine* (February 2001), p. 202.

Page 189 "And at that point, . . ." Oprah Winfrey, "Oprah Talks to Dr. Phil," *O: The Oprah Magazine* (February 2001), p. 202.

Page 190 "A peace settled . . ." Oprah Winfrey, "Oprah Talks to Dr. Phil," *O: The Oprah Magazine* (February 2001), p. 202.

Page 190 "I said to her, . . ." Oprah Winfrey, "Oprah Talks to Dr. Phil," *O: The Oprah Magazine* (February 2001), p. 198.

Page 190 "Ignoring hospital rules, . . ." From the biography *Dr. Phil Getting Real* on the A&E Television Network.

Page 190 "Being a father . . ." From the biography *Dr. Phil Getting Real* on the A&E Television Network.

Page 191 "Where were you . . ." Phillip C. McGraw, *Self Matters* (New York: Simon & Schuster, 2001), p. 6.

Page 191 "I screwed up . . ." Phillip C. McGraw, *Self Matters* (New York: Simon & Schuster, 2001), p. 6–7.

Page 191 "Don't you realize . . ." Phillip C. McGraw, *Self Matters* (New York: Simon & Schuster, 2001), p. 306.

Page 192 "We made a decision, . . ." Phillip C. McGraw, *Self Matters* (New York: Simon & Schuster, 2001), pp. 306–307.

Page 192 "I can't stand . . ." As reported on www.drphil.com.

Page 192 "She is a very family . . ." Interview with Karen Tingle.

Page 192 "It's always been . . ." David Tarrant, "L.A. Can't Get Fill of Dr. Phil," *Dallas Morning News* (February 17, 2003).

Page 193 "Yet she was still . . ." Phillip C. McGraw, *Life Strategies* (New York: Hyperion, 1999), p. 279.

Page 193 "The whole place . . ." Oprah Winfrey, "Oprah Talks to Dr. Phil," *O: The Oprah Magazine* (February 2001).

Page 194 "I would listen to her . . ." Phillip C. McGraw, *Relationship Rescue* (New York: Hyperion, 2000), p. 260.

Page 194 "I could see . . ." *Entertainment Tonight* (January 22, 2002), interview featuring Phil and Robin McGraw.

Page 194 ". . . she'd come in . . ." *Entertainment Tonight* (January 22, 2002), interview featuring Phil and Robin McGraw.

Page 194 "We love each other . . ." As reported on www.drphil.com.

Page 195 "I'm not real . . ." Cecelia Goodnow, "Phil McGraw Draws Raves for 'No Bull' Approach to Rescuing Relationships," *Seattle Post Intelligencer* (March 4, 2000), p. C1.

Page 195 "Years ago . . ." Phillip C. McGraw, *Relationship Rescue* (New York: Hyperion, 2000), p. 136.

Page 195 "I remember once . . ." Phillip C. McGraw, *Relationship Rescue* (New York: Hyperion, 2000), p. 136.

Page 196   "I'm just going . . ." "Worst Spouse in America," *Dr. Phil* (May 7, 2003).

Page 196   "When I married her, . . ." Oprah Winfrey, "Oprah Talks to Dr. Phil," *O: The Oprah Magazine* (February 2001).

Chapter 15

Page 197   "Jay can get . . ." *Larry King Live,* CNN (October 5, 2002), interview with Larry King.

Page 197   "But I always knew . . ." *Larry King Live,* CNN (July 13, 2002), interview with Larry King.

Page 199   "I'm proudest when . . ." *People,* "The Top 50 Bachelors" (June 24, 2002), p. 64.

Page 199   "I think his parents . . ." Interview with Chris DeBello.

Page 199   "I love the opportunity . . ." *Larry King Live,* CNN (July 13, 2002), interview with Larry King.

Page 199   "These days, . . ." Martha Irvine, "Move over Dad: When It Comes to Advice for Teens, Straight-Talking Psychologist's Son Is in the Driver's Seat," Associated Press Worldstream (November 2, 2001).

Page 199   "He came across . . ." Interview with Helen Anders.

Page 200   "My dad is . . ." Jay McGraw, *Life Strategies for Teens* (New York: Simon & Schuster, 2000), p. 25.

Page 201   ". . . doesn't get it. . . ." Jay McGraw, *Life Strategies for Teens* (New York: Simon & Schuster, 2000), p. 58.

Page 201   "I was a horrible . . ." Martha Irvine, "Move over Dad: When It Comes to Advice for Teens, Straight-Talking Psychologist's Son Is in the Driver's Seat," Associated Press Worldstream (November 2, 2001).

Page 202   "If he couldn't eat . . ." Martha Irvine, "Move over Dad: When It Comes to Advice for Teens, Straight-Talking Psychologist's Son Is in the Driver's Seat," Associated Press Worldstream (November 2, 2001).

Page 202   "Robin McGraw used to ask . . ." Interview with former CSI employee.

Page 202   ". . . like an English class lecture, . . ." Jay McGraw, *Life Strategies for Teens* (New York: Simon & Schuster, 2000), p. 35.

Page 202   "When you bring home . . ." Jay McGraw, *Life Strategies for Teens* (New York: Simon & Schuster, 2000), p. 92–93.

Page 202 "When I was cruising . . ." Jay McGraw, *Life Strategies for Teens* (New York: Simon & Schuster, 2000), p. 55.

Page 202 "I think I heard . . ." Jay McGraw, *Life Strategies for Teens* (New York: Simon & Schuster, 2000), p. 55.

Page 203 "For these people, . . ." Jay McGraw, *Life Strategies for Teens* (New York: Simon & Schuster, 2000), p. 73.

Page 203 "I was faced . . ." Jae-Ha Kim, "Get Real with Dr. Phil," *Chicago Sun-Times* (February 10, 2001), p. 30.

Page 203 ". . . always let us . . ." Jae-Ha Kim, "Get Real with Dr. Phil," *Chicago Sun-Times* (February 10, 2001), p. 30.

Page 204 "He turned it on . . ." Interview with Skip Hollandsworth.

Page 204 "I grew up . . ." Jae-Ha Kim, "Get Real with Dr. Phil," *Chicago Sun-Times* (February 10, 2001), p. 30.

Page 205 "I thought it would . . ." Waliya Lari, "Helping Teens Help Themselves," *Daily Texan* (February 8, 2001).

Page 205 "I spent a lot of time . . ." Waliya Lari, "Helping Teens Help Themselves," *Daily Texan* (February 8, 2001).

Page 205 "If one class's book . . ." Waliya Lari, "Helping Teens Help Themselves," *Daily Texan* (February 8, 2001).

Page 205 "Looks like something . . ." Joanne Good, "Hopes and Fears—Generation Y Has Its Say: Secret Life of Teens Goes to the Experts, Teens Themselves," *Edmonton Journal* (May 16, 2001), p. E4.

Page 205 "We're not trying . . ." Martha Irvine, "Move over Dad: When It Comes to Advice for Teens, Straight-Talking Psychologist's Son Is in the Driver's Seat," Associated Press Worldstream (November 2, 2001).

Page 206 "The book's very formulaic . . ." Interview with Helen Anders.

Page 206 "The dad got in . . ." Interview with Dan Coughlin.

Page 206 "Phil has always said . . ." Interview with Skip Hollandsworth.

Page 207 ". . . but what family member . . ." Interview with Chris DeBello.

Page 207 "But he also knew . . ." Interview with Chris DeBello.

Chapter 16

Page 209 "I mean, what . . ." *Donahue*, MSNBC (September 16, 2002), interview with Phil Donahue.

Page 210   Dialogue between Lauri, Nick, and McGraw from "Cheaters," *Dr. Phil* (December 9, 2002), syndicated by King World Productions.

Page 211   "It's the psychological . . ." Mark Donald, "Analyze This," *Dallas Observer* (April 13, 2000).

Page 211   "No one changes . . ." Mark Donald, "Analyze This," *Dallas Observer* (April 13, 2000).

Page 211   "I think about myself . . ." *Donahue,* MSNBC (September 16, 2002), interview with Phil Donahue.

Page 212   "You know, you go . . ." *Dateline NBC,* NBC-TV (September 13, 2002), interview with Jane Pauley.

Page 212   "I don't look at . . ." *KRON News at 9,* KRON-TV (November 25, 2002), interview with Henry Tennenbaum.

Page 212   "Let me tell you, . . ." *Gayle King Can Talk to Anyone: Dr. Phil,* Oxygen (January 21, 2003), interview with Gayle King.

Page 212   "I don't mean . . ." *Donahue,* MSNBC (September 16, 2002), interview with Phil Donahue.

Page 212   "Let me tell you, there ain't . . ." Marc Peyser, Vanessa Juarez, and Ana Figueroa, "Paging Dr. Phil," *Newsweek* (September 2, 2002), p. 50.

Page 213   "In my view . . ." Phillip C. McGraw, *Life Strategies* (New York: Hyperion, 1999), p. 23.

Page 213   "Have they been living . . ." Interview with Allison Conner.

Page 214   "I view his program . . ." Interview with Nancy Levin.

Page 215   "I just wonder . . ." Interview with Denise Hayes.

Page 216   "We have exclusionary . . ." *KRON News at 9,* KRON-TV (November 25, 2002), interview with Henry Tennenbaum.

Page 216   "He is practicing psychology . . ." Interview with Carole Lieberman.

Page 216   "It's not unlike . . ." Interview with Robert Simmermon.

Page 217   "There is some theater . . ." *Larry King Live,* CNN (October 5, 2003), interview with Larry King.

Page 217   "I know this . . ." *Larry King Live,* CNN (October 5, 2003), interview with Larry King.

Page 217   "Sometimes it's Jerry Springer . . ." Interview with Robert Simmermon.

Page 218   "I've watched a number . . ." Marc Peyser, Vanessa Juarez, and Ana Figueroa, "Paging Dr. Phil," *Newsweek* (September 2, 2002), p. 50.

Page 218 "I'm not for everybody, . . ." Marc Peyser, Vanessa Juarez, and Ana Figueroa, "Paging Dr. Phil," *Newsweek* (September 2, 2002), p. 50.

Page 218 "You see a lot . . ." *Gayle King Can Talk to Anyone: Dr. Phil,* Oxygen (January 21, 2003), interview with Gayle King.

Page 218 "Now, there will be . . ." Lynn Elber, "Psychologist, Oprah Protégé Flying Solo," Associated Press (September 12, 2002).

Page 219 "He addresses problems . . ." Interview with Carole Lieberman.

Page 219 "Bembeneck, according to her attorney, . . ." Jessica Hansen, "Bembeneck hurts foot in escape out of Los Angeles Window," *Milwaukee Journal Sentinel* (November 17, 2002), p. 152.

Page 220 "Na-na-na-na. . . ." "Debate Dr. Phil—Part 2," *Dr. Phil* (April 11, 2003), syndicated by King World Productions.

Page 220 "There are millions . . ." "Dr. Phil's Vault," *Dr. Phil* (May 28, 2003), syndicated by King World Productions.

Chapter 17

Page 221 "I get underwear . . ." "Phil McGraw: Sexiest Self-Help Guru," *People* (November 26, 2001).

Page 222 "Honestly, I've never . . ." "Be My Guest," *Dr. Phil* (April 28, 2003), syndicated by King World Productions.

Page 222 "*NSYNC happened to be staying . . ." From the biography *Dr. Phil Getting Real* on the A&E Television Network.

Page 223 "I want to know . . ." "It Must Be True . . ." *Week* (June 27, 2003), p. 16.

Page 223 "Fess up here. . . ." *Dateline NBC,* NBC-TV (September 13, 2002), interview with Jane Pauley.

Page 223 "I thought it was Jeffrey Tambor . . ." *Today,* NBC-TV (May 16, 2003), interview with Katie Couric.

Page 223 "She could be vulnerable . . ." *Dateline NBC,* NBC-TV (May 13, 2003).

Page 224 "We produced them . . ." *Late Show with David Letterman,* CBS-TV (February 17, 2003).

Page 225 "I'm thinking of going . . ." Michael McIntee, "Tuesday, February 13, 2003/Show #1952," *Wahoo Gazette* (February 13, 2003), the *Late Show* web site, available from http://www.cbs.com/latenight/lateshow/exclusives/wahoo /archive/2003/03/archive13/shtml, accessed August 7, 2003.

Page 225 "He's man enough . . ." *Late Show with David Letterman,* CBS-TV (February 17, 2003), interview with David Letterman.

Page 226 "They [*Late Show* producers] like to do . . ." "Be My Guest," *Dr. Phil* (April 28, 2003), syndicated by King World Productions.

Page 227 "Dr. Phil, if you're out there, . . ." Tim Rogers, "The Unstoppable Phil McGraw," *D* (April 2003), p. 16.

Page 227 "McGraw rented his first place . . ." Ruth Ryon, "Hot Property: He Flirted, Now Dr. Phil's Ready for Commitment," *Los Angeles Times* (December 29, 2002).

Page 227 "A few months later, . . ." Skip Hollandsworth, "Love Thy Self-Help," *Texas Monthly* (September 2003), p. 122.

Page 227 ". . . a 12,000-square-foot . . ." Ruth Ryon, "Hot Property: He Flirted, Now Dr. Phil's Ready for Commitment," *Los Angeles Times* (December 29, 2002).

Page 228 "To keep roots . . ." Alan Peppard, "Leeza Opens up Her Purse," *Dallas Morning News* (January 20, 2003), p. 25A.

Page 228 " . . . get up, go to . . ." David Tarrant, "L.A. Can't Get Fill of Dr. Phil," *Dallas Morning News* (February 17, 2003).

Page 228 "He'd much prefer . . ." David Tarrant, "L.A. Can't Get Fill of Dr Phil," *Dallas Morning News* (February 17, 2003), p. 1E.

Page 228 "I don't feel like . . ." *Larry King Weekend,* CNN (May 17, 2003), interview with Larry King.

Page 229 "My lifestyle has not changed . . ." *Today,* NBC-TV (April 29, 2003), interview with Jill Rappaport.

Page 229 "It comes with . . ." David Tarrant, "L.A. Can't Get Fill of Dr. Phil," *Dallas Morning News* (February 17, 2003), p. 1E.

Page 229 "An avid tennis player, . . ." "USA Tennis Florida Rubs Elbows with Celebrities at Chris Evert Pro-Celebrity Classic" (December 3, 2002), USA-Tennis Florida web site, available from http://www.usatennisflorida.usta.com /communitytennis/fullstory.sps?iNewsid=25038&itype=11 4&icategoryid=229, accessed August 7, 2003.

Page 230   "McGraw and his teammates . . ." Press release, Mercedes-Benz cup web site (December 26, 2002), available from http://www.Mercedes-benzcup.com/Mediacoverage /release01-03sampras.asp, accessed August 7, 2003.

Page 230   "I really wanted . . ." *Today,* NBC-TV (April 29, 2003), interview with Jill Rappaport.

Page 231   "I've rewritten all my lines. . . ." "Be My Guest," *Dr. Phil* (April 28, 2003), syndicated by King World Productions.

Page 231   "I bet that broke . . ." "Be My Guest," *Dr. Phil* (April 28, 2003), syndicated by King World Productions.

Page 231   "I'd never met him . . ." "Be My Guest," *Dr. Phil* (April 28, 2003), syndicated by King World Productions.

Page 232   "To me a star . . ." David Tarrant, "L.A. Can't Get Fill of Dr. Phil," *Dallas Morning News* (February 17, 2003).

Chapter 18

All quotes relating to McGraw's "Life Laws" were taken from *Life Strategies* by Phillip C. McGraw (New York: Hyperion, 1999).

INDEX